RIT - WALLACE LIBRARY
CIRCULATING LIBRARY BOOKS

OVERDUE FINES AND FEES FOR <u>ALL</u> BORROWERS

*Recalled = $1/ day overdue (no grace period)
*Billed = $10.00/ item when returned 4 or more weeks overdue
*Lost Items = replacement cost+$10 fee
*All materials must be returned or renewed by the duedate.

Power Tools Recharged

125+
Essential Forms
and Presentations
for Your School Library
Information Program

JOYCE KASMAN VALENZA

POWER TOOLS

Recharged

125+
Essential Forms
and Presentations
for Your School Library
Information Program

JOYCE KASMAN VALENZA

ILLUSTRATED BY EMILY VALENZA

AMERICAN LIBRARY ASSOCIATION
CHICAGO
2004

The paper used in this publication meets the minimum requirements of American National Standard for Information Sciences—Permanence of Paper for Printed Library Materials, ANSI Z39.48-1992. ∞

Library of Congress Cataloging-in-Publication Data
Valenza, Joyce Kasman.
    Power tools recharged : 125+ essential forms and presentations for your school library information program / Joyce Kasman Valenza.
        p.   cm.
    Rev. ed. of: Power tools. 1998.
    Includes bibliographical references.
    ISBN 0-8389-0880-2 (alk. paper)
    1. School libraries—Administration—Forms.
2. Media programs (Educational)—Administration—Forms. 3. School libraries—Activity programs.
4. School libraries—Marketing. I. Valenza, Joyce Kasman. Power tools. II. Title.
Z675.S3V315 2004
025.5′678—dc22   2004005853

Printed in the United States of America

08 07 06 05 04   5 4 3 2 1

Contents

2

Program Administration   71

3

Measuring the Impact of Our Programs   141

4

Instructional Tools for Information Literacy   177

5
Student Tools for Information Literacy   259

Introduction

When *Power Tools* was published in 1997, the Web was in its infancy, teacher-librarians were struggling to get their arms around a new information landscape, and *Information Power,* our national standards for information literacy, was just emerging in final revised form.

Since 1997 the information landscape has changed dramatically. And the need for information skills had never been clearer. Teacher-librarians have new mandates, new roadmaps, and new vision.

Though I have been a librarian for twenty-eight years, I have never felt more passionate about my mission. I fear if we don't reach the current generation of learners, we lose an opportunity to prepare information-literate citizens, citizens for whom information that is good enough is *not* good enough, citizens who understand the value of information professionals in their academic, professional, and personal lives.

Great challenges face teacher-librarians today, challenges that position us to become change agents for our students, teacher colleagues, administrators, and larger communities. Our roles are growing increasingly important in the school culture. We are rightly becoming the information technology experts in our buildings; leaders in the areas of searching, information access, evalua-tion, and communication; protectors of intellectual property; and defenders of intellectual freedom.

School reform movements stress instructional strategies that point to the need for stronger library information programs. More than ever, teacher-librarians and classroom teachers are engaging in new partnerships—in inquiry-driven research, interdisciplinary approaches, critical thinking, project- and problem-based learning, and collaborative, hands-on, authentic activities. Federal and state initiatives and the national standards movement stress accountability, and teacher-librarians must determine their roles in helping their schools achieve.

We have daunting jobs. Teacher-librarians must manage staff; develop policies; build and maintain dynamic collections; design, implement, and assess instructional units; and plan and promote our programs while integrating information skills; performing readers' advisory services; planning in-service activities; providing guidance to students, faculty, and parents; and staying ahead of the technology curve. To meet these challenges, we must continually *retool.*

There is little time to be as effective as we would like in all areas of our service. The day is not long enough to manage, collaborate, instruct, and promote and lead change at the level to which most of us aspire.

Ironically, at this time when the need for school library information programs appears greatest, we are faced with threats to our funding and our programs. It is essential for any professional to document his or her achievements and success. In an era of accountability and short funding, libraries must report their achievements to their stakeholders, ensuring that the school community develops a clear view of the importance of our evolving roles and our direct impact on learners.

Power Tools: Recharged updates the original handbook-toolkit for teacher-librarians to reflect the current information landscape and new expectations and demands of school information professionals. Most sections have been completely revised. The project features a completely new presentation section and a new focus on documenting and measuring the impact of the library program.

Power Tools Recharged is a toolkit designed to help simplify your job, to give you a way not only to manage, but to lead change when there is no time to create from scratch. During these past twenty-eight years, I've had a wonderful and wide assortment of library positions. With each position I found myself beginning from scratch, reinventing the wheel. *Power Tools Recharged* presents customizable, ready-to-use forms and tested ideas that will

- help you manage, promote, and assess your program;
- increase the effectiveness of your program while reducing your workload;
- help you help your students and faculty partners develop information skills; and
- help teachers integrate information skills into the whole-school program.

I've included just about everything I need to get me through the average year—library passes and style sheets, organizers to help students gather and analyze information, templates to help you create annual reports and acceptable-use policies, evaluation forms for Web resources, a mass-assignment alert for your local public library, job descriptions, rubrics for research papers and multimedia presentations, and much more. I am grateful to very generous colleagues who have contributed their own field-tested work.

Though *Power Tools Recharged* includes a number of tools designed to enhance information literacy skills, *Power Research Tools* (American Library Association, 2002), the companion volume to this work, provides a far wider array of such resources. The combined tools in both these works should get you through almost any day.

The last chapter of *Power Tools Recharged* consists of six slide presentations, suitable for a variety of constituent groups. They clarify the role of the library information specialist in light of current educational trends and new information technologies, and they explain behaviors and skills critical to learners.

Every library program is different. Every teacher-librarian has a different teaching style. Using the files on the included CD-ROM, you can easily customize the documents to meet the needs of your own program. Put "your library name here." Add your own graphics. Grab graphics from the slides and move them to the documents. Edit and re-create. Use and improve. Add to this notebook your own important forms and program ideas so you have them all in one convenient place.

Power Tools Recharged frees you to focus on the essentials—ensuring that library work is learner-centered, that the library information center functions as a laboratory for learners, that instruction is planned collaboratively with classroom and subject-area teachers, and, most importantly, that our students are developing their own *power tools* for the future: strong information skills.

Acknowledgments

This book is a mirror of a library program, and a library program is essentially a collaborative effort.

Whatever we are able to achieve at Springfield is in large part because of the members of our faculty and staff who continue to value the type of active learning that can happen only when a school has a strong library information program.

Thanks to our principal, Joe Roy, for his vision and leadership and to K–12 Language Arts Coordinator Carol Rohrbach, who spreads the gospel of information literacy and our shared high expectations for student work across discipline from K–12. Thanks to all my inspiring teacher colleagues but especially Michael Wagman, Veronica Sweeney, and Ken Rodoff, who regularly work to invent new learning strategies with me.

My assistants and dear friends Michele Kennedy and Jo Ann Supplee continually ask "How can we help you?" of me and more importantly of our staff and our students. Their service approach is critical to our program and allows me to focus my efforts on teaching and learning.

Thanks to Patrick Hogan and Laura Pelehach for trusting me to understand the needs of my colleagues and to Dianne Rooney for her deft touch in designing sense of my messy pages.

Thanks also to the many professionals off whom I bounce so many ideas, notable among them Doug Johnson, Bob Berkowitz, Sara Johns, and Terry Young.

Thanks also to my family—Dennis, Emily, and Matthew—who sacrifice, each in his and her own ways, for the cause of information literacy.

Communicating Your Program

Imagine you had the budget of your dreams and a beautiful new facility. Imagine you designed the perfect information skills curriculum and knew your collection inside out. Would any of this matter if your clients, patrons, and users chose not to visit?

An effective communications program is as essential a component to your program as a fine curriculum and a decent budget. People need to know who you are and what you do, and they may not. Most classroom teachers and administrators did not learn about dynamic, state-of-the-library information center programs in their preservice preparation.

Students, teachers, administrators, parents, and the larger school community should—no, must—understand your goals and what you can offer. They must feel welcome in your facility. The library can be the heart and the brain of a school, the center of its culture. What you do, or do not do, can affect the entire school program. The tone you set can spread through the entire building. You also determine how children and young adults will view libraries and librarians when they leave school. You make a difference in the instructional effectiveness of your building and your faculty.

Our importance as a profession and the importance of our facilities, though dear to us, may not be clear enough to the communities we serve. In these times of cutbacks, with some administrators viewing libraries as nonessential and others feeling that the Internet is an adequate replacement for a library media center, you cannot have too many friends.

Whenever possible avoid "no." Your goal is to get to "yes." Provide classroom teachers and administrators the materials they need to shine. Go the extra mile to get a student that hard-to-find article or book. Help parents and community members with their personal information needs. All of these activities promote your program, our profession, and student achievement. Communicate your abilities and your worth.

1-1
Teacher-Librarians: A Field Guide to an Evolving Species

Originally published in the *Classroom Connect Newsletter* (April 2002), this article explains the current and evolving role of the teacher-librarian in the information literate school culture. You may use it for parent or school board meetings or distribute it to new teachers.

1-2
Top Ten Things Baby Teachers Should Know about School Libraries

Doug Johnson's supportive letter is just the thing a new teacher would welcome that very first week. It presents you as colleague and partner.

1-3
Top Ten Things Teachers Should Know to Better Understand Student Network Behavior and the Web

This collected list of what teachers need to know should help avoid shoddy research efforts and promote learning and on-task behavior during Internet-based assignments and laboratory-based lessons.

1-4
Letter to Parents: Ch-ch-ch-ch-changes . . .

For a school that values inquiry and thesis-driven research, this letter explains "the changes" to parents and clarifies why a child's report on a planet, country, or president probably didn't make the grade. Parents can be excellent allies in promoting students' information literacy.

1-5
The Principal's Manual for Your School Library Media Program

The American Association of School Librarians' brochure aims to help principals work with their teacher-librarians and faculty to plan and assess their school's library media program. It also functions as a tool to help principals gain a better understanding of what to expect from a state-of-the-art library information program.

1-6
Book Talk Tips

One of your best strategies for promoting reading and allowing your students to better get to know you is the book talk. These little *book commercials* really allow you to express your creativity and your enthusiasm for books.

1-7
Starting a Student Book Club

Everyone is joining! Why shouldn't your student book lovers have an opportunity to get together, share their passions for reading and discussion, and develop a shared reading history? The tips offered in this document are designed to guide you through start-up to thoughtful discussion. The generic questions at the end of the document will help get discussions going for nearly every reading.

1-8
The Authors' Wish List

Toni Buzzeo, teacher-librarian and an author herself, pulls together tried-and-true tips for hosting a successful author visit.

1-9
Current Awareness Service

Our teachers love this service aimed at keeping them up-to-date in their fields of interest. We send them tables of contents of their favorite journals, and they return the pages, having circled any articles of interest. We deliver copies of the circled articles in their mailboxes.

1-10
Thought You'd Like to Know . . .

Materials do no one any good just sitting there. They need to be promoted off the shelves. New materials especially seem to lose some of their shine once they're shelved for the first time. Every time an order arrives, send those likely to be most interested a notice so they can immediately preview the material.

1-11
How Can We Help?

Distribute this at the beginning of the school year or the beginning of each semester. It will help to plan purchases and avoid surprises that occur long after the budget is spent. These forms may be useful in encouraging more teachers to plan cooperative units with you and help you to schedule more timely information skills instruction.

1-12
Join Us in Improving Our Library! (Faculty Committee)

In some schools it may be beneficial to gather program support through the development of a faculty library–information center committee. Such committees allow you to receive formal feedback relating to the effectiveness of the program and facility. They may also help you to establish schoolwide programs, facilitate fund-raising, and promote library use among learners and other faculty members. You may choose to hold monthly meetings or host them only once or twice a year.

1-13
Dear Language Arts/Social Studies/ Science/Health Teacher

Distribute these letters to classroom teachers at the beginning of the school year or whenever you feel you've lost touch. These are meant as skeletons. Substantially customize the letters to reflect the strengths of your own collection, and periodically update the web links.

1-14
Welcome to Your Library Information Center (Student/Parent Brochure)

Have these brochures available during student orientation, and distribute them at parent-teacher organization meetings. The brochure provides students with a written reminder of the services you offer and fine and behavior policies. Parents may be surprised to discover the scope of the resources you provide for their students and will appreciate the contact information. Communicate that the fax number can be used to transmit a late form or an assignment mistakenly left at home.

1-15
The School Library: Your Partner in Learning and Instruction (Faculty Brochure)

Use this brochure with new teachers or distribute it with your September newsletter. It explains the ways you support and partner with faculty and explains our information literacy standards.

1-16
What Is Plagiarism? (Brochure)

As part of your academic integrity campaign, these brochures can help you and your teachers communicate policy and inform students of school-wide expectations for ethical research attitudes and behaviors.

1-17
Request for Donation of Library Technology

What do your local businesses do with their current equipment when they are about to upgrade? They may just be looking for a good home and a tax break, and your letter may be arriving at just the right time. Though you shouldn't expect any powerful state-of-the-art gems, you should make it clear that you are looking for late model equipment, not items they just couldn't bear to trash. For many of us, a few workstations to alleviate the word-processing demand could be a welcome gift.

1-18
Gift Book Program

Gift book programs can help build a needy program, allow students to feel pride in their library, and encourage relationships with parents and community members. This letter and form will help you promote your program and establish guidelines to ensure the gifts you receive are valuable additions to your collection.

1-19/1-20
Bookplates: Birthday Book and Memorial Book

These plates created in Microsoft Publisher format will enable easy customization of bookplates recognizing gifts received.

1-21
Mass-Assignment <u>Alert!</u>

As a courtesy, fax this form to your local public library when you get notice that a *big one* is coming. This will allow the public library staff to prepare for the onslaught and try to divide materials more equitably among their patrons. It also will contribute to better relations between you and your public library colleagues.

1-22
Community Resource File

This was a file I kept up regularly in the days I was a public librarian. Such a file can also be useful in a school setting. You may use it to identify speakers for programs or the right people to recommend for a particular district committee. Your students may want to conduct e-mail (or personal) interviews with the many hidden experts in your community.

1-23
Technology Information Night

Use this form to help you promote an event to share your district's technology vision, exemplary student work, and district policies with your community.

1-24
Wanted: Library Volunteers

Even if you have paid assistants, you may need some extra hands for special projects. Distribute this letter to parents at the beginning of the school year, and keep those names on file.

1-25
Wanted: Library-Tech Squad Members

My staff and I are often too busy to keep up with paper, cartridge, and toner changes. When a teacher has a tech problem, he or she often runs into the library for crisis help. Having a group of responsible students trained and "on call" can be a valuable time-saver. They can help you keep your web site up-to-date, and they can set up the headphones for the visiting Spanish class. With training, these students may even help you guide other students as they produce research projects with PowerPoint, Publisher, or html editing software. They are likely to feel an investment in the program and very positive about their service to the school. Their training is well worth your time.

1-26
Library Web Site Organizer

A school library web site presents you as an information professional and is essential in guiding students, faculty, and community members to the best resources on the Web. It also provides broad access to your tips sheets, advice, style guides, lessons, and policy statements twenty-four hours a day. This outline will help you plan what to include, but you may not want to cover all the areas listed. Select a focus that best meets the needs of your community, one that is manageable. Visit School Libraries.Net at http://www.school-libraries.net for advice and examples of best practice.

Teacher-Librarians
A Field Guide to an Evolving Species

WHY A FIELD GUIDE?

Not long ago, we had the largest influx of new teachers our high school has seen in several years. This group gave me an interesting, informal, research base. Not one of these recently credentialed, technology-confident professionals knew who I was. They were stunned when I offered to develop resource Web pages for their classes. They were confounded when I offered to block time to collaborate on a WebQuest or to help them design assessments for research projects. They were nearly overcome when I offered to help them with research for their own graduate courses. Not one of them had been prepared to come into their new buildings and find a teaching partner in the library. Not one of them understood my role as the teacher-librarian in the school community.

So I feel a strong need to introduce my colleagues and myself to teachers everywhere who have not been regular readers of library journals and to those who, for a variety of unfortunate reasons, have not seen a working model of today's dynamic school library.

FIELD GUIDE INTRODUCTION

I am your librarian. You may think you know me, but if you met me when you yourself were in high school, it's time for a completely new introduction. Things have changed. Today's libraries are the places "where the rubber meets the road," where all the technology skills learned in computer labs and the content learned in classrooms are applied in research and communication efforts. In a wired school, librarians are the information specialists: the Web site developers, database experts, technology leaders, upholders of intellectual freedom, protectors of intellectual property, and technology trainers and integrators.

Today's teacher-librarians address the digital divide by providing both physical and intellectual access to technology. We organize the Web for teachers and students, providing signage and convenient access, much in the same way that we've always organized the physical space of our library facilities. We advocate for student access to information, as we model and demonstrate respect for intellectual property. We select high-quality online databases that lead students to content in journals, newspapers, broadcast sources, and reference works. In partnership with teachers, we design instruction and assessment. And, yes, we also promote reading and literacy in its broadest sense.

RELEVANCE OF THE SPECIES

I have heard people argue the relevancy of physical libraries and librarians in a growing virtual world. Working with young people on a daily basis, I know how critical human interaction is. I know that students don't know what they don't know. And dependence on the free Web and the new independence that the Web gives student researchers often results in substantial research "holes." I know that a student's research improves when he or she poses a question to a human rather than a fictional butler. I know that thoughtful research is a training ground for adult life and that good research habits require creativity, training, and much practice, and that research involves careful strategies and materials beyond the free Web. I know that topical research—merely finding and retelling information in a state, president, or country report—has no relevance in an information-rich landscape. I know how to help teachers change the questions to make research a meaningful learning experience. I know how to design Web-based instruction and how to design assessment tools that measure students' use of information technologies, as well as their mastery of content standards. I know that I have expertise in database searching that my teaching colleagues will never have time to develop. And I know that it is my responsibility to ensure that my students and faculty develop skills of information literacy, so that they know how to access, evaluate, analyze, organize, document, and communicate information in effective and ethical ways.

For those who argue that libraries are an unnecessary expense in a digital information landscape, I would argue that a good teacher-librarian is one of the best educational bargains around. In a nutshell, librarians help learners learn and librarians help teachers teach.

From the Official Field Guide, allow me to formally introduce my species.

TEACHER-LIBRARIAN (MAGISTER LIBRARII)

Alternate names: School Librarian, School Library Media Specialist, Library Information Specialist

Habitat: School buildings (and, by virtual reach to the school community, wherever they can log in)

Description: Physical descriptions vary, though species is predominantly female. Most examples are extremely friendly and highly skilled in information technology.

ROLES OF THE TEACHER-LIBRARIAN

According to *Information Power* (American Library Association and Association for Educational Communications and Technology, 1998), the teacher-librarian can be identified as having the following four roles and responsibilities:

1. As teacher, the teacher-librarian collaborates with "members of the learning community to analyze learning and information needs, to locate and use resources that will meet those needs, and to understand and communicate the information the resources provide." These duties include curricular leadership in helping both staff and students develop

techniques and skills in accessing, evaluating, and using "information from multiple sources in order to learn, to think, and to create and apply new knowledge."

2. Working with the entire school community as instructional partner, the teacher-librarian "works closely with individual teachers in the critical areas of designing authentic learning tasks and assessments and integrating the information and communication abilities required to meet subject matter standards."

3. As information specialist, providing leadership and expertise: "Working in an environment that has been profoundly affected by technology, the teacher-librarian both masters sophisticated electronic resources and maintains a constant focus on the nature, quality, and ethical use of information available in these and in more traditional tools."

4. As program administrator providing management expertise, planning, and evaluation: "the library media specialist is an advocate for the library media program and provides the knowledge, vision, and leadership to steer it creatively and energetically in the twenty-first century."

ENDANGERED STATUS

The subspecies of Teacher-Librarian indigenous to North America is classified as threatened in several states, in spite of research-based evidence citing its importance in student achievement and in the learning chain (see Library Research Service studies of Colorado, Pennsylvania, and Alaska at http://lrs.org/). Habitat degradation may result from the shortsightedness of bureaucrats and administrators who fail to understand the importance of the species as a human link between technology and knowledge. Additional threats exist from administrators who maintain that Web access is an acceptable substitute for a library program.

The abandonment of funding for school libraries and the elimination of the species are national problems, particularly critical in poor urban areas, resulting in a negative impact on the habitat and learning environments of young people. "Nearly 30 years ago, as student populations in the New York City public schools began to turn from ethnic white to black and brown, the city started to dismantle its school libraries," wrote Jonathan Kozol in his book *Ordinary Resurrections*. Kozol described the library divide, decrying the embarrassing inequities as a "form of theft that is too often irreversible." He contended, "It is a conscious act of social demarcation: a shameful way of building barriers around a child's mind, of starving intellect, of amputating dreams."

OTHER INFORMATION ABOUT THE SPECIES

Teacher-Librarians are among the friendliest, most flexible, and compatible creatures you will find in a school environment and will generally work tirelessly to help students and teachers. But, beware: Teacher-Librarians can be dangerous when:

Their library budgets are cut, despite the increasing costs of balancing print and electronic collections that serve entire school communities.

They are required to shift their focus from learners to clerical tasks (see "Library Aides" for a description of that entirely different species!).

They function predominantly as providers of "prep" periods for teachers, and are thus diminished in curricular relevance and effectiveness in delivering authentic instruction in information literacy.

Students' access to information is significantly threatened.

Students and faculty confront them with blatant lapses in information ethics.

Related Species: Public librarians, available after school and weekends, and academic librarians also have vested interests in information literacy and the broader literacy of young people.

Breeding: Most teacher librarians have both educational certification and library credentials, often a Masters in Library Science. Most have continued training in information technology through formal coursework, professional conferences, and reading.

Signs: Tracks of this species include a strong school Web presence; balanced, high-quality print and electronic collections including age-appropriate subscription databases; and high, school-wide

standards for authentic, inquiry-driven student research and ethics.

SOUNDS OF THE SPECIES

In state-of-the-art electronic field guides, readers are exposed to songs, calls, and other sounds of the species being studied. I asked a few of our best *specimens* to make their own sounds to help me describe the species more accurately. Listen to what these representatives of the species have to say:

On Partnerships with Teachers

"What I try to stress is that I am there to help teachers and to help their students to be successful," said Mary Alice Anderson, Media Specialist at Winona (MN) Middle School, who believes it is particularly important for librarians to connect with new teachers. Anderson, who teaches courses at Winona State University, wonders about new teachers' lack of knowledge about librarians. "Most of the people who take technology courses learn technology rather than the information literacy viewpoint," noted Anderson. "New teachers come in not knowing what a media specialist is. They apologize for taking my time and I have to explain that that is what my job is. That helping them is what I want to do, and what I am here to do. They'll apologize for not knowing something, but we're all learning this together. Nobody expects anyone to be an expert."

On Reaching beyond the Library

Like most of us, Anderson sees her job reaching well beyond the walls of her library. Many of us extend our services 24/7 through the resources and guidance of our Web pages. Anderson notes this reach often applies to critical building-wide support. "I was just thinking about tech support—how much I provide because we don't have enough technicians," said Anderson. "Are there teachers who don't think of the media specialist as someone who can help them and might be able to help them faster than the technicians who serve multiple buildings? Do teachers think of a media specialist as working in a specific place—the media center—rather than working in the entire school?" Anderson emphasizes that the librarian represents a program rather than a place. "And what we buy, what we do is for everyone, the entire school."

On Curricular Leadership and Flexibility

"The librarian is one person in the school who knows the whole curriculum," said Sara Kelly Johns, Library Media Specialist, Lake Placid (NY) Middle/Senior High School District. "She is able to co-teach with a large group of people who have widely varied teaching styles, and she can have fun doing it." One of the habits of the species Johns has noticed is flexibility. "He or she comes today with a plan and consistently reprioritizes it. The day is about reacting to the constantly shifting needs of students and teachers—having to deal with one teacher planning for next month, at the same time as you are dealing with another teacher going with the teachable moment for tomorrow. The school librarian is never bored."

On Students' Need for New Literacy Skills

Johns noted that there have been big changes in the ways students do research. "When there was a topic, fifteen years ago, kids were scratching for information. They had to search and search. Now there is so much information out there that kids must know how to evaluate and use information ethically. They need to ask better questions. Not to accept information just because it is quick and easy. They need to find the search engines that give the best results. They need to understand that articles in a database are often more reliable than material on a self-published Web site. They have to know how to evaluate the expertise of an author. They need to produce work with their own voices. And just like classification of mammals in biology class, these are skills that have to be taught."

"Multiple-media literacies—historical literacy, information literacy, visual literacy, cultural literacy, scientific literacy—are the 'new basics' of our teaching in the 21st century," said Librarian and Curriculum Coordinator Debbie Abilock of the Nueva School in Hillsborough (CA). "I see our teaching of technology, research, primary sources, and Web scanning as comparable to teaching the age-old school tasks of basic reading and writing—and they are as essential to critical and creative problem-solving as basic print literacy. Reading styles and speeds must adjust to the

demands of different tasks—from nonlinear skimming of hypertext to visual analysis of GIS data layers. However, these dynamic forms of literacy present librarians and students with new challenges. What does it mean to comprehend meaning in representations that integrate text, visuals, and sound? How do I assess saliency in an information-overloaded world? What is authority and credibility in the Internet's self-publishing environment? How can I identify bias and assumptions in the alluring world of visual media? How does my own teaching and writing change to fit new media?" Abilock noted that many of her own Web pages are "designed to challenge both me and my students to answer these questions—not with rules, but with strategies."

On Ethical Use of Information Technologies

"The school librarian is the perfect person to help students and teachers think about the ramifications of technology use," said Frances Jacobson, Librarian at University of Illinois Laboratory High School. "It's because we teach technology differently. From e-mail conversations, to plagiarism, to hacking, to what it means to be a responsible citizen in a wired environment, we focus teachers and students on the ethical uses of educational technology. For us, it's not just teaching 'how'; it's teaching 'why.' We teach the process, the transferable skills. We help kids make intellectual connections relating to information—who it belongs to, how to share it, and how to contribute in their own voices."

On Information Technology Leadership

Mike Eisenberg, Dean of the Information School at the University of Washington and developer of the Big6 information problem-solving system, sees the species as functioning as the CIO (Chief Information Officer) of the school. "Every organization needs one—someone who sees the big picture and can talk to users as well as techies, someone who can manage it all—the administrative, information, and instructional sides."

"I am feeling that our technology consultant role underlies all that we do," said Peter Milbury, librarian at Chico (CA) High School, co-moderator of the LM_NET discussion list of more than 14,000 school librarians, and Webmaster of his own

1-1D

award-winning school library Web site. "Unless we are fluent in the use of the kinds of technology that allow students to access and present information successfully, we are not able to fully perform our jobs. This is because information is so wedded to technology. The major medium for information access today is the Web. Thus, it is absolutely essential that school librarians are comfortable with finding information on the Web, both free and fee-based."

"The library media specialist is rapidly changing from being an information desert guide—helping learners locate scarce resources—to being an information jungle guide—helping learners evaluate and select resources of value," said Doug Johnson, Director of Media and Technology in the Mankato Schools. "It's not finding the hidden waterholes anymore, as much as being able to tell the good ones from the bad ones."

As a species, librarians continue to evolve. Our continued evolution is focused on learning in an information-rich world, on staff development, educational partnerships, constructivist strategies that move students well beyond topical research, ethics, evaluation and searching skills, and new media literacies. The Internet cannot replace libraries. In fact, new technologies make the need for new guidance all the more obvious. Those boxes and wires we put in our classrooms and labs will have little meaning unless information professionals select quality resources for them. The technology itself has little value unless teachers in partnership with librarians help students to effectively and ethically locate, analyze, evaluate, synthesize, and communicate information.

SOURCE: By Joyce Kasman Valenza. Adapted from an article that first appeared in the April 2002 issue of the *Classroom Connect Newsletter,* volume 8, number 7. © Classroom Connect, Inc. Classroom Connect is an award-winning provider of professional development programs and online instructional materials for K–12 education. http:// www.classroom.com. (800) 638-1639.

Top Ten Things Baby Teachers Should Know about School Libraries

"Head for the Edge," April/May 2003
Doug Johnson
dougj@doug-johnson.com

Dear First Year Teacher,

Welcome to school. Is it ever nice to see your fresh, smiling face! I hope some of your eagerness and enthusiasm rubs off on the rest of us who have been here awhile. (A couple of us still yearn for the days of the one room school.)

I am the school media specialist, or librarian, if you prefer. I answer to both. I recognize that your teacher preparation may not have given you much information about or experience with working with me or using our library's resources effectively. There is also a pretty good chance that the school library you used during your own school days was different from our program here.

To help get things off on a positive spin, here are a few things I'd like you to know about the library, our program and me that can help us both form a great partnership.

1. The librarian doesn't own the library. You and your students do. You can recommend materials and have a voice in library policy making. Volunteer to become a member of our school's library advisory committee.

2. The library should be considered an "intellectual gymnasium." It's not a student lounge, study hall or baby-sitting service. The students in the library, including the ones you send, should have a reason for being there. Whether for academic purposes or personal use, students should be in the library because they need the library's resources, not just because they need to be somewhere.

3. The best resource in the library is the librarian. I can help you plan a project, solve a technology problem, find professional research, give insight into an ethical problem, or answer a reference question. And if I can't do it, I will help you find someone who can. I can help find interlibrary loan materials you need that are not in the school library itself. Helping others gives me a huge sense of satisfaction so please never hesitate to ask me.

4. Planning is a good thing. Advanced planning with me will greatly increase your and your students' chances for success with projects that require information resources. A well-planned research unit or technology project will greatly decrease frustrations for everyone involved. With my experience, I can let you know what strategies work and don't work.

5. Recognize that the library provides access to both print and electronic information. I can determine which one best suits your and your students' needs. Students do not always realize that print resources are the best for many purposes. It breaks my heart to watch a student spend a frustrating hour trying to find the answer to a question on the Internet that could have been answered with a print resource in minutes.

6. The librarian can be helpful in evaluating the information found on the Internet. One of the greatest challenges of using the Internet is determining whether the facts and opinions found there are credible. I have the training and tools to do just that. And it is my mission to teach students effective evaluation skills as well.

7. The librarian can help create assessments for your students' projects. The findings of research projects presented in electronic form, conclusions drawn from primary resources, and research that calls for higher-level thinking to be demonstrated all call for good authentic assessment tools rather than a simple gut-reaction comments or an objective test. I can help you find examples of these sorts of tools as well as help you create and administer them yourself. Let's work together to make your students' learning experiences as meaningful as possible.

8. The librarian can be your technology support center. I'm no technical guru, but I can help you and your students with technology applications. Need to use a scanner or digital camera? I can show you how. Need to create a multimedia presentation? Let me give you a quick lesson. Looking for effective ways to search the web? Ask me. I'm not a technician, but I can sometimes help locate that kind of help for you as well.

9. The library can help your students' performance on standardized reading tests. Research has proven that children become more adept at reading by extensively practicing reading at or just below grade level. The library contains a wide range of material in print format that students can use to improve reading skills. And I can help match just the right book or magazine with just the right reader. If you need a book talk for your class or help with a student struggling to find something of interest, just say so.

10. The librarian will be your partner when trying new things. It's been said that some teachers during their career teach one year, thirty times. Can you imagine how long those thirty years must have seemed? If you need somebody to share the glory or the shame of a new unit, activity, or methodology, I'm the one.

I hope your next thirty years will be exciting and gratifying. You'll be influencing the lives of hundreds, if not thousands of kids in incredibly positive ways.

The subtitle of my professional standards document is *Building Partnerships for Learning*. I have truly taken that concept to heart. I am here to help you and your students do things you can't do alone.

Again, welcome,

Your library media specialist

SOURCE: Reprinted with permission of Doug Johnson. From *Library Media Connection*, "Head for the Edge," April/May 2003. Linworth Publishing.

Top Ten Things Teachers Should Know to Better Understand Student Network Behavior and the Web

1. **Life exists beyond the "free Web."**
Understand that students should be looking beyond the "free Web" for their materials, to full-text databases, and yes, books. Students (or anyone else) may generally prefer fewer clicks and fewer steps. But if we are to encourage habits of scholarship, we need to move students beyond what is merely convenient to search for the best. Very often this type of search will lead them to the many online subscription services (the premium channels!) that we pay for and make available under "Catalogs and Databases" on the library website. You may want to direct students to start at the Virtual Library because, in many cases, it will save them time.

2. **Expect quality; it is out there.** Force students to defend their sources, especially those from the "free Web." Simply ask them to explain how they got to the source and why they chose to cite it. The materials in our subscription services, to varying degrees, come prefiltered for quality. They have already gone through the publishing process and have been approved by a variety of editors and publishers. The free Web, on the other hand, though it has much of value to offer, is an unfiltered, self-publishing medium. Its sources require critical evaluation! Annotations are not asking too much when it comes to free Web sources.

3. **Analyze URLs on the free Web** when you evaluate a Works Cited page and when you work with students in the lab. *Sites created by free hosting services like Geocities, AOL Members, and Tripod should raise a red flag.* Sites including a "~" are generally created by an individual who may be part of a larger institution, organization, or service. These sites vary greatly in quality. If a site is an .edu, confirm whether it is maintained by a university department, professor, freshman, or middle school students. Dismiss most K–12 sites as nonscholarly, especially for high school use. Remember, anyone can buy any domain, with the exceptions of .mil and .gov. If a site is an .org, rather than a .com, it is not necessarily superior in content.

4. **Beware/aware of shifting windows.** When in a lab setting, recognize that students tend to open multiple windows with the intent of hiding some—fantasy sports, chat, games, etc. You can check to see if your students are on task by peeking at the bottom task bar to see which windows are currently open.

5. **Discourage personal downloads.** Our high-speed network makes it tempting for students to download music, video, games, and application files at school. When downloaded to student folders, these files take up excessive server space. They can slow the network down, compromising its limited bandwidth, especially during busy times of the day. Reserve downloads for academic use.

6. **Update your virus definitions weekly.** Protect your machine! Viruses are hidden in many types of files. They generally come from downloads and e-mail attachments. You may pick them up from an infected disk. See our network administrator if you need instructions.

7. **Check regularly for plagiarism** and let your students know that you do. The best preventative measure is to expect an environment valuing academic integrity and to design projects that require original thought and don't lend themselves to cutting and pasting. To check for plagiarism, you can paste short selections of more unique text, surrounding by quotation marks, into full-text

search engines like Alltheweb.com or Google. Your school might subscribe to a prevention service like turnitin.com.

There is no perfect answer or system. Many "invisible Web" sources and databases won't be caught by a search engine or check service. You will not catch all offenders, but if your students know how highly you value academic integrity, that you check for suspected plagiarism, and that you know where to check, they will likely be deterred. You can find additional strategies for battling plagiarism at VirtualSalt: Anti-Plagiarism Strategies for Research Papers (http://www.virtualsalt.com/antiplag.htm) and a rather long list of paper mills/cheat sites at http://www.coastal.edu/library/mills2.htm.

8. **Understand frames.** On a Web page, frames may *disguise* where you really are. Frames split your browser into two or more windows. They often load Web pages from another source into a window without revealing the source address. If you are in Google Image Search or Ask Jeeves, or other frame-based site, you will want to "remove frames" in order to see where your image or text is actually originating. Look for a "Remove Frames" button. Students should be aware of this issue too. We want our students to evaluate the "true source" of their sources. Still confused? See me for a demo.

9. **Log-off.** Do not leave your account logged on and walk away from your machine! This is like leaving your grade book open, or an upcoming exam in plain view on your desk.

10. **Have students log-off too.** Students should be concerned about security too! They should never "share" their passwords or leave their files or accounts open. Students are accountable for their passwords and for what is in their folders.

Feel free to contact me for more information,

Your teacher-librarian

A Letter to Parents

Ch-ch-ch-ch-changes . . .

As parents you may have noticed some changes in the type of research challenges we are presenting to students, and the expectations we have for their research products. And you've probably wondered, *what's going on?*

The big picture

Information has never been more available. Students must now evaluate information in ways never required of us when we were in school. The journal articles and books we spent hours finding were prefiltered for quality by editors and publishers and selected by librarians. Now the acts of locating and accessing information are turbo-charged and, because the Web is a self-publishing medium, the evaluation process is squarely in the hands of students. The Web affords students a great deal of independence, often removing adult consultation from the research process. Developmentally, students may be unaware of the "research holes" or the important sources missing from their projects. They may not distinguish sources of high quality from those of dubious value. Their facility with word processing and their ability to manipulate digital content may tempt them to produce cut and paste efforts, without the student's own original voice.

The response

We are in the midst of a whole-school/district initiative focused on student research, specifically linked to the national standards for information literacy, as well as standards for technology and content area learning, and directly concerned with enhancing student achievement.

As a faculty, we are teaching students to discern and use resources of high quality both online and off. We expect balance in student source lists. For some topics it makes sense to use the *free* Web exclusively. For most, it does not. I estimate that a whopping 90% of the books on our library shelves are not on the "free web." You'll notice I am careful to label the part of the Web that most students access through standard search engines as "the free web." Beyond this relatively small part of the Web, our students have access to a wealth of full-text books, journal and newspaper articles, documents, and broadcast transcripts through online subscription services that we promote when they visit with their classes and make available to them at home through passwords.

As a faculty, we also expect students to engage in thoughtful research based on inquiry. You are not likely to see your students engaged in *topical research. Topical* projects like the traditional country, the state, the planet, the president or the element report are not likely to be *ingested* into a student's system. Instead you are likely to see your students asked to develop essential questions—questions that do not have easy answers. Questions that inspire them to compare, analyze, debate, evaluate, judge, predict, construct, or propose a solution. (Instead of write a report about a disease, students will likely be asked to defend which major disease is most worthy of government research funding.) Often we will ask students to develop a thoughtful thesis—a clear, specific assertion relating to the assigned topic that the student will support with strong evidence. To succeed in this task, the student writer's voice must be heard through his or her careful analysis. Cut and paste efforts are unlikely to make the grade.

Research projects are not mere busy work. In addition to training students to be effective writers, the research process trains students for adult problem solving and decision making. It prepares students for the world of academics and the world of work and helps students prepare to answer such questions as:

Which car should I buy and how much should I pay?

Which candidate will best represent my interests?

How can I convince my boss to accept my proposal?

Whom should I believe?

So, what's a parent to do?

You can help us address our information literacy initiative by helping your student create quality research products and by encouraging your student to reflect on his or her work. For many children, the Web has increased their feelings of self-efficacy, practically removing adults from the research process. Above all,
you can help us by *intruding.*

Please:

- Ask your student if he or she has used subscription databases in his/her research. Make sure your student has a password list. (Because our state and our own school pay for these *premium channels,* it would be a waste for them to watch *basic cable* all day.) Students who rely on the free Web *only* ignore such wonderful databases as *EBSCOHost, GaleNet, AP Photo Archive, SIRS,* and *Facts.com,* with their high-quality book, magazine, newspaper, and reference article content. Most of these databases are available from our library web page. If you'd like to learn more about them, please give me a call!

- Ask to help as your student brainstorms potential research questions and thesis statements. If your student needs to develop a working thesis, can it pass five tests?

    1. Does it inspire a reasonable reader to ask, "How?" or "Why?" (It should!)

    2. Would a reasonable reader respond with "So what?" or "Who cares?" (He or she shouldn't!)

    3. Does it include general phrasing and sweeping words such as "all" or "none" or "every"? (It shouldn't!)

    4. Does it lead the reader toward the topic sentences (the subtopics needed to prove the thesis)? (It should!)

    5. Can the thesis be adequately developed in the required length of the paper or project? (It should!)

- Ask to check students' works cited and works consulted pages for balance and quality. Have they used the Web exclusively? Have they ignored books? Of the websites they have cited, how many appear to have been produced by universities, museums, and recognizable organizations? Do any of them have suspicious domain names, like Geocities or AOL Members? Good researchers search for credibility, authority, accuracy, and relevance. Good searchers are fussy!

- Look for "research holes." Quite simply, kids don't know what they don't know. Though the Web gives them great independence, they may not recognize the best words to use in a search and they may not recognize the best documents in a result list when they see them. However clever they are, in your travels as an adult, you are likely to know things your thirteen-year-old does not. Encourage your student to research with "peripheral vision," to be on the lookout for these related terms, names, and organizations. In a subscription database that means using the controlled language, or thesaurus, to find the appropriate subject headings. In a search engine, that means browsing through annotations for additional vocabulary or making use of features like "more like this" and "similar pages" when they appear near really good results. Suggest names or events or keywords worth searching that might not necessarily be in your student's realm of knowledge. If you suspect important content has been overlooked, it is likely the teacher will too.

- Is your student in a search engine rut? Is he or she relying on a certain "fictional butler" way too much? All search boxes are not the same. Students have a wide variety of search options: search engines; a growing number of *smarter* search engines (*Google, Vivismo, Wisenut, Teoma,* and many more); specialized search engines (like *Scirus,* for science); and subject directories like KidsClick! or Librarians' Index to the Internet—for the one-concept search or when they want to get to the good stuff quickly.

- Did your student document all non-original ideas—quoted, paraphrased or summarized? For further information on how to responsibly borrow the ideas of others, our online style sheet is available at: (insert your own link here).

- If you proofread your students' work, can you hear their own voices—their own original thoughts and analyses—among the quotes?

- And finally, does your student need to put the laptop down and get a lift to a library? It's not all on the Web. Don't allow your students to ignore the value of books and other print content. A two-page printout cannot compete with in-depth biography, scholarly nonfiction, or contemporaneous reporting of the history of the last few decades produced BDE (Before the Era of Digitization).

Sincerely,

Your Teacher-Librarian

The Principal's Manual

For YOUR

School Library Media Program

American Library Association
American Association of School Librarians
50 E. Huron St.
Chicago, IL 60611-2795

Read Before Operating:

✔ Student achievement is our bottom line.

✔ The school library media program puts your state and national learning standards into action.

✔ The school library media program supports and strengthens the curriculum.

✔ Reading for learning, reading for pleasure, reading is for life.

✔ The school library media program bridges the digital divide.

✔ The school library media program is an ongoing process. It is a program that develops and changes with your school improvement plan.

✔ The school library media program is the heart, the hub of your school learning community.

Non-Profit Org.
U.S. Postage
PAID
Permit No. 3226
Chicago

For Optimal Operation:

✔ Building and district administrative support

✔ Time structured to ensure that collaboration around instructional issues becomes an important part of the school day and school week

✔ Participation in curriculum planning

✔ Inservicing teachers in information access and delivery of information literacy instruction to students

✔ Flexibility in scheduling classes and opportunities to encourage reading and spontaneous research

✔ Involvement of parents and cooperation with the public library

Troubleshooting:

ACCESS THESE RESOURCES

Adcock, Donald C., ed. *A Planning Guide for Information Power: Building Partnerships for Learning.* Chicago: American Association of School Librarians, a division of the American Library Association, 1999. Complete with rubric, guides your library media program planning process. To order, call 800-545-2433, then press 7.

American Association of School Librarians Web site: http://www.ala.org/aasl. Be sure to check out the Learning Through the Library and Facts & Figures links.

American Association of School Librarians and Association for Educational Communications and Technology. *Information Power: Building Partnerships for Learning.* Chicago: American Library Association, 1998. THE guiding document for effective school library media programs. To order, call 800-545-2433, then press 7.

_____. *Information Literacy Standards for Student Learning.* Chicago: American Library Association, 1998. These standards can be applied to state and national learning standards. Covers general aspects of student learning as well as information literacy standards. To order, call 800-545-2433, then press 7.

Library Research Service (Denver, CO) Web site: http://www.lrs.org. This site includes recent research on the impact of school library media programs on student achievement using test scores.

National Study of School Evaluation. *Program Evaluation: Library Media Services.* Schaumburg, IL: National Study of School Evaluation, 1998. Excellent tool assessing your program AND guiding its progress. To order, call NSSE at 800-THE-NSSE (800-843-6773).

Seidel, Kent, Ph.D., ed. *Assessing Student Learning: A Practical Guide.* Cincinnati, OH: Alliance for Curriculum Reform, 2000. CD-ROM of best practices in subject area student assessment. To order, call ACR at 513-761-2271.

Your state department of education Web site. Check out the grants and other resources and services that are available to school library media programs.

From the office of the
American Association of
School Librarians (AASL)

TO: The Principal

FROM: American Association of
        School Librarians (AASL)

RE: The Principal's Manual

It is the season to look around, regroup, and plan ahead. What needs a fresh start? What needs repair? What needs just a little fine tuning?

The enclosed Principal's Manual is designed to guide you in assessing and planning for your school library media program. AASL offers this manual as an aid as you prepare with your school library media staff, district administrators, teachers, students, and parents for the next school year.

There are valuable tools that will assist you every step of the way. So take your manual in hand and enjoy the journey!

▶ Remove along perforation. ▶

Specifications:

STAFF

State-certified school library media specialist(s)

Clerical support

School learning community volunteers including parents, students, and community members

RESOURCES

Funding supportive of acquiring new print materials and subscribing to online sources

Collection development that includes withdrawing outdated materials from the library media collection

FACILITIES

An inviting space that encourages students to enter and enjoy learning

Hardware and software and the requisite space and electrical support

Planning for maintenance and for future expansion

How to order extra parts

Seek Grant Funding and Other Resources: Check out your state department of education Web site

Some Assembly Required:

STEP 1. Walk down to your library media center. Interact with the school library media specialist, the teachers, and the students. Have a seat, take a moment, think about what you see and hear and feel.

STEP 2. Take this Principal's Manual in hand when you meet with your library media specialist. Share the goal of developing a vision of your school library media program. Ponder these questions together:

- ✔ What is our mission?
- ✔ How can we work together as partners to achieve this mission?
- ✔ How can we encourage collaboration with teachers?
- ✔ How can the library media specialist become more involved with the curriculum?
- ✔ Think backwards – what information skills do we want our students to have when they leave our school?

STEP 3. Consider your library media center budget. Just for starters, bolster your non-fiction collection for all grades. Connect with other principals to receive the best online database prices. Does your library media center facility need attention? Do you have furniture to support your multimedia hardware?

STEP 4. Encourage your library media specialist to network with local school library media groups, your state library media organization, and the American Association of School Librarians. We need to share and learn from each other in this changing world of information and instructional technology. Your students and teachers will benefit from every workshop and conference attended by your school library media specialist.

Developed by Gail Bush for the
American Association of School Librarians,
a division of the American Library Association
50 E. Huron St., Chicago, IL 60611-2795
800-545-2433 ext. 4386 aasl@ala.org
Developed and distributed through a grant from the Bound to Stay Bound Books Foundation

Book Talk Tips

Book talks are commercials for books. They are one of our best vehicles for pitching our wares. They can take forms as countless as those ubiquitous and highly effective television spots. And they can be great outlets for our professional creativity.

Don't slack! Try not to talk books you haven't read or haven't read in many years. Kids can easily uncover *blurb slackers!*

Grab 'em and don't let go! Engage them right away with a compelling opening. Close strong too!

Mix it up! Include a little something for everyone. Mix fat and skinny books. Mix a fair combination of *boy* and *girl* interests. Include a couple of nonfiction titles in a predominantly fiction talk. Throw in a classic, though you may want to avoid labeling it as such. Mix up your talking strategy too. Use a variety of techniques—demonstration, quotes, dramatization, etc. Interesting pacing works well for this type of presentation. Some talks may be more detailed than others. Two sentences may be all you need to sell some titles.

Theme it! Though there are occasions you'll want to talk books of one genre exclusively, think broad themes. Vary your themes and groupings of books. Interpret ideas and concepts in your talks— challenges, friendship, particular moods, types of characters, plots, and settings across genre.

Organize! Keep outlines of your talks on large index cards. Though you want to talk directly rather than read to the students, you'll often need a cheat sheet. You can clip the cards on the back of book to remind you of characters' names and details and page numbers. Keep these cards on file. They can be shuffled later for inclusion in a variety of other talks.

Be loose! Students love to interact. Be prepared to leave your *script* and ad-lib and accept input.

Prepare! Be able to speak from memory. You want to convey your enthusiasm with your eyes, facial expression, and body language. Consider visiting a class in advance of your talk and asking students about personal favorites.

Gauge your effect! Watch their body language. If you or your audience is bored, drop the offending book and move on to the next title. After the talk, rethink and refine your approach to that book.

Create a handout! Avoid the confusion of "which one was the one . . .?" Bring a list of the books—authors and titles—you will be talking with brief identifying notes.

Multiply! Attempt to gather multiple copies of the books you plan to talk, either by buying or borrowing from other schools in your district. Consider bringing reserve sign-up sheets for each book to create fair waiting lists. All book copies are limited when you do a successful talk. Be prepared to note "if you liked" titles, other books in a series, and other titles by the same author. When you are book talking several classes in one day, you'll want to include a variety of selections, or by the end of the day, you can expect a lot of frustrated kids.

Dramatize! If it suits the book (and your personality) get into character. Invent dialogue. Talk in the voice of a character and tell a little bit of your story or describe an exciting incident. Bring the audience in to the experience of a character. "Imagine you are home alone . . . " If it works for you, grab a puppet.

Prop it up! Items related to a book inspire curiosity and create a visual or audio focus for your talk. A Vermeer print might be just right to show for *Girl with a Pearl Earring*. Other books might cry out for a bell or a candy bar. Occasionally you might run a muted video clip behind you with a piece of historical footage.

Quote! Don't go overboard in length, but a gripping passage or fascinating bit of dialogue can go a long way to sell a book. Avoid reading for more than a minute.

Tease! Pique their interest, but don't tell too much. Never reveal an ending. End each talk with a clincher. Leave 'em wanting more.

Be creative! Have fun talking the books you love. Experiment with a variety of approaches.

Read professionally! Learn from the experts. Get books by Joni Bodart, Caroline Feller Bauer, Hazel Rochman, and Patrick Jones. Visit the websites of Nancy Keane (http://nancykeane.com/booktalks/) and Jennifer Hubert (http://tln.lib.mi.us/~amutch/jen/index.html) for ideas and tips or Teen Reads (http://www.teenreads.com).

Starting a Student Book Club

Why start a book club?

Everyone is joining a book club. In living rooms, schools, libraries, bookstores, restaurants, even in front of their computers, folks of all ages who crave a bit of intellectual stimulation, and some quiet pleasures, are discussing books and developing a shared reading history. Many of our students are craving this same opportunity. And what better activity for a teacher-librarian to sponsor than a book club!

Among the most rewarding features of a book club is the closeness that its members develop. Club members often share deep personal experiences. These contributions contribute to group cohesiveness and support. Book club members feel pride in their independent learning and shared reading histories. They enjoy the unique opportunity in their young lives to get together with others who share their passion for reading.

How do you start?

As with any other school club, put your posters out when school starts. Spread the word among your most likely suspects, including your most voracious readers and those kids not affiliated with lots of other clubs. If you can find two great leader-type kids, plant the idea with them and let them begin to create their own buzz among their friends. Spread the word among parents at PTA meetings and through your informal contacts. Use the language arts department to help you select students who might most enjoy this activity. Don't aim for one "type" of kid. Readers come in all shapes and sizes. (In one school club, a concentration of my membership came from the wrestling team.)

Hold meetings at regular times. Busy students tend to like to plan their lives around predicable patterns. Investigate student schedules as you plan. If many of

the members of your club are also in band, you'll want to avoid band rehearsal days and times.

Hold a brief organizational meeting to have members get to know each other and you as club sponsor. Use a short reading for the first discussion meeting. Poems and short stories work well. You'll need time during that first meeting to conduct organizational tasks.

Maintain a bulletin board announcing meetings and posting reviews and covers of upcoming readings. Devote space on the library website to Book Club News and Reviews. Consider delegating bulletin board and Web page responsibilities to reliable students.

Bigger is not necessarily better for this club. Don't aim for a huge membership. While the ideal size for a book club varies, with clubs of more than ten or twelve members it can be difficult to ensure that everyone gets an opportunity to contribute.

Order the books well in advance of the meeting. Some titles may be difficult for your local bookstore to obtain in bulk on short notice.

Seek help: Perhaps another teacher, perhaps a very special parent friend? Two alternate club sponsors can help ensure the conversation is lively by contributing questions when student questions run dry and provide a break when the stress of various school year events compete with readings.

Mix it up! Not everyone loves mystery or science fiction. Some readers crave nonfiction. A school book club is likely to include a mix of grades, genders, and interests. Make sure it's clear that every book is not going to be universally loved. Remind students that it is both mind-expanding and good for the soul to be exposed to books they would not ordinarily pick up, books outside their areas of interest and comfort. Brace yourself! At each meeting, someone is likely to express extreme disappointment. Avoid making it the same member each time. Remind students that there are both *good* reads and *powerful* reads. Book clubs are not necessarily about pleasure reading, although members may very often enjoy the readings. Mix it up by sometimes including videos, short story or poetry readings, or even reading a particularly powerful document. Mix lighter and more challenging readings. Mix classics with hot new stuff. You might even consider having the club meet you at a movie theater if an appropriate film premieres and it is truly ripe for discussion.

About leading: You or your club will have to determine the leadership style of the group. You will need someone to lead each meeting. Will the adult sponsors take the responsibility? Will you have upperclassmen or the whole group take responsibility for leadership in turns? In a school book club, club officers may take turns leading or make leadership decisions.

Leadership responsibilities might include gently reminding members to let others speak and encouraging more shy contributors. In a school book club, you may have to work to get the voices of younger students heard. You will need to turn the subject back to the book in case discussion gets uncomfortably or inappropriately personal. Even if a student is chosen to lead the discussion, have around ten open-ended questions prepared just in case your leader runs out of steam!

There are no stupid questions. There are no right or wrong answers. Every club member brings something different and valuable to the table and can enrich our understanding of the reading. Even if you have a list of wonderful questions, the best discussions are often spontaneous. Allow for free flow if the students take off in an exciting direction you hadn't planned, as long as it is in some way relevant. Avoid teaching. This is a club; don't impose curriculum.

Decide on meeting logistics

Options for meeting times might include lunch breaks, after school, or evenings (our facility is open Wednesday nights). Consider how much time you will schedule between meetings. If you are reading books of weight, meeting every month or every six weeks is reasonable. For middle school groups with shorter readings, perhaps every two or three weeks might work. Be sensitive to student stress periods. You may want to skip meetings around midterms, finals, or major project deadlines (like History Day, Science Fair or Senior Thesis). Be sensitive to holidays.

Middle and high school students need sustenance when they discuss literature! If you decide food is an essential, will you share the snack responsibilities? The library seems like the perfect space. If you have a private classroom, it might make the snack issue more workable. Of course, you'll want to arrange chairs in a circle or around tables to promote discussion.

Selecting the readings

Not every *New York Times* best seller works well for a high school or middle school book club.

Caution: One of the adults involved should read each selection in advance to ensure that it is appropriate for the grade or maturity level of the group. Selecting books from award-winning lists for children and young adults provides some guidance, but only you can assess the reading tastes and sensibilities of your own group. Decide on a title selection policy. Students will want input and will question fairness if their suggestions are never acknowledged.

You might try to search the Web for similar groups that have posted reading lists. Solicit old favorites from among group members.

Pick at least two or three books in advance, whether they're chosen by the adult sponsor or consensus of the group. Nothing is more frustrating than spending huge quantities of club meeting time arguing over book choices. You want to spend your limited time talking books!

Use your suggestions to create survey forms and voting lists and tally the lists outside of meeting time. Try to negotiate more than one reading when you make these selections. (For reading suggestions and guides, see the Web resources below!) When you suggest readings, seek and bring copies of reviews to help sell the titles. Bring a copy of the book to pass around. Unless your group is fairly homogeneous (for instance, a middle school mother-daughter club), attempt to select books that meet the diverse interests of your group and that will not totally frustrate your younger or weaker readers.

The outside world and school culture may inspire reading choice. One year our students wanted desperately to visit the Holocaust Memorial Museum in Washington, D.C. I agreed that our club could plan and sponsor the trip if our focus for the year was Holocaust literature. If world events focus student attention on a particular area of our troubled world, consider an engaging memoir, biography, or historical fiction title.

Acquiring and funding the books: It may be difficult to fund all the readings for all students. In some clubs students may buy their own books. Try to find titles that are available in paperback. Contact the local bookstore and see if you can get an educators' discount or if they will make special arrangements for book club leaders. Contact the PTA to see if grant money is available. You may not need to totally fund the books. We use funding for half the cost of books and charge students a fairly modest five dollars. Consider pairing your club with another local club and try swapping sets of books for readings that might interest both clubs.

What is a good book for discussion?

You'll want to select books that are in some way "mind-expanding." Good books have complex characters challenged by choices and situations. Good book choices inspire students to uncover universal truths and explore the personal relevance of these truths. Good books have interesting messages and employ elegant use of language. Avoid escape or formulaic titles, which rely on plot alone and offer no ambiguity. Ambiguity makes for fabulous discussion! Be prepared. When a member of the group recommends a bland or formulaic title, you'll have a bit of tap dancing to do in explaining why it might not be the best choice.

Consider scheduling readings that will make interesting comparisons, for instance, various retellings of fairy tales, books that involve an epic quest, or books on the Middle East. For instance, one year we discussed both Donna Jo Napoli's *Beast* (a retelling of *Beauty and the Beast*) and Gregory Maguire's *Confessions of an Ugly Stepsister* (a retelling of *Cinderella*). Another year we selected several titles with civil rights themes.

What are the responsibilities of a good book club member?

- Read the reading! Nothing is more frustrating to those who actually read the book than attending a meeting full of book slackers and posers. Sure, there will be an occasional meeting when you may not have finished the book, but you owe it to your fellow club members to come prepared to talk. Book Club is a commitment, not just an opportunity to socialize.

- Mark interesting, confusing, or impressive sections. Mark heavily! Use sticky notes if you cannot mark up the book!

- Write questions as you read and as you reflect on what you've read. Some clubs require that every member come with at least one good question at every meeting.

- Look at interesting dialogue. Questions like "What does Jim mean when he says . . .?" often fuel discussion.

- You are not allowed to say, "I hated this book!" without explanation. You may say, "I wish the author had better developed the protagonist! I just couldn't feel any sympathy for her." Be open. It is very possible to have a great discussion around a book you didn't particularly like.

- As you read, compare the reading to other books, poems, or plays you have already read.

- Listen and respond thoughtfully to the comments of other club members. Begin your comments with words like "I agree with what Sally just said! You know there's more evidence pointing to this on page 13, when the character says . . ."

- Avoid dominating the discussion.

- Be prepared to read interesting, elegant, or confusing passages aloud.

- If you are a veteran member, try to encourage new members to express themselves.

- Remember, you have something to contribute even if you don't fully understand the work. You have something to say even if you are shy!

- While personal response may add significantly to the discussion, aim for a balance in your comments with direct reference to the reading.

- Have fun!

General questions for any book discussion

- What most impressed you about this reading? Describe your reading experience.

- How does your own life experience contribute to your understanding of this reading?

- Were there parts of the work, particular paragraphs you found confusing?

- What theme or themes does this work ask us to examine?

- What do you believe is the author's message?
- What questions do you think the author expects us to ask? What questions is the author asking him/herself?
- What voice did the author choose for this work? (First person, omniscient narrator, alternating perspectives, etc.) How many narrators are there? Why did the author choose this particular voice or voices? Can we trust the voice?
- How did the language, choice of words, and sentence structure contribute to the reading?
- Why did the author choose the title? Does the title add to our understanding of the work? Were chapter titles meaningful?
- How and why did the author structure the work as he or she did? Did the sequencing make sense? Did he or she use flashbacks or other sequencing devices? How did these devices affect your understanding of the plot, theme, character, or mood?
- What did you think of the characters? Did you empathize with (care about) them? Why or why not? Why did they behave as they did? If you could put yourself in their places, would you respond similarly or differently? How did you feel about the choices they made? What are their flaws and strengths? Do the characters grow through the course of the work?
- Does the dialogue ring true? Why or why not?
- How important is setting, time, or place in this work?
- Were there parts of this reading where you appreciated unusual or elegant use of language?
- Did the author use quotes before a chapter or are they integrated in the work? Do these quotes enhance your understanding or appreciation of the work?
- Is there a clear plot and subplot? Does the subplot contribute to your understanding of the reading?
- How does this book fit into the literary genres or movements you know of?
- Was the story credible?
- What do you feel were the flaws of this reading?
- What kind of imagery does the author use? Does he or she use particular symbols or extended metaphors? Do these strategies enhance your appreciation or understanding?
- Are any broader social issues being discussed than what appears on the surface of the plot? Does the author make his or her points effectively?
- How does this reading compare with our other readings or works you have read on your own? Is it similar to books by the same author, set in the same time or place, with similar characters and themes, or in the same genre? If you have seen a film adaptation of this book, how did it compare?
- Are there any "what if" questions that strike you? For instance, what happens to these characters after the last page?
- Were you satisfied with the resolution?

Preparing to lead

As a teacher-librarian, you have perhaps more tools than any other type of discussion leader. Research the author in Wilson's *Current Biography* or in *Wilson Biographies* or Gale's *Contemporary Authors,* off- or online. Look for criticism in GaleNet's *Literature Resource Center* or any of Gale's book series of criticism. The For Students series, *Novels for Students, Poetry for Students, Short Stories for Students, Drama for Students,* offer great context and provide excellent choices for readings. For newer works, seek book reviews on Amazon.com and any of your journal and newspaper databases. Book club reading guides abound on the Web. Seek them out as you plan your own questions.

Book Club Resources and Reading Guides

ALA Best Books for Young Adults
http://www.ala.org/yalsa/booklists/bbya

American Library Association for Parents, Teens, and Kids (click on appropriate book award)
http://www.ala.org/parents/index.html

Alex Awards (Young Adult)
http://www.ala.org/yalsa/booklists/alex

Amazon.com Reading Groups
http://www.amazon.com (search for Reading Groups)

Barnes & Noble BookBrowser: The Guide for Avid Readers
http://www.bookbrowser.com/

Book Group List
http://www.iland.net/~awahl/

BookMuse (Powell's)
http://www.bookmuse.com

BookSpot
http://www.bookspot.com

HarperCollins Reading Group Guides
http://www.harpercollins.com/hc/readers/index.asp

HarperCollins Teaching Guides
http://www.harperchildrens.com/hch/parents/
teachingguides/

Houghton Mifflin Readers Guides
http://www.houghtonmifflinbooks.com/readers
_guides/

KidsReads
http://www.kidsreads.com

Morton Grove Public Library Thinking Out Loud Book
Club Guides
http://www.webrary.org/rs/TOL.html

Multnomah Talk It Up!
http://www.multcolib.org/talk/index.html

Penguin Putnam Great Books Guides (Click on
"Discussion Guides")
http://www.penguinputnam.com

Random House Reading Group Guides
http://www.randomhouse.com/reader
_resources/browsetitle/

Reading Group Choices
http://www.readinggroupchoices.com

Reading Group Guides
http://www.readinggroupguides.com

Scholastic Discussion Guides
http://teacher.scholastic.com/authorsandbooks/
discguide/index.htm

SimonSays (Click on "Reading Guides")
http://www.simonsays.com

Teen Reads
http://www.teenreads.com

Vintage Reading Group Guides
http://www.randomhouse.com/vintage/read/
list.html

The Authors' Wish List

(Compiled by The POD, an on-line group of children's writers)

SCHEDULING

- Contact the author to confirm the author visit!

- Never ask the author to do additional sessions after details of the visit have been agreed upon.

- If the author has 15 minutes between sessions, do not let students use that time to get their books signed. The author needs those 15 minutes to catch his or her breath, race to the restroom, get a drink, and sit down for a minute. Speaking to large groups of kids demands high energy, and the author can't do it nonstop without a break.

- If you expect an author to do extra things, such as "read something to the entire student body" or "tell us how reading has changed your life," tell her or him before the visit so that she or he can be prepared.

PREPARING THE STUDENTS

- Students must be familiar with the author's books. If possible, prepare students by reading all of the author's work with or to them. Otherwise, select several books to share, beginning well in advance of the visit.

- The best school visits occur when preparations infuse the curriculum.

- Read *Terrific Connections with Authors, Illustrators, and Storytellers* and "The Finely Tuned Author Visit." *See references.

PHYSICAL ARRANGEMENTS

- Prepare to introduce the author in a fun and lively way. The librarian or teacher who does this job is basically the warm-up band to get the kids fired up.

- If the author is speaking in a large room, such as an auditorium or gym, you must provide a microphone for the students' questions. It's impossible to hear students unless they are in the first few rows. (An alternative to a student microphone is to provide the author with a lapel mike and room to move to the person who is speaking.)

- If possible, have the students wear name tags. It is a tremendous help to the author both during the presentation and while signing.

- Do not leave students alone with the visiting author. Authors are not hired to be babysitters. Likewise, if a teacher or librarian sees students disrupting, he or she should not be afraid to interrupt the session to remedy the situation. It is not the author's job to teach manners.

CREATURE COMFORTS

- Provide someone, either an adult or an older student, to act as the author's host for the day. The host should greet the author, make introductions to teachers and staff, and guide the author from place to place.

- Provide ongoing hot tea with lemon or cold water for the author's voice.

- Make time for a midmorning snack.

- Allow enough time to get from one class to the next and for bathroom breaks.

- Plan for a real lunch rather than cafeteria food.

- Don't plan evening activities that run late if the author is visiting your schools for a week. The author needs the evening to rest and regroup for the next day.

BOOK SALES AND SIGNINGS

- Do not assume that an author will bring books to sell at a school visit. Many authors do not sell their own books and feel very uncomfortable being put into the position of doing so. Check with the author in advance.

- If the author does not sell her or his own books, order books on the day the author confirms. You can never order books too early. The biggest mistake schools make is waiting too long to order.

- Double-check with booksellers or jobbers providing books to be sure that all titles are available.

- Provide a reasonably comfortable adult-size chair and table for the signing.

- Do not allow students to ask the author to sign slips of paper or body parts. Most authors will provide signed bookmarks or provide a master sheet so the school can make them. That way, each child can take home something signed by the author whether or not they buy a book.

- If it's a young authors conference and the students have written their own books, let them know that the author cannot sign hundreds of their books as well as her or his own.

- Schedule an hour or more during which the author is in the library without a group. During this time, each class in turn can send students with books to sign. This gives the students the opportunity to visit with the author while their book is being signed, and it solves the problem of too many restless kids waiting for their turn.

- Provide an adult to help at the signing table. It's hard for the author to keep an eye on all the visual aids brought while the kids are picking them up and looking at them unattended.

- There will always be students who want to buy books after the author's visit. Most authors will leave a few signed bookplates for that purpose, so make sure books are still available for sale after the event.

PAYMENT

- Pay the author's stated fee and do not try to negotiate a lesser fee.

- Author visits are exhausting and the fee is well earned.

- If you need the author's Social Security number or an invoice before a school-district-issued check can be processed, tell the author in advance so that the check can be ready the day of the visit.

- Don't make the author ask to be paid. This is awkward. Know that the author expects to be paid at the end of the day. There is nothing worse for the author than having to say, "Um, well, do you have my check?"

ACCOMMODATIONS AND TRANSPORTATION

It is generally not a good idea to ask an author to stay in a private home. Many authors find it impossible to relax in someone else's home. They often feel they must be entertaining when they'd really rather not talk to anyone after talking all day. However, it is appropriate to verify that this is the author's preference.

If you have arranged for someone to pick up the author, be sure the driver arrives on time. The author will need time to catch his or her breath and set up materials before beginning presentations for the day.

Provide someone to transport the author, when necessary, between morning and afternoon schools so that s/he arrives on time.

References

Buzzeo, Toni. "The Finely Tuned Author Visit." *Book Links* 7 (March 1998): 10;15.

SOURCES: Buzzeo, Toni, and Jane Kurtz. *Terrific Connections with Authors, Illustrators, and Storytellers.* Libraries Unlimited, 1999. Reproduced with permission of Greenwood Publishing Group, Inc., Westport, CT.

Current Awareness Service

Yes, I'd like to participate in the library's current awareness service. Please send the table of contents of my favorite journal(s) to me on a regular basis. Later, I can request copies of articles that look interesting by circling them and returning the table of contents page(s) to the library.

Please send the contents page(s) for the following journals:

Teacher's Name _____

Please return this form to the library information center.

- -

Current Awareness Service

Yes, I'd like to participate in the library's current awareness service. Please send the table of contents of my favorite journal(s) to me on a regular basis. Later, I can request copies of articles that look interesting by circling them and returning the table of contents page(s) to the library.

Please send the contents page(s) for the following journals:

Teacher's Name _____

Please return this form to the library information center.

Thought You'd Like
to Know . . .

FYI!! FYI!!

TO:

FROM: The Library Information Center

DATE:

We thought you'd like to know the following new

☐ print resource   ☐ software   ☐ media item(s)   ☐ subscription database has arrived!!!

Please stop by and take a look!

Thought You'd Like
to Know . . .

FYI!! FYI!!

TO:

FROM: The Library Information Center

DATE:

We thought you'd like to know the following new

☐ print resource   ☐ software   ☐ media item(s)   ☐ subscription database has arrived!!!

Please stop by and take a look!

How Can We Help?

?!??? ??????

Please complete the following form and return it to the library information center.

Teacher _____ Date _____

Course Title _____ Semester _____

Grade/Level _____

We'd like to make it easier for you to teach your course. We can provide bibliographies and students pathfinders to guide your students. We can help brainstorm ideas for projects and help you teach and assess them. We can also keep you filled in when new materials arrive. Please let us know which areas you are planning to cover in your course, especially if you've changed your plans since previous semesters!

Please list any specific materials you would like to see purchased for this course.

If any of your units will involve student library work, please let us know if you'd like us to

___ place materials on reserve or one special limited loan
     Please specify:

___ address, reinforce, and/or develop instruction around particular information literacy skills
     Please specify:

___ prepare formal bibliographies and/or book talks
     Relating to:

___ bookmark relevant Web sites or create a Web page to guide students to quality online resources
     Relating to:

___ create a pathfinder identifying the best research strategies and the best resources in all formats
     for this project
     Please specify:

Please stop by and we'll set up a time to further plan resources, instruction, and assessment!

Join Us in Improving Our Library!

The School Library Committee ensures that your library information center best meets our students' needs and that our current program continues to grow and thrive. Please consider joining. The committee will meet on a monthly or as-needed basis.

Responsibilities of the Library Information Center Planning Committee

1. Work with the teacher-librarian to establish immediate and long-range goals and priorities for the library information center program.

2. Recommend additional resources—technologies, print and media resources.

3. Recommend additional services and activities and procedures to ensure accessibility to the broad learning community.

4. Offer input on library information center policies and procedures for staff and students and suggest revision.

5. Serve as a support group or liaison for the library information center in the community (for example, at board meetings).

6. Volunteer to help organize school-wide projects promoting reading, information skills, and technology integration—for example, read-ins, literacy nights, and family technology nights.

7. Support and advise others regarding library-related policies—intellectual freedom, materials selection, copyright, academic integrity/plagiarism.

8. Participate in policy reconsideration and revision.

9. Advocate for support of the library information center program and its users—for example, by providing insight into the effects of budget cuts on learners or by presenting information on parent nights.

10. Participate in regularly evaluating the library information center program and planning new services and activities.

11. Assist in identifying and addressing needs.

12. Plan media- or technology-related staff development activities.

Please consider joining us and serving learners in your school by helping to build a stronger library information center.

- -

Please return this form to the library.

Yes, I am interested in joining the _____ School Library Information Center Committee.

Teacher/Administrator/Student/Parent Name_____ Date _____

Dear Language Arts Teacher,

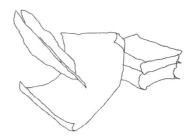

I look forward to meeting your classes this year!

    I wanted to share with you some general resources that you may not be aware are available in our library. You may want to add your own favorite web sites to these lists. Please stop in and we'll discuss your program. Together we'll plan resource-based, inquiry-driven units connecting information skills to your content-area goals. Feel free to stop in for a tour or demonstration of any of our online and electronic products.

Let me know how I can help,

Your teacher-librarian

PRINT REFERENCES

Library of Literary Criticism of English and American Authors

Contemporary Literary Criticism, Twentieth-Century Literary Criticism, Nineteenth Century Literary Criticism

Magill's Survey of World Literature and Survey of American Literature

World Literature Criticism

Beacham's Encyclopedia of Popular Fiction

American Writers

Novels for Students, Poetry for Students, Drama for Students

Library of Literary Criticism of English and American Authors

Look for volumes of the *Understanding Series,* which deals with specific major titles, around the reference area in the numbers 810, 812, 813

Literary Lifelines

Major 20th Century Writers: A Selection of Sketches from Contemporary Authors

American Writers

Modern American Women Writers

Contemporary Authors

Twentieth Century Authors

Encyclopedia of World Biography

Note: An index to the Gale series of reference books is available on the Web at http://www.galenet.com/servlet/LitIndex.

SUBSCRIPTION DATABASES

GaleNet's *Literature Resource Center, Biography Resource Center, Contemporary Authors,* and *Scribner's Writers Series*

Wilson Biographies

Literature Online

Roth's Lit Finder

ONLINE RESOURCES

Journals

KAIROS: Journal of Rhetoric, Technology and Pedagogy http://english.ttu.edu/kairos

NCTE Journals http://www.ncte.org/pubs/journals

General Education Gateways

About.com Elementary Educators http://k-6educators.about.com

About.com Secondary http://7-12educators.about.com

Blue Web'n http://www.kn.pacbell.com/wired/bluewebn

Discovery School Lesson Plan Library http://school.discovery.com/lessonplans

edHelper.com (lessons, webquests, worksheets) http://www.edhelper.com

Education World Teacher Resources http://www.educationworld.com

FREE: Federal Resources for Educational Excellence http://www.ed.gov/free

GEM The Gateway http://thegateway.org

Kathy Schrock's Guide for Educators http://discoveryschool.com/schrockguide

Marco Polo http://www.marcopolo-education.org

National Geographic Education http://www.nationalgeographic.com/education

New York Times Teacher Connections http://www.nytimes.com/learning/teachers/index.html

PBS TeacherSource http://www.pbs.org/teachersource

SearchERIC.org http://www.searcheric.org

Tom March's BestWebQuests.com http://bestwebquests.com

WebQuests http://webquest.sdsu.edu

Outstanding Gateways for Language Arts

ERIC Language Arts Resources http://www.eduref.org/cgi-bin/res.cgi/Subjects/Language_Arts

Language Arts: FREE (Federal Resources for Education) http://www.ed.gov/free/s-lanart.html

NCTE http://www.ncte.org

Online Poetry Classroom http://www.onlinepoetryclassroom.org

ReadWriteThink http://www.readwritethink.org

Web English Teacher http://www.webenglishteacher.com

Professional Organizations

National Council of Teachers of English http://www.ncte.org/homepage

International Reading Association http://www.ira.org

Center on English Learning & Achievement (CELA) http://cela.albany.edu

Standards

Standards for the English Language Arts (NCTE/IRA) http://www.ncte.org/about/over/standards

English Language Arts Standards (ISTE-NETS) http://cnets.iste.org/currstands/cstands-ela.html

Standards for English Language Arts (IRA and NCTE)
http://www.reading.org/advocacy/elastandards/index.html

Developing Educational Standards (for both state and national standards)
http://edstandards.org/StSu/ELA.html

McREL's Standards Database http://www.mcrel.org/standards-benchmarks

Nine Information Literacy Standards for Student Learning http://www.ala.org/aasl/ip_nine.html

Outstanding Language Arts Websites

Carol Hurst's Children's Literature Site http://www.carolhurst.com

Children's Literature Web Guide http://www.ucalgary.ca/~dkbrown

Database of Award-Winning Children's Literature http://www.dawcl.com

EDSITEment http://edsitement.neh.gov

Grammar Bytes http://www.chompchomp.com/menu.htm

Guide to Grammar and Writing http://ccc.commnet.edu/grammar

Instructional Materials in Writing http://www.cln.org/subjects/writing_inst.html

Internet Public Library: A+ Guide to Research and Writing http://www.ipl.org/teen/aplus

Literature Circles http://www.literaturecircles.com/index2.htm

Literature Circles Resource Center http://fac-staff.seattleu.edu/kschlnoe/LitCircles

Michigan Teacher Network: English/Language Arts Education http://mtn.merit.edu/english.html

Paradigm Online Writing Assistant http://www.powa.org

Purdue OWL: Handouts http://owl.english.purdue.edu/handouts

Purdue OWL: The Writing Process http://owl.english.purdue.edu/handouts/general/index.html

Gale Free Resources (Literary Index, Glossary of Literary Terms, How to Write a Term Paper)
    http://www.gale.com/free_resources/index.htm

American Library Association Book Awards (Click on Awards and Scholarships Book/Media Awards)
    http:///www.ala.org

Read Write Think http://www.readwritethink.org

S.C.O.R.E. Cyberguides http://www.sdcoe.k12.ca.us/SCORE/cyberguide.html

S.C.O.R.E. Language Arts http://www.sdcoe.k12.ca.us/SCORE/cla.html

Newbery Medal Home Page http://www.ala.org/alsc/newbery.html

On-Line Books Page http://onlinebook.library.upenn.edu

On-Line English Grammar http://www.edunet.com/english/grammar/index.html

Resources for American Literature http://www.cwrl.utexas.edu/~daniel/amlit/index.html

Traci's Lists of Ten http://www.tengrrl.com/tens

Web English Teacher http://www.webenglishteacher.com

VIDEOS

American Short Story Collection

Voices and Visions Series

And many video adaptations of great literary works

Dear Social Studies Teacher,

I look forward to meeting your classes this year!

   I wanted to share with you some general resources that you may not be aware are available in our library. You may want to add your own favorite web sites to these lists. Please stop in and we'll discuss your program. Together we'll plan resource-based, inquiry-driven units connecting information skills to your content-area goals. Feel free to stop in for a tour or demonstration of any of our online and electronic products.

                         Let me know how I can help,

                         Your teacher-librarian

PRINT REFERENCES

Books

   Land and Peoples

   Encyclopedia of Bioethics

   Pro Con Series

   Information Aids Series

   Encyclopedia of Social Issues

   Taking Sides Library

   Grolier Pro/Con

   Encyclopedia of Bioethics

   Bioethics for Students

   Notebooks behind the Desk: Issues and Controversies on File, CQ Researcher

Journals

   Current History

   Scholastic Update

   National Geographic

   Newsweek

   Time

   U.S. News and World Report

ONLINE RESOURCES

Journal

   World & I http://www.worldandi.com

Subscription Databases

   Gale's Student Resource Center Gold

   SIRS Researcher and Government Reporter

EBSCOhost

Opposing Viewpoints Resource Center

Issues and Controversies

CQ Researcher

Facts.com

ABC-CLIO History and Geography Databases

Standards

Social Studies Standards http://www.socialstudies.org/standards

National Standards for History http://www.sscnet.ucla.edu/nchs/standards

Eighteen National Geography Standards http://www.ncge.org/publications/tutorial/standards

Developing Educational Standards (for both state and national standards)
   http://edstandards.org/Standards.html

McREL's Standards Database http://www.mcrel.org/standards-benchmarks

Nine Information Literacy Standards for Student Learning http://www.ala.org/aasl/ip_nine.html

Professional Organizations

National Council for Geographic Education http://www.ncge.org

National Council for the Social Studies http://ncss.org

National Center for History in the Schools http://www.sscnet.ucla.edu/nchs

Education Gateways

Blue Web'n http://www.kn.pacbell.com/wired/bluewebn

GEM The Gateway http://thegateway.org

New York Times Teacher Connections http://www.nytimes.com/learning/teachers/index.html

About.com Secondary http://7-12educators.about.com

About.com Elementary Educators http://k-6educators.about.com

Education World Teacher Resources http://www.educationworld.com

Discovery School Lesson Plan Library http://school.discovery.com/lessonplans

edHelper.com (lessons, webquests, worksheets) http://www.edhelper.com

FREE: Federal Resources for Educational Excellence http://www.ed.gov/free

Kathy Schrock's Guide for Educators http://discoveryschool.com/schrockguide

Marco Polo http://www.marcopolo-education.org

National Geographic Education http://www.nationalgeographic.com/education

PBS TeacherSource http://www.pbs.org/teachersource

SearchERIC.org http://www.searcheric.org

Tom March's BestWebQuests.com http://bestwebquests.com

WebQuests http://webquest.sdsu.edu

Outstanding Social Studies Web Sites to Investigate

About.com Geography http://geography.about.com

ERIC Social Studies Resources http://www.eduref.org/cgi-bin/res.cgi/Subjects/Social_Studies

EconEdLink http://www.econedlink.org

EDSITEment http://edsitement.neh.gov

EuroDocs http://www.lib.byu.edu/~rdh/eurodocs/homepage.html

Historical Atlas of the 20th Century http://users.erols.com/mwhite28/20centry.htm

History and Politics Out Loud http://www.hpol.org

History Channel http://www.historychannel.com

History Place.com http://www.historyplace.com

Learning Page: Library of Congress American Memory http://lcweb2.loc.gov:8081/ammem/ndlpedu/index.html

NARA Digital Classroom http://www.archives.gov/digital_classroom/index.html

National Geographic Xpeditions http://www.nationalgeographic.com/xpeditions

National Geographic Education http://www.nationalgeographic.com/education

Our Documents http://www.ourdocuments.gov

Oyez: A Supreme Court WWW Resource http://oyez.at.nwu.edu/oyez.html

Primary Source Pathfinder http://mciu.org/~spjvweb/primary.html

Professional Cartoonist (Editorial Cartoons with lesson plans) http://www.cagle.com/teacher

Social Issues Pathfinder http://mciu.org/~spjvweb/issuespath.html

Social Studies School Service Online Activities
http://socialstudies.com/c/@9crDOmMTkGTpA/Pages/activities.html

Teach with Movies: A New Tool for Parents and Teachers http://teachwithmovies.org

Teaching History Online (lots of simulations) http://www.spartacus.schoolnet.co.uk/history.htm

Teaching with Documents http://www.edteck.com/dbq

SPECIAL AREAS

Maps

American Memory Maps Collections http://memory.loc.gov/ammem/gmdhtml/gmdhome.html

Color Landform Atlas of the United States http://fermi.jhuapl.edu/states/states.html

Historical Atlas of the Twentieth Century http://users.erols.com/mwhite28/20centry.htm

National Atlas http://nationalatlas.gov

National Geographic's Map Machine http://plasma.nationalgeographic.com/mapmachine

Places in the News http://memory.loc.gov/ammem/gmdhtml/plnews.html

MapQuest http://mapquest.com

Maporama http://www.maporama.com/share

MultiMap.com http://uk2.multimap.com

Perry Casteneda Library Map Collection http://www.lib.utexas.edu/maps/index.html

TopoZone http://www.topozone.com

United Nations Cartographic Section http://www.un.org/Depts/Cartographic/english

Biographical

Biographical Dictionary http://www.s9.com/biography

Biography.com http://www.biography.com

Gale (free resources) http://www.galegroup.com/free_resources

Who2? http://www.who2.com

Grolier's American Presidency http://gi.grolier.com/presidents

POTUS http://www.ipl.org/div/potus

President of the United States http://www.whitehouse.gov/history/presidents/index.html

Presidents of the United States http://www.presidentsusa.net

Presidents Index http://odur.let.rug.nl/~usa/P

Nations, Travel

Amnesty International http://www.amnesty.org/ailib/aireport

Atlapedia Online http://www.atlapedia.com

CIA World Factbook http://www.odci.gov/cia/publications/factbook/index.html

Country Reports.org http://www.countryreports.org

Economist Country Briefings http://www.economist.com/countries

General Travel Sites http://mciu.org/~spjvweb/maps.html

Human Rights Watch http://www.hrw.org/hrw

INCORE: Internet Conflict Data Service http://www.incore.ulst.ac.uk/cds/countries/index.html

InfoNation (United Nations comparisons) http://www.cyberschoolbus.un.org/infonation/info.asp

Library of Congress Country Studies http://lcweb2.loc.gov/frd/cs

Library of Congress's Portals to the World http://www.loc.gov/rr/international/portals.html

Lonely Planet's Destinations http://www.lonelyplanet.com/destinations

State Department's Background Notes http://www.state.gov/r/pa/ei/bgn

World Statesmen.org http://www.worldstatesmen.org

Worldwide Gazetteer http://www.gazeteer.com

Your Nation http://www.your-nation.com

Fifty States

ClassBrain.com State Reports http://classbrain.com/artstate/publish

50 States and Capitals http://www.50states.com

Internet Public Library's Stately Knowledge http://www.ipl.org/div/kidspace/stateknow

Stateline.org http://www.stateline.org

GOVERNMENT

Ben's Guide to U.S. Government for Kids http://bensguide.gpo.gov

FirstGov: Your First Click to U.S. Government http://www.firstgov.gov

KidsGov http://www.kids.gov

U.S. HISTORY

American Cultural History: The Twentieth Century http://www.nhmccd.edu/contracts/lrc/kc/decades.html

From Revolution to Reconstruction . . . and What Happens Afterwards http://odur.let.rug.nl/usanew

SOCIAL ISSUES

Multnomah County Library Homework Center http://www.multnomah.lib.or.us/lib/homework/sochc.html

Internet Public Library Social Issues and Social Welfare Resources http://www.ipl.org/ref/RR/static/soc80.00.00.html

Poynter.org http://poynter.org/dj/shedden

Public Agenda Online http://www.publicagenda.org

Incore Country Guides http://www.incore.ulst.ac.uk/cds/countries/index.html

Out There News: Megastories http://www.megastories.com/index.shtml

VIDEOS

Schlessinger United States History Series

A & E Biography Series

Dear Science Teacher,

I look forward to meeting your classes this year!
   I wanted to share with you some general resources that
you may not be aware are available in our library. You may
want to add your own favorite web sites to these lists. Please stop
in and we'll discuss your program. Together we'll plan resource-
based, inquiry-driven units connecting information skills to your content-area goals.
Feel free to stop in for a tour or demonstration of any of our online and electronic products.

Let me know how I can help,

Your teacher-librarian

PRINT REFERENCES

Books

Gale's Encyclopedia of Science

McGraw Hill Encyclopedia of Science and Technology

New Book of Popular Science

Journals

Discover

Futurist

National Geographic

Science News

Oceans

Popular Science

Science

Scientific American

Omni

Science on File

Today's Science on File

Environment

ONLINE RESOURCES

Journals

CNN Science and Space http://www.cnn.com/TECH/space

Discover Magazine http://www.discover.com

Nature http://www.nature.com/nature

Popular Science http://www.popsci.com/popsci

Science News Online http://www.sciencenews.org

Science Magazine Online http://www.sciencemag.org

Scientific American http://www.sciam.com

USA Today Health and Science http://www.usatoday.com/news/health/front.htm

Why Files: Science Behind the News http://whyfiles.org

Standards

AAAS Benchmarks Online http://www.project2061.org/tools/benchol/bolframe.htm

Eisenhower National Clearinghouse National Standards http://www.enc.org/professional/standards/national

National Educational Technology Standards http://cnets.iste.org

National Science Education Standards http://stills.nap.edu/html/nses

State Frameworks http://www.enc.org/professional/standards/state

Developing Educational Standards (for both state and national standards)
   http://edstandards.org/Standards.html

McREL's Standards Database http://www.mcrel.org/standards-benchmarks

Nine Information Literacy Standards for Student Learning http://www.ala.org/aasl/ip_nine.html

National Organizations

ENC (Eisenhower National Clearinghouse): A Math and Science Teacher Center http://www.enc.org

AAAS Project 2061 (Initiative to advance literacy in science, math and technology)
   http://www.project2061.org

Science Search Engines

Scirus http://scirus.com

Education Gateways

Blue Web'n http://www.kn.pacbell.com/wired/bluewebn

GEM The Gateway http://thegateway.org

New York Times Teacher Connections http://www.nytimes.com/learning/teachers/index.html

About.com Secondary http://7-12educators.about.com

About.com Elementary Educators http://k-6educators.about.com

Education World Teacher Resources http://www.educationworld.com

Discovery School Lesson Plan Library http://school.discovery.com/lessonplans

edHelper.com (lessons, webquests, worksheets) http://www.edhelper.com

FREE: Federal Resources for Educational Excellence http://www.ed.gov/free

Kathy Schrock's Guide for Educators http://discoveryschool.com/schrockguide

Marco Polo http://www.marcopolo-education.org

Math Forum http://mathforum.org

National Geographic Education http://www.nationalgeographic.com/education

PBS TeacherSource http://www.pbs.org/teachersource

SearchERIC.org http://www.searcheric.org

Tom March's BestWebQuests.com http://bestwebquests.com

WebQuests http://webquest.sdsu.edu

Science Gateways

Access Excellence @ the National Health Museum http://www.accessexcellence.org

Biology Project: University of Arizona http://www.biology.arizona.edu

Center for Science Education http://cse.ssl.berkeley.edu

National Geographic Education http://www.nationalgeographic.com/education

New York Times Lesson Plans: Science http://www.nytimes.com/learning/teachers/lessons/science.html

Science Education Gateway (National consortium of scientists, museums, and educators focus on space and aviation science) http://cse.ssl.berkeley.edu/segway

Physical Science Information Gateway http://www.psigate.ac.uk/newsite

Exploratorium Museum of Science, Art and Human Perception http://www.exploratorium.edu

FirstGov for Science http://www.science.gov

NASA Explores: Express Lessons and Online Resources http://www.nasaexplores.com

NOVA Online: Science Programming on Air and Online http://www.pbs.org/wgbh/nova

Science Learning Network http://www.sln.org

Science Net Links (Part of the excellent Marco Polo program) http://www.sciencenetlinks.com

SCORE Science (lessons, standards, and resources from Schools of California On-line Resources for Education California schools) http://scorescience.humboldt.k12.ca.us

Whelmers http://www.mcrel.org/whelmers

Eisenhower Network http://www.mathsciencenetwork.org

Nobel e-Museum http://www.nobel.se

VIDEOS

Schlessinger Science Library

NOVA Series

Discovery Series

National Geographic Series

Dear Health Teacher,

I look forward to meeting your classes this year!

I wanted to share with you some general resources that you may not be aware are available in our library. You may want to add your own favorite web sites to these lists. Please stop in and we'll discuss your program. Together we'll plan resource-based, inquiry-driven units connecting information skills to your content-area goals. Feel free to stop in for a tour or demonstration of any of our online and electronic products.

Let me know how I can help,

Your teacher-librarian

PRINT REFERENCES

Books

CIBA Medical Illustrations

Diseases

Grolier's Wellness Library

Marshall Cavendish Family Medical Encyclopedia

New Our Bodies, Ourselves

Journals

Current Health

ESPN

Prevention

Psychology Today

Sports Illustrated

ONLINE RESOURCES

Journals

ESPN http://espn.go.com/main.html

Physical Education Digest http://www.pedigest.com

Prevention http://www.prevention.com

Runner's World http://www.runnersworld.com

Sports Illustrated for Kids http://www.sikids.com

Sports Illustrated Online http://sportsillustrated.cnn.com

Track & Field News http://www.trackandfieldnews.com

Databases

SIRS Researcher

EBSCOhost

GaleNet

Standards

Developing Educational Standards (for both state and national standards)
http://edstandards.org/Standards.html

McREL's Standards Database http://www.mcrel.org/standards-benchmarks

National Standards for Physical Education
http://www.aahperd.org/naspe/publications-nationalstandards.html

Professional Organizations

AAHPERD: American Alliance for Health Physical Education Recreation and Dance http://www.aahperd.org

AAHE American Association for Health Education http://www.aahperd.org

National Association for Health and Physical Education http://www.aahperd.org/naspe/template.cfm

Educational Gateways

Blue Web'n http://www.kn.pacbell.com/wired/bluewebn

GEM The Gateway http://thegateway.org

New York Times Teacher Connections http://www.nytimes.com/learning/teachers/index.html

About.com Secondary http://7-12educators.about.com

About.com Elementary Educators http://k-6educators.about.com

Education World Teacher Resources http://www.educationworld.com

Discovery School Lesson Plan Library http://school.discovery.com/lessonplans

edHelper.com (lessons, webquests, worksheets) http://www.edhelper.com

FREE: Federal Resources for Educational Excellence http://www.ed.gov/free

Kathy Schrock's Guide for Educators http://discoveryschool.com/schrockguide

Marco Polo http://www.marcopolo-education.org

Math Forum http://mathforum.org

National Geographic Education http://www.nationalgeographic.com/education

PBS TeacherSource http://www.pbs.org/teachersource

SearchERIC.org http://www.searcheric.org

Tom March's BestWebQuests.com http://bestwebquests.com

WebQuests http://webquest.sdsu.edu

Health Gateway Sites

ERIC Resources for Health Education http://www.eduref.org/cgi-bin/res.cgi/Subjects/Health

ERIC Resources for Physical Education http://www.eduref.org/cgi-bin/res.cgi/Subjects/Physical_Education

Healthfinder http://www.healthfinder.gov

KidsHealth http://www.kidshealth.org

PE Links 4 U http://www.pelinks4u.org

Sports Media: Physical Education for Everyone http://www.sports-media.org

Go Ask Alice! http://www.goaskalice.columbia.edu

PE Central: The Web Site for Health and Physical Education http://www.pecentral.org

Health Search Engine

Scirus (Science search engine) http://scirus.com

Outstanding Health Web Sites to Investigate

Ask Alice: Columbia University Health Question and Answer Service
   http://www.cc.columbia.edu/cu/healthwise/alice.html

Centers for Disease Control http://www.cdc.gov

CNN Interactive: Health Main Page http://www.cnn.com/HEALTH

Girl Power http://www.girlpower.gov

KidsHealth from the duPont Hospital for Children http://www.kidshealth.org

WebMD http://webmd.org

K-12 Physical Education

National Association for Sport and Physical Education http://www.aahperd.org/naspe

NOAH: New York Online Access to Health http://www.noah-health.org

PE Central http://pe.central.vt.edu

Physical Education Resources http://www.mcrel.org/lesson-plan/health/index.asp

PubMed http://www.ncbi.nlm.nih.gov/PubMed

U.S. Department of Health and Human Services http://www.hhs.gov

Visible Human http://www.nlm.nih.gov/research/visible/visible_human.html

VIDEO

Drug Information Library

Springfield Township
High School

Welcome to Your Library Information Center

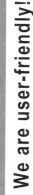

"The mission of the library media program is to ensure that students and staff are effective users of ideas and information." *Information Power* 1998

We are user-friendly!

Teacher-Librarians Are "Information Consultants."

You are not alone! Ask us:

- for research advice
- to help you brainstorm research ideas
- to help your find *the best* print or online resources for your projects
- for a recommendation for a great read
- for help with Web and database searching
- for help with your personal information needs and interests

1234 Information Way
Library Land, PA 12345

(555) ***_****
Fax: (555) ***_****
Email: librarian@school.org
Website: http://libraryweb.htm

Let us help you connect!

Online Databases
GaleNet/UXL
bigchalk
SIRS Researcher
SIRS Government Reporter
EBSCOhost
New York Times
Facts On File

Ask your teacher-librarian for a password list to use these resources from home.

Remember our Virtual Library is available from home:

1-14A

Let us help you learn!
@ the library, we can connect you with:

- a good book
- magazines and newspapers
- online databases to use at school or at home
- personal research consultation and searching tips
- documentation advice (how to cite!)
- interlibrary loan (get materials from other libraries)
- reference books
- videos, DVDs, CDs, audiocassettes
- note sheets, organizers, and bibliography formats for preparing research projects
- resources for and help with multimedia production and presentation: scanners, html software, digital cameras, video cameras
- and much more!

Library Rules
- Be considerate of others who are working
- Use a quiet voice
- No food or drinks
- Appropriate language only
- When others are waiting for workstations, limit your time online
- Show care when using all library resources

Please respect the rights of other library users to study and learn.

THE BIG SIX: Steps in the Research Cycle

Task Definition
- What is the problem to be solved?
- What types of information are needed to solve the problem?

Information-Seeking Strategies
- What are the possible sources of information?
- Which are the best of all the possibilities?

Location and Access
- Where are these sources?
- Where is the information in each source?

Use of Information
- What information does the source provide?
- How can you extract the information you need?

Synthesis
- How does the information from all the sources fit together?
- How is the information best presented?

Evaluation
- Was the information problem solved?
- If the problem had to be solved again, what would you do differently?

With permission from Michael B. Eisenberg and Robert E. Berkowitz, The Big6 Model. Big6 website http://www.big6.com

1234 Information Way
Library Land, PA 12345
Phone: (555) ***_****
Fax: (555) ***_****
Email:

Library facts

Library Hours
Mon. through Thur. 7 a.m.–4 p.m.
Fri. 7 a.m.–3 p.m.

Staff: Teacher-librarian:

Library Assistants:

Phone:

Fax:

E-mail:

Loan period

Books:	4 weeks (except reserves)
Magazines:	overnight
Videos/DVDs:	overnight (see librarian)
Reference:	library use only!
Fines:	5¢ per day for overdue titles
	25¢ per day for overnight items
Photocopies:	10¢ per page

The School Library: Your Partner in Learning and Instruction

Developing Information Literate Students

Inspiring Lifelong Learning

Helping Teachers Teach—

Because Student Achievement is the Bottom Line!

Your Friendly School Library

1234 Information Way
Library Land, PA 12345
Phone: (555) ***-****
Fax: (555) ***-****
Email: librarian@school.org

Promoting standards for learners:

Nine Information Literacy Standards for Student Learning

Information Literacy
The student who is information literate:

Standard 1: accesses information efficiently and effectively.

Standard 2: evaluates information critically and competently.

Standard 3: uses information accurately and creatively.

Independent Learning
The student who is an independent learner is information literate:

Standard 4: pursues information related to personal interests.

Standard 5: appreciates literature and other creative expressions of information.

Standard 6: strives for excellence in information seeking and knowledge generation.

Social Responsibility
Standard 7: The student who contributes positively to the learning community and to society is information literate and recognizes the importance of information to a democratic society.

Standard 8: The student who contributes positively to the learning community and to society is information literate and practices ethical behavior in regard to information and information technology.

Standard 9: The student who contributes positively to the learning community and to society is information literate and participates effectively in groups to pursue and generate information.

Excerpted from Chapter 2, "Information Literacy Standards for Student Learning," of *Information Power: Building Partnerships for Learning.* Copyright © 1998 American Library Association and Association for Educational Communications and Technology. ISBN 0-8389-3470-6.

The teacher-librarian can help you:

- design instruction and assessment
- obtain resources to support instruction and student research
- master and integrate information technology and information skills
- design Web-based instruction
- create Web pages, bibliographies, online instructional units, WebQuests

Faculty loan policy:

Staff members may borrow materials for an entire semester. If another staff member or student requests an item, we will notify you and "negotiate."

Please return any materials when you are finished with them so others may use them.

How you can help us:

- Notify the teacher-librarian as soon as possible about any upcoming resource-based class projects
- Tell us if you wish materials placed on reserve
- Meet with the teacher-librarian for planning sessions before bringing your class in for a project
- Reserve class space in the library as far in advance as possible. We book fast!
- Share copies of your assignment sheet and any assessment tools and handouts you plan to use
- Remain with your students and supervise their behavior while they are in the library information center
- Provide passes for students who may need to visit the library during class time

We have resources for your students:

- passwords for our high-quality subscription databases
- note-taking resources
- bibliographic style sheets
- graphic organizers
- research rubrics for multimedia presentations, debates, speeches, etc.
- project consultation!

Here's what we can do:

- Collaboratively plan, teach, and assess research activities for your students
- Recommend and obtain curricular resources to extend your classroom resources
- Present book talks for your classes
- Prepare bibliographies, Web pages, and pathfinders to support student research
- Prepare reading lists
- Gather needed materials from other libraries
- Provide in-service training in information literacy and information technologies
- Help you produce instructional materials
- Integrate information skills into your units of study
- Provide guidance on documentation and the ethical use of information
- Provide bibliographic style sheets for students
- Provide AV media and equipment
- Teach curriculum-related information skills with you
- Brainstorm project ideas and instructional strategies
- Place materials on reserve so they will be more equitably available to all students for the length of a project

Ask us for a:

- journal list
- list of media materials
- list of available databases with passwords
- list of great websites on areas you'll be covering

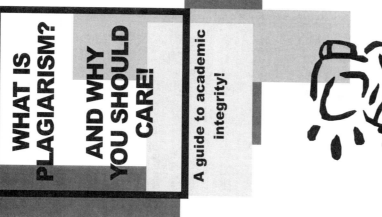

WHAT IS PLAGIARISM?

AND WHY YOU SHOULD CARE!

A guide to academic integrity!

Your Favorite High School Library

About In-Text/In-Project Documentation

What it is: The brief information in in-text documentation should match full source information in the Works Cited page

Purpose: to give immediate source information without interrupting the flow of a paper or project.

Why bother? The academic world takes in-text documentation seriously. Readers look for *authority* in your writing.

Inaccurate documentation is as serious as having no documentation at all.

How to do it: Parenthetical citations are usually placed at the end of a sentence.

- Cite the author's last name and the page number in parentheses. (Smith 72)

- In the absence of an author, cite the title and the page number. (Citing Sources 72)

- If you are using more than one book by the same author, list the last name, comma, the title, and the page. (Smith, Citing Sources 72)

- If you identify the author and title in the text, just list the page number: *According to Smith in Citing Sources, citing is critical when you refer to statistics* (72).

- When citing a Web source in-text, you are not likely to have page numbers, just include the first part of the entry. (Smith)

Confused? Check our school style sheet or consult your teacher-librarian for more information!

You can borrow from the works of others!

As long as you document when you:

Quote: Quotes are the exact words of an author, copied directly from a source, word for word. Quotations must be cited!

Paraphrase: When you rephrase the words of an author, putting his/her thoughts in your own words. When you paraphrase, you rework the source's ideas, words, phrases, and sentence structures with your own. Paraphrased material must be cited!

Summarize: When you put the main idea(s) of one or several writers into your own words, including only the main point(s). Summaries are significantly shorter than the original and take a broad overview of the source material. Summarized material must be cited!

Remember to keep careful records of your sources and quotes *as you research*. It may be very hard to retrace your research steps!

1-16A

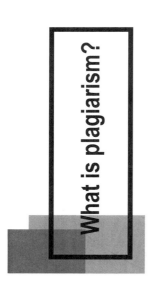

What is plagiarism?

Plagiarism is the act of presenting the words, ideas, images, sounds, or other creative expression of others as your own.

IF: you have included, copied or downloaded the words and ideas of others in your work and neglected to cite,

IF: you have turned in someone else's work,

IF: you have had help you wouldn't want your teacher to know about,

You have probably plagiarized!

Remember, your teachers expect honesty! They know your work; they consult with each other; they check suspicious work in Web search tools.

Two types of plagiarism:

Intentional

- Copying a friend's work
- Buying or borrowing papers
- Cutting and pasting blocks of text from electronic sources without documenting
- Media "borrowing"

Unintentional

- Careless paraphrasing
- Poor documentation
- Quoting excessively
- Failure to use your own "voice"— your work should be original!

Academic Integrity Counts!

- Education is not an "us vs. them" game!
- When you copy, you are cheating yourself; you limit your own learning!
- The consequences are not worth the risk! Your academic reputation follows you.
- Giving credit to authors whose ideas you use is the right thing to do!
- Citing gives the information you present authority.
- Citing makes it possible for your readers to locate your source.
- Cheating is unethical behavior.

It's not worth the possible consequences:

- "0" on the assignment
- Parent notification
- Referral to administrators
- Suspension or dismissal from school activities— sports and extracurricular
- Note on student record
- Loss of reputation in our school community

But do I have to cite everything?

NO! Facts that are widely known and information and judgments that are considered "**common knowledge**" do NOT have to be documented!

If you see a fact in more than five sources, it is likely to be "common knowledge."

You don't need to cite when you are writing about your own experiences, observations, conclusions, and reactions.

When in doubt, cite!

Request for Donation of Library Technology

(Your Library address)

(Date)

(Local business owner)

Dear _____ ,

Our library is in need of *recent model* hardware and peripherals for student research, as well as for word processing, database, spreadsheet, desktop publishing, and presentations. If you plan to upgrade any of your current equipment in the near future, please consider a donation to our facility. Your gift would benefit both students and faculty members. We would be happy to announce your gift in the area newspapers.

Please feel free to contact me any time to discuss your possible cooperation.

Thank you for your time and consideration.

Sincerely,

Teacher-Librarian

Gift Book Program

Dear Parents and other Friends of the _____ Library,

   In partnership with the PTA, the _____ School Library is conducting a Special Occasion/Birthday Gift Book Program. The program helps grow our library collection while formally commemorating special days and people in the lives of our students.

   We welcome your participation! Consider adding a book to our collection:

*   to honor your child's birthday
*   in honor (or memory) of a grandparent, special friend, family member
*   to honor a special teacher
*   as part of your holiday giving

   To reduce the chance of duplication, and ensure the integrity and vitality of our school's collection, please help us select books in the following ways:

*   Select a book from our library's wish list and send a check in the amount of the price of the book you selected. A copy of the wish list is at the circulation desk and posted on our website. We can also e-mail or fax the list to you. Please pick both a first- and second- choice title in the event that we have an overlapping gift choice.
*   Ask to see a copy of age-appropriate award-winning booklists from our state and national library associations.
*   Make a donation toward the purchase of new books in the amount of your choice. You may contact the teacher-librarian to discuss book choices—titles, genre, etc.

   A bookplate will be placed in your gift book and your child will have the opportunity to be the first borrower!

   Please make all checks payable to_____

   We thank those parents who have generously supported the library by donating books through the Birthday/Gift Book Program. We hope others will join this effort. If you have questions contact us

by phone number _____

or e-mail _____

   Respectfully,

   Teacher-Librarian

LIBRARY GIFT PROGRAM FORM

Please return this completed form with any donations or checks. We will acknowledge your generous gift with a letter, note your gift in the next library newsletter, and place a bookplate in your gift book.

Child's Name _____ Grade ____

Homeroom/Room_____ Date_____

Parent's/Donor's Name _____ _____ Phone

Parent's mailing address: _____

- -

OCCASION OF GIFT

_____ Birthday _____ Memorial _____ Non-specific gift   Other _____

- -

BOOK SELECTION

_____   I am enclosing the library's book wish list, indicating 1st and 2nd choices and have included a check for $ _____

_____   Please arrange for my child to choose a gift selection with the help of the teacher-librarian. Enclosed is check for $ _____

_____   I would like to discuss gift options with the teacher-librarian, please contact me by _____

Notes _____
_____
_____

- -

INFORMATION FOR BOOK PLATE

(Fill in for books donated in honor of someone's birthday.)

Birthday Date: _____ (If gift is in honor of a birthday)

Honored Birthday Student: _____ Presented by: _____

(Fill in for books donated in honor or in memory of a person or occasion other than a birthday.)

In honor of: _____ or In memory of: _____

Presented by: _____

Suggested wording: _____

- -

ANNOUNCEMENTS OR ACKNOWLEDGMENT

Acknowledgments will be sent for memorial gifts and gifts honoring an occasion.
Please provide a mailing address if you would like a formal acknowledgment:

For further information regarding our gift book program, please contact the teacher-librarian:

Phone: _____

E-mail: _____

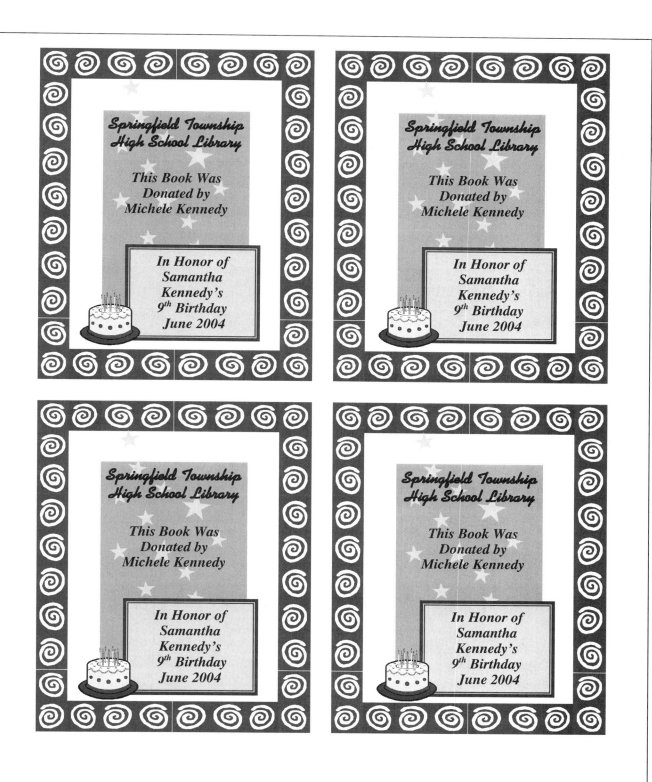

SPRINGFIELD TOWNSHIP HIGH SCHOOL LIBRARY

In Memory
James Smith

Beloved Student
and Friend

Donated by the
STMS/STHS PTA

June 2004

SPRINGFIELD TOWNSHIP HIGH SCHOOL LIBRARY

In Memory
James Smith

Beloved Student
and Friend

Donated by the
STMS/STHS PTA

June 2004

SPRINGFIELD TOWNSHIP HIGH SCHOOL LIBRARY

In Memory
James Smith

Beloved Student
and Friend

Donated by the
STMS/STHS PTA

June 2004

SPRINGFIELD TOWNSHIP HIGH SCHOOL LIBRARY

In Memory
James Smith

Beloved Student
and Friend

Donated by the
STMS/STHS PTA

June 2004

Mass-Assignment **Alert!**

TO: _____, Public Librarian

FAX #:

DATE:

Dear Public Library Colleague,

We wanted to alert you to a major research project that has been assigned in our school. You may want to keep some of your material on reserve to meet student demand and to more equitably distribute your resources. Here are some details you may find helpful.

Teacher _____ Subject/Class _____

Grade _____ Date Due _____

Project/Assignment _____

Expected Product _____

A copy of the student assignment sheet follows for your convenience. Please feel free to contact us with any questions.

Teacher-Librarian _____

School _____

Phone _____

E-mail _____

Fax # _____

Community Resource File

help mentors
support
advice

Dear Community Member,

Our school district is in the process of establishing a community resource file. We are seeking people who would be willing to share their professional expertise or other talents with our students. The database we create will allow us to identify potential speakers, people willing to be interviewed as part of a student research project, and electronic mentors who might be available to answer student e-mail questions or participate in an online chat with a class. A copy of the database will be on file in each of the district's school library information centers.

If you would like to serve as an educational resource person, please complete the following questions and return this form to any of our school library information centers.

- -

Name _____   Date _____

Work Phone _____   Home Phone _____

E-mail _____

Briefly describe your special talents, hobbies, or area(s) of expertise. _____

_____

_____

_____

_____

_____

_____

_____

_____

Credentials (optional) _____

_____

_____

I would be interested in working with students in grades ___ K–2 ___ 3–5 ___ 6–8 ___ 9–12 ___ all

Attention parents: Please attend the school district's . . .

TECHNOLOGY INFORMATION NIGHT

Our school district is hosting an evening to provide parents with information about the use of technology in our instructional program. We are convinced that our integration of a variety of technologies is bringing exciting opportunities to your children by increasing their global awareness, fostering creativity and production, enhancing reading and writing, improving research skills, presenting career options, and encouraging lifelong learning. Please join us for a demonstration of some of our favorite resources and learn about

- student opportunities for research, communication, publishing, multimedia production, and collaboration
- research strategies that will empower students to find information efficiently and effectively
- our district's Acceptable Use Policy—guidelines for appropriate behavior
- how you can support our efforts at home

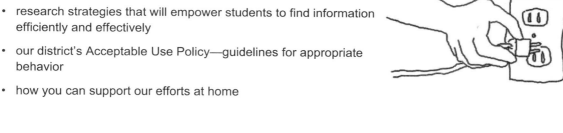

When:

Where:

To register:

For more information:

    Phone:

    E-mail:

WANTED:
Library Volunteers

Our library information center is in need of your support. Even if you can spare just one hour per week, you can help us provide a stronger library program for your children. Volunteering in the library information center will also allow you to learn more about your child's school experience and give you an opportunity to observe our classes in action.

Please check any activities in which you'd like to participate.

☐ shelving

☐ filing

☐ circulation

☐ database entry

☐ helping to maintain the library website

☐ preparing displays/bulletin boards

☐ fund-raising

☐ helping students with computer projects

☐ helping students with research projects

☐ other. Please suggest:

Time(s) and day(s) available _____

_____

Any special talents you might be able to contribute to our program _____

_____

_____

_____

_____

_____

_____

Name _____

Home Phone _____ Work Phone _____

E-mail _____

Please return this form to school with your child.

WANTED:
Library-Tech Squad Members

Attention students:

We are looking for some talented, dedicated, and trustworthy students to join our Library-Tech Squad. If you have a free period, or some time before or after school, and you wish to make a contribution to your library and your school, please consider joining.

Duties will include:

setting up labs for class visits

evaluating websites and software

checking and updating Web page links

installing software

upkeep of printers—changing cartridges, paper, etc.

emergency visits to teachers' rooms

guiding other students and teachers in use of online resources, technology, and audiovisual materials

Training sessions begin _____

- -

Please sign me up for the Library-Tech Squad!

Name _____ Grade _____ Homeroom _____

Free periods _____

Special talents _____

_____

_____

_____

_____

_____

_____

_____

Please return this form to the library.

Library Web Site Organizer

Back Reload Forward Bookmark Home Stop

Your School Library
Address
Phone Fax E-Mail
Hours
Library Information Specialist(s)

1. Essential Information
   - school district icon
   - name of library and librarian
   - address
   - phone
   - fax
   - e-mail link
   - hours

2. Library mission statement/Information literacy goals and related sites/your curriculum or links to the integrated library curriculum. Link to *Information Power* or state standards pages.

3. Introductory text including the mission of this web site: Example: We hope that this site will provide access to quality information resources to support learning for the entire school community 24/7.

4. To guide you (policies, procedures, and handouts)
   - acceptable use policy
   - academic integrity policy
   - about copyright and intellectual property
   - style sheets customized to your resources
   - tips for in-text/in-project documentation
   - research tips (evaluation, searching strategies: Boolean, phrase searching, truncation, etc.)
   - recommended search engines
   - recommended subject directories and gateways

5. Online catalog (link to the OPAC for both school and home use) and links to appropriate other catalogs (other district, public and academic libraries), statewide holdings database

6. Databases: link to your subscription services. Make sure students have passwords or separate links for remote use

7. For students: curricular resources arranged by subject or teacher, unit, or assignment

8. For teachers
   - links to lesson plan gateways
   - links to standards and curricular resources (rubrics, clipart, graphic organizers)
   - links to educational research: journals, ERIC resources, databases

9. For parents (family-related sites)
   - research tips for parents
   - how to help your child with homework and projects

10. Sites for general reference
    - reference portals
    - online encyclopedia
    - maps / atlases
    - biographical tools
    - dictionaries and thesauri
    - almanacs
    - "This day in history sites"

11. Reading
    - reading lists and reading suggestions
    - student reviews
    - local and national awards, appropriate to age level

12. Library newsletter (pdf?)

13. Library annual report (pdf?)

14. Links to local colleges (if high school)

15. Other great school library sites (for your use mostly!)

16. Student book reviews

17. Local history, news, resources

18. Student publications / exemplary work

19. New and noteworthy! (print or electronic materials)

20. Sites for the college search and career (if high school)

21. Recent and upcoming programs and events (visiting author, Teen Read Week, etc.)

2

ram Administration

It's those routine activities that create the groundwork needed to keep a library running effectively and serve learners and faculty. In this section, you'll find many of the essentials: the planning documents, passes, instructions for the substitute, model policies, collection development advice, and job descriptions.

2-1
Checklist of Administrative Tasks: An Annual To-Do List for Teacher-Librarians

This list of ideas will guide new teacher-librarians as they enter the rhythm of a typical school year. Add your own essential tasks as they apply to events in your own building.

2-2
Class Visit Planning Form

When classroom teachers plan in advance, you can develop instruction and assessment more carefully and identify, gather, and purchase appropriate materials. Use this form to help you conduct an interview prior to a class visit. Planning will also give you an opportunity to create Web pages and pathfinders to guide students to recommended materials. We attach a copy of this form to our September newsletter and have plenty on hand at the desk. Because of the skills/standards check-off

section, these forms help document the scope and effect of our information skills instruction on the school community.

2-3
Teacher-Librarian Job Description

These criteria, based on professional responsibilities outlined in *Information Power,* will guide administrators as they look to hire new professional teacher-librarians.

2-4
Interview Questions for Teacher-Librarians

When your district is hiring a new teacher-librarian, whether or not you are on the interview committee, volunteer to help prepare the questions. Those in charge of the interview may not know the most critical questions to ask.

2-5
Library Assistant/Paraprofessional Job Description

This form describes the qualities you are likely to be looking for in an assistant. Use it also to announce a job.

2-6
Interviewing the Library Assistant/Paraprofessional

Having the right assistant is critical to the success of your program, to what you are able to accomplish, and it is essential to your own happiness. These questions will guide you as you interview clerical staff and assess the abilities and attitudes of library assistant/paraprofessional candidates.

2-7
Dear Teacher-Librarian Substitute

Leave this letter in a folder and attach your plans. Often a library substitute will have no clue about what work might be done during slow times. Your staff should help your substitute get started.

2-8
Academic Integrity Policy for Student Research

Students are less tempted to plagiarize when they understand that the entire school team values honesty and academic integrity. This policy describes the responsibilities of both teachers and students in developing a culture of academic integrity and lists possible consequences for dishonest research behavior.

2-9
Material Selection Policy

Each school district should establish a collection-development policy, a framework for development and growth of a balanced quality collection that meets the needs of its school community. The policy ensures that staff, students, and the community understand the scope and purpose of the library collection and provides continuity when the staff of a facility changes. It should establish priorities for purchases and budget allotments. Districts must set criteria for selection and weeding to minimize personal bias and provide the community with a balanced collection. It is essential to have a policy in place in the event of a challenge. Having a selection policy available allows the complainant to see that you are professional and systematic in your approach to collection building. It will also allow you time to alert your administrators of the situation. Collection policies should be

board approved and should cover all the schools in a district.

2-10
Citizen Request for Reconsideration of Materials

It is important for the teacher-librarian to defend the collection against challenges. The opinions of one citizen or parent do not generally represent the sentiment of an entire community. That citizen's complaint should not deter others from their right to access to materials. A citizen's complaint form should be attached to your selection policy. If a citizen is serious about challenging material, he or she must complete a form that will be submitted to a challenge committee for evaluation. Often complaints go no further than a verbal exchange, but if a problem should arise, the form begins an official process.

2-11
Weeding and the Teacher-Librarian

Weeding is probably one of the toughest jobs a librarian must do. It is time-consuming, and it temporarily removes us from our work with learners. However, weeding is what keeps our collections vital and attractive. Weeding ensures materials are current, accurate, and relevant to the school program. It allows students and staff to more easily find the quality materials and provides for better use of space. The result is a more effective library program. This document offers a rationale for weeding, tips for de-selection, and "critical Cs" to consider as you examine individual items.

2-12
Suggestion for Library Purchase

Don't assume you are the only one keeping up with the review media. However well you know the curriculum, you must rely on the true content experts to help you make collection decisions. Make sure you survey the faculty regularly to see if they have any suggestions for purchase. I try to do this at the end of the school year, when the new budget seems at its biggest and I am excited about preparing purchase orders. Remember to request previews of electronic and online products whenever possible to avoid large-item budget disappointments.

2-13
Itemized Budget Proposal Worksheet

Even if you are given a block amount of money each year without question, it would still be a good strategy to inform those who do your building's "pie slicing" of what you need, how you plan to spend your funding, how those items you select support and enhance your program, how they further your mission, and how they will impact learners. If you find it useful, calculate costs per learner.

2-14
Rules for Library Workstations

You may need to establish priorities and rules for cooperative behavior for your busiest areas. Sometimes rules have to be set to avoid crowding and socializing in areas where a great amount of work has to occur within a short time period.

2-15
Library Assignment Pass

When teachers send small groups of students to the library, you'll want to make sure they all "arrive safely," and you may want to verify their reason for visiting.

2-16
Library Class Time: Appointment Slip

Like in the typical doctor's office, library "no-shows" also present problems. These appointment slips function as reminders to classroom teachers who have just signed up for library time.

2-17
Shelving Guide

If you're lucky, you'll have students and adult volunteers helping you with the never-ending task of getting books and other materials back on the shelves. This guide will help train your devoted helpers to do it right and remind them of the importance of accuracy in shelving.

2-18
Guidelines for Showing Films in the Classroom

This policy explains Fair Use and copyright in regard to showing videos in the classroom, whether the videos are rented, purchased, copied, or borrowed from the library. The policies also clarify prohibitions against recreational showings in school.

2-19–2-21
Policy for Using R-Rated Films in the Classroom, Teacher's Request to Use R-Rated Video, and Letter to Parents regarding Use of R-Rated Video

Especially at the high school level, teachers will likely be interested in showing popular videos that may have been labeled "R." Examples of video materials currently carrying an R rating include such high quality films as *Glory*, *Schindler's List*, *Elizabeth*, and *The Joy Luck Club*. Clearly, students may benefit from viewing and discussing such materials, especially when they directly relate to their course of study. Parents and administrators should be informed when teachers plan to show such videos to students. If a parent objects, a teacher should provide an opportunity for the student to "opt out" of the video showing and provide an alternate, equally valid assignment. Provide teachers with these model forms and letters to facilitate communication with parents and ensure there is no miscommunication between teachers and administrators. Consider setting up and serving on an Academic Standards Committee that reviews R-rated films for relevance and value to the curriculum as a systematic way of approving films and backing colleagues against potential film challenges. With students also showing excerpts of videos in class projects, the policy offers guidelines that should avoid embarrassing surprises.

2-22
Policy on District-Provided Access to Electronic Information, Services, and Networks (Model Acceptable Use Policy)

It is likely that the district's teacher-librarians will have significant input in drafting and revising policies for network and Internet use. Some districts insist on signed parental permissions and signed student acknowledgements of their responsibilities. The policy is based on a model developed by the Indiana Department of Education (http://ideanet.doe.state.in.us/olr/aup/aupmod.html) and incorporates permission forms used at Springfield Township. All highlighted material was edited or not originally part of the Indiana document.

2-23
Weekly Schedule Sign-Up Form

This form works as a scheduling tool for our block-scheduled facility and the spaces available for class visits. Customize it to meet the needs of your own schedule and space.

2-24
Library Equipment Sign-Outs

If you circulate materials other than books and media, you might need to develop a weekly sign-out form for equipment. It is possible that you might not have time to check the circulation system when a teacher absolutely has to know where the digital camera is *this minute.* Put this form on a clipboard at the circulation desk to quickly put your finger on who has what when.

2-25
Library Weekly Schedule

Customize this form and use it as a reminder to teachers who have signed up for the upcoming week. Deposit it in the appropriate mailboxes, or e-mail it on Thursday or Friday. It will help you avoid pesky no-show behavior.

2-26
Drop-In Students (Form)

Use this form to keep track of those students who are visiting on their own, not with their classes. The form can protect students if they are accused of cutting or not being where they should be. Their signature assures that the student arrived in the library, where they presented a pass.

2-27
MARC Checklist

This checklist, by expert cataloger Candy Blessing of Ephrata High School (PA) and of Mansfield University's graduate library program, lists critical MARC fields and subfields to be included in bibliographic and holdings records for books and non-print materials that are included in your library's electronic cataloging system.

2-28
Vendor Barcode Log

This log, also suggested by Candy Blessing, is used to record the barcode ranges assigned to different vendors in vendor profiles or on particular orders. Also use the form to log generic barcodes ranges ordered in bulk from major vendors for materials that are cataloged manually.

2-29
Import/Export Log

Use Candy Blessing's log to keep track of the MARC records imported from various sources including materials vendors, cataloging outsourcing vendors (AccessMARC, Marcive, etc.), and copy cataloging locations (Access PA, Library of Congress, etc.). The log is also useful to track records that were exported for such varied reasons as items to be repaired, edited, or enhanced with MARC Magician and items to be shared with other libraries and for a deletion log of the records that were exported and then deleted from the catalog.

2-30
Library Fax Cover Sheet

Cover your faxes and identify yourself.

Checklist of Administrative Tasks: An Annual To-Do List for Teacher-Librarians

AUGUST

- Visit and sort summer mail. (Avoid being overwhelmed next month!) Try to get paid time for your support staff to help.
- Get bulletin boards in order.
- Assess facility for cleanliness to see if all equipment and furniture is in the right place. Retrieve missing and borrowed items. (Things tend to shift over the summer.)
- Check boxes against purchase orders.
- Create "Welcome Back" brochures and newsletters for students, teachers, and parents.
- Prepare the OPAC for circulation with the school district calendar.
- Prepare or update orientation lessons.
- Prepare list of online databases with remote access passwords for faculty and students. Check vendor invoices and correspondence for any changes since last year's list.
- Send letters to invite back veteran volunteers.
- Recruit new volunteers.
- Distribute curriculum-mapping documents in classroom teachers' mailboxes.
- Create or update forms and passes. Review any changes in policies or procedures and inform staff.
- Prepare orientation activities.
- Greet custodians and ask (gently) about any critical cleaning or furniture/equipment moving issues. Follow up with e-mail.
- Order materials for Banned Books Week.
- Examine samples of standardized tests looking for opportunities to design instruction keyed to information-type skills tested.

SEPTEMBER

- Prepare for the grand opening!
- Schedule appropriate student orientations with faculty.
- Distribute an upbeat(!) newsletter for teachers with updated media and database lists and any forms they will need to get started. Invite collaboration!
- Stop by the local public library with appropriate resource materials.
- Check the public library schedule of events to promote with students and teachers.
- Prepare or update policies for circulation, computer use, etc.
- Get class sign-up conference sheets ready for *early bird* teachers.
- Orient and train new volunteers.
- Catalog and process new materials.
- Submit annual goals to principal.
- Approach principal (in-person or by memo or e-mail) with initial plans for any major events—book fairs, author visits, etc.—and include associated costs.

- Join any building/district committee that seems relevant to your mission or interesting to you personally.
- Recruit new and veteran student aides.
- Solicit new members for the Faculty Advisory Committee.
- Submit forms to ensure permission to attend state and national professional conferences.
- Prepare a list of professional magazines for faculty use—distribute Current Awareness Program reminder form.
- Greet the art teachers. Ask sweetly for any emergency supplies you may need. Solicit and welcome any displays of student work. Your facility will be much enhanced by any such exhibits!

Bulletin Board Themes: Welcome back, Labor Day, Hispanic Heritage Month, Banned Books Week, Study skills, Teachers' or students' favorite summer reads, Library Card Sign-up Month, International Literacy Day

Literary Birthdays: Richard Wright (4), Paul Fleischman (5), Jack Prelutsky (8), Jon Scieszka (8), Mildred Taylor (13), Tomie DePaola (15), Robert McCloskey (15), H. G. Wells (21), Stephen King (22), F. Scott Fitzgerald (24), William Faulkner (25), Shel Silverstein (25)

OCTOBER

- Ask to attend the various department meetings.
- Determine any curricular changes to be addressed with new materials or instruction.
- Invite faculty in to examine new resources and discuss upcoming units and assist with weeding the collection in their areas of expertise.
- Conduct initial surveys relating to reading interests, user satisfaction, self-efficacy, creating a baseline for comparison later in the year.
- Catalog and process new materials.
- Orient new faculty members (host them during lunch, free periods, or after school). Discuss services and resources specific to their programs. Suggest future meetings to plan instruction.
- Host the first meeting of the Faculty Advisory Committee.
- Host a Teen Read Week activity.
- Attend parent night and PTA meetings. Prepare packets for parents that include introductory brochures, database password lists, your academic integrity policy, school style sheet, etc. Consider proposing author visits, grants, and book fairs to parents at these events.

Bulletin Board Themes: Teen Read Week, Halloween (bats, spiders, witches, etc.), Autumn, Harvest, Mysteries, International School Library Day, Computer Learning Month, Consumer Information Month, Discoverer's Day/Columbus Day, United Nations Day, National Book Month

Literary Birthdays: Karen Cushman (4), Frank Herbert (8), R. L. Stine (8), John Lennon (9), Oscar Wilde (16), Eugene O'Neill (16), Arthur Miller (17), Phillip Pullman (19), Bruce Brooks (23), Sylvia Plath (27), Dylan Thomas (27), Katherine Paterson (31)

NOVEMBER

- Consider hosting a mock election with the social studies department.
- Browse fall/winter vendor catalogs for promising new titles to discuss with departments.
- Host an activity for Children's Book Week.

- Ask volunteers to read shelves.
- Offer to host a faculty meeting and request a few minutes to discuss and display new materials and databases.

Bulletin Board Themes: Thanksgiving, Immigrants/Pilgrims, Native American Heritage Month, Elections/politics, Harvest, Children's Book Week, Veteran's Day, American Education Week, Family Literacy Day

Literary Birthdays: Stephen Crane (1), Albert Camus (7), Bram Stoker (8), Fyodor Dostoyevsky (11), Kurt Vonnegut Jr. (11), Robert Lewis Stevenson (13), Daniel Pinkwater (15), Margaret Atwood (18), Charles Schultz (26), William Blake (28), Louisa May Alcott (29), Madeline L'Engle (29), C. S. Lewis (29), Jonathan Swift (30), Mark Twain (30)

DECEMBER

- Buy small holiday gifts for volunteers.
- Consider a holiday reception, breakfast, or luncheon for volunteers.
- Distribute reminders about end-of-semester overdues.
- Prepare for holiday break by turning off all electronic equipment.

Bulletin Board Themes: Holidays (Christmas, Chanukah, Kwanzaa), Winter, Gifts, New Year, Human Rights Day (10)

Literary Birthdays: David Macaulay (2), Joseph Conrad (2), Walt Disney (5), Emily Dickinson (10), Melvil Dewey (10), Nostradamus (14), Jane Austen (16), Jerry Pinkney (22), Avi (Wortis) (23), Rudyard Kipling (30)

JANUARY

- Update teachers about new materials.
- Follow up on midterm graduates—library obligations, etc.
- If teachers are retiring or leaving/transferring at midterm, send notices to inspire return of library materials.
- Second semester curriculum updates—meet with as many teachers as possible, especially new teachers, to discuss changes or refinements in curricular units.
- Update principal about progress toward meeting annual goals.
- Consider presenting at PTA meeting regarding improving student research, new electronic resources, etc.
- Host a *marking party.* Invite faculty to grade finals in the library. Offer snacks, music, a collegial environment.

Bulletin Board Themes: Martin Luther King's Birthday, Snowflakes, Winter Olympics, Resolutions, National Book Month, National Hobby Month

Literary Birthdays: J. D. Salinger (1), Isaac Asimov (2), Carolyn Haywood (3), J. R. R. Tolkien (3), Jacob Grimm (4), Sherlock Holmes (6), Zora Neal Hurston (7), Robert Cormier (17), A. A. Milne (18), Edgar Allan Poe (19), Virginia Woolf (25), Lewis Carroll (27), Lloyd Alexander (30)

FEBRUARY

- Analyze focused sections of your collection for upcoming purchasing.
- Target teachers you did not collaborate with first semester for unit planning in the new semester.

- Celebrate Library Lovers Month.
- Order materials for National Library Week.

Bulletin Board Themes: Black History Month, Valentine's Day/Love around the World, Romance! Groundhog Day, Chinese New Year, Presidents Day, Job Shadow Day

Literary Birthdays: Jerry Spinelli (1), Langston Hughes (1), James Joyce (2), Ayn Rand (2), Joan Lowry Nixon (3), James Michener (3), Charles Dickens (7), Laura Ingalls Wilder (7), Jules Verne (8), Alice Walker (9), Judy Blume (12), Jacqueline Woodson (12), Jane Yolen (12), William Sleator (13), Chaim Potok (17), Robert Newton Peck (17), Toni Morrison (18), Amy Tan (19), W. E. B. DuBois (23), Wilhelm Grimm (24), Cynthia Voight (25), Victor Hugo (26), John Steinbeck (27), Donna Jo Napoli (28)

MARCH

- Check budget, begin to reconcile purchase orders, and plan to spend any remaining funds. Funds sometimes freeze in March!
- Begin to solicit teacher input for consideration file for next year's budget.
- Host a Read-Across-America activity.

Bulletin Board Themes: Women's History Month, Beginning of spring, Wind/kites, Read Across America (March 2), National Craft Month, National Nutrition Month, Music in Our Schools Month, March Madness (basketball), Freedom of Information Day

Literary Birthdays: Dr. Seuss (2), John Irving (2), Sid Fleischman (16), Virginia Hamilton (12), Lois Lowry (20), Louis Sachar (20), Randolph Caldecott (22), Robert Frost (26), Tennessee Williams (26), Julia Alvarez (27)

APRIL

- Begin developing budget for next year—examining categories for expenditure: supplies, databases, print materials, professional dues.
- Host a Book Fair celebrating National Library Week or School Library Media Month.
- Consider inventorying a section or two of your collection. Read shelves first.
- Get appropriate presents (or flowers) for your assistants and other very special administrative assistants in the school or district!

Bulletin Board Themes: Earth Day, April Fools Day, National Library Week, School Library Media Month, Zoo and Aquarium Month, Shakespeare's birth and death, National Poetry Month, Young People's Poetry Month, Rain, Flowers, Rebirth, Easter/Passover, School Library Media Month, National Library Week, TV Turn-off Week, World Book and Copyright Day, International Children's Book Day (April 2), Administrative Assistants' Day, National Volunteer Week, El Día de los Niños/ El Día de los Libros

Literary Birthdays: Anne McCaffrey (1), Hans Christian Anderson (2), Washington Irving (3), Maya Angelou (4), Richard Peck (5), Booker T. Washington (5), William Wordsworth (7), Gary Soto (12), Charlotte Brontë (21), William Shakespeare (23), Lois Duncan (28)

MAY

- Begin your major campaign (notices, posters, letters home, etc.) to retrieve problem overdue materials. Remind teachers to return materials they no longer need.

- Set and publicize the last date for all loans and the last date for returns—regular loans? Graduating class? Interlibrary loan? Faculty?
- Work with Language Arts Department to finalize summer reading lists. Post reading list on Web page and share with public libraries and bookstores.
- Promote books on the summer reading list. Begin a summer loan campaign and set the date due.
- Create an overdue list and run overdue notices.
- Communicate with the office about consequences for students who neglect to return materials and procedures and send list of fines and lost materials.
- Distribute overdue notices to students and send friendly reminders to teachers with outstanding materials. Offer to extend loans to teachers for summer use.
- For elementary- and middle-schoolers, ask the local public librarian to promote the public library's summer programs.
- Begin to prepare annual report.
- Inventory supplies and equipment to assess needs for next school year.
- Check vendors' prices for regularly ordered items for next year's budget.
- Schedule summer cleaning projects with custodial staff.
- Examine consideration file and survey faculty by e-mail for final input on materials before preparing purchase orders.
- Assess subscriptions—magazines and newspapers, databases, standing orders—for level of use. Decide on renewals.
- Prepare purchase orders and enter orders in database.
- Reconcile any outstanding purchase orders with Central Office and with the vendors. Are there funds left? Should you transfer funds from one budget code to another? Can you transfer them to next year?
- Analyze results of standardized tests, and target areas of need for instruction in such areas as reading, writing, analysis, problem solving, information processing.

Bulletin Board Themes: Flowers, Spring, Mother's Day, Asian Pacific Heritage Month, Older Americans Month, National Teacher's Day, May Day, Cinco de Mayo, Physical Fitness Month, Memorial Day, National PTA Teacher Appreciation Week, Get Caught Reading Month

Literary Birthdays: Todd Strasser (5), Milton Meltzer (8), Caroline B. Cooney (10), Christopher Paul Curtis (10), L. Frank Baum (15), Paul Zindel (15), Bruce Coville (16), Gary Paulsen (17), Malcolm X (19), Arnold Lobel (22), Arthur Conan Doyle (22), M. E. Kerr (27), Walt Whitman (31)

JUNE

- Conduct end-of-year surveys relating to reading interests, user satisfaction, skills self-efficacy. Compare with surveys conducted earlier in the year.
- Run statistical reports and complete annual report.
- Distribute annual report to building and main office administrators, board members, and PTA officers.
- Submit report to principal addressing progress toward meeting goals. Thank him/her for support over the past school year.
- Purge graduating class from the database. Promote other classes in the database.
- Write thank-you notes to volunteers.

- Set up calendar for upcoming school year in database.
- Inventory collection or additional portions of collection. Read shelves first; consider weeds as you inventory!
- Collect and inventory outstanding equipment—digital cameras, projectors, etc.
- Arrange for summer cleaning and repair of equipment.
- Straighten up—shelve everything left on book trucks, take down bulletin boards and displays, remove materials from shelves and desktops for more effective summer cleaning.
- Enter new students in the OPAC (get disk from elementary or middle school if possible).
- Take your staff out to lunch or dinner!

Bulletin Board Themes: Summer reading, Good luck, graduates! Father's Day, Flag Day, Beach, Travel

Literary Birthdays: Thomas Hardy (2), Frederico Garcia Lorca (5), Cynthia Rylant (6), Nikki Giovanni (7), Carolyn Meyer (8), Maurice Sendak (10), Nat Hentoff (10), Ann Frank (12), Brian Jacques (15), Chris Van Allsburg (18), Jean Paul Sartre (21), George Orwell (25), Eric Carle (25), Pearl Buck (25)

THROUGHOUT THE YEAR

- Look for opportunities to speak to community groups, and attend department or grade meetings.
- During slower times read and weed your shelves. Keep them alive and interesting to users.
- Continue to keep your website alive and valid, a place your users want and need to visit.
- Create pathfinders for major students projects and to address student and faculty research needs.
- Maintain a consideration file of teacher requests and items that would support curricular and student needs.
- Communicate library news with regular (monthly or quarterly) newsletters—print, e-mail, or web-based.
- Offer to collaborate with teachers to create online units or WebQuests to spark up units in need of spark.
- Send updates to your administrators and faculty relating to their personal research needs and interests. Give them what they want before they know they need it. (For instance, if your principal is interested in data-driven management, send copies of any related articles as they come in.)
- Solicit student work from teachers for display. What better way to illustrate your contribution to the learning process!
- Assess teachers' teaching and learning needs and develop in-services or informal meetings to address those needs.

Class Visit Planning Form

Course Title _____ Teacher _____

Today's Date _____ Visit Date(s) _____ Period(s) _____

Grade _____ Level _____ Number Assigned Sections _____

1. Briefly describe the project/activity _____

   _____

   _____

   _____

2. Content goals/Standards _____

3. Information skill goal(s)/standard(s): Circle all that apply:

   Defining problem   Locating/Searching   Analyzing   Documenting/Ethical Use

   Organizing/Synthesis   Communicating   Evaluating/Reflecting

   Other_____

4. Assignment begins _____ Assignment is due _____

5. How will students define the research problem/question/thesis?

   ❏ Students will select ideas from suggestions on an assignment sheet. (Please attach a copy of your assignment sheet or other student handouts.)

   ❏ Students will independently develop questions/theses for research.

6. What types of materials will students be using?

   ❏ Free Web   ❏ Online Subscription Databases   Specify_____

   ❏ Periodicals   ❏ Books   ❏ CD-ROMs   ❏ Audiovisual DVD, Video, etc.

   List any specific or major resources you'd like the students to use:

   List any materials you would like excluded from use:

7. Expected product(s) _____

_____

8. How will the final product be assessed? (Shall we work on a new rubric? Please attach a copy of your rubric or assessment tool you have already developed.)

9. Would you like the teacher-librarian to help you prepare a Web guide page or pathfinder to guide students to resources?

   ❏ Yes   ❏ No   ❏ Let's work on it together!

   Suggestions _____

10. Do your students require any special technology preparation or presentation? (e.g., Software loaded, Web sites created, bookmarks gathered, or software introduced?)

11. Are there learning differences that may need to be addressed for this assignment? Please share here or stop in to chat.

12. If you plan to put materials on reserve, which type of loan would you prefer? Which materials should be set aside?

    Type of loan: ❏ Normal circulation   ❏ Overnight   ❏ Room use

    Other (list): _____

13. Would you recommend we notify the public library of this assignment?

    ❏ Yes   ❏ No

    Any specific advice:

14. Notes, suggestions, plans, stuff we should discuss?

Teacher-Librarian Job Description

SUMMARY

The mission of the school library information program is "to ensure that students and staff are effective users of ideas and information." It is the job of the teacher-librarian to accomplish this mission as outlined in *Information Power, Building Partnerships for Learning* (American Association of School Librarians and Association of Educational Communications and Technology, Chicago: 1998).

The teacher-librarian serves the learning community by presenting a clear and creative vision for the school library program. He or she supports the educational philosophy and objectives of the school district by engaging in three key roles to facilitate effective delivery of the curriculum: program administration, learning and teaching, and information access and delivery.

The teacher-librarian plans, arranges, administers, and implements the library information center program. She or he organizes, establishes, and supervises routines and procedures for the smooth operation of the library information center. The teacher-librarian is the school's information technology expert. He or she has technological expertise in electronic information resources, library-management software, and electronic resources available in the content areas. The teacher-librarian instructs students in the skills necessary to effectively access, evaluate, analyze, synthesize, and communicate information in traditional and emerging formats. The teacher-librarian creates and maintains an atmosphere that encourages student and faculty use. She or he updates personal expertise by keeping aware of best practice, belonging to professional organizations, and studying and analyzing library, media, and educational trends. The teacher-librarian's role is one of an educator, administrator, and information consultant, a professional who is expected to take a leadership role in implementing the school's educational program.

EDUCATIONAL REQUIREMENTS

The qualified teacher-librarian is both an instructional and knowledge manager. He or she holds professional credentials in education, as well as in library science.

The American Association of School Librarians' position statement on preparation of school library media specialists recommends:

> School library media specialists have a broad undergraduate education with a liberal arts background and hold a master's degree or equivalent from a program that combines academic and professional preparation in library and information science, education, management, media, communications theory, and technology. The academic program of study includes some directed field experience in a library media program, coordinated by a faculty member in cooperation with an experienced library media specialist. Library media specialists meet state certification requirements for both the library media specialist and professional educator classifications. While there may be many practicing library media specialists who have only an undergraduate degree and whose job performance is outstanding, the master's degree is considered the entry-level degree for the profession.

The graduate degree is earned at colleges and universities whose programs are accredited by appropriate bodies such as the American Library Association (ALA), the National Council for the Accreditation of Teacher Education (NCATE), or state education agencies.

DUTIES AND RESPONSIBILITIES

Program Administration

Establishes and evaluates annual and long-range goals for the library information program, seeking input from the learning community

Prepares grant proposals when appropriate

Participates in curriculum planning meetings

Plans, administers, operates, supervises, and evaluates the library information center, developing policies to ensure efficient operation and optimal service and revising policies when appropriate

Prepares and administers the library budget, keeping records of all expenditures

Plans and maintains a relevant professional library to promote the professional development of the faculty and administrative staff

Maintains an efficient system of classifying, cataloging, and circulating all library materials; instructs teachers and students in the use of the library system

Develops policies and coordinates procedures for challenged materials

Develops and disseminates policies relating to appropriate use of resources, such as the Internet and school network, intellectual freedom, intellectual property, and academic integrity

Serves as member of the school media and technology committees

Maintains schedule flexible and accessible to learners and faculty

Maintains an environment that encourages learning and fosters use, encouraging appropriate conduct of students using the facility

Supervises and trains paraprofessional, clerical, or technical staff members

Through service on building and district committees, participates in curriculum development and implementation

Maintains cooperative relationships with local public and academic libraries and other community organizations

Prepares schedules, with input from teachers and building administrators, for integrated information skills instruction

Keeps records of student use, circulation, purchases, and losses; provides regular reports on the library as required by the administration and as needed for planning purposes

Trains and supervises library clerks, para-professionals, and adult and student volunteers

Supervises the regular inventory of library materials, evaluates the collection, weeds obsolete and worn materials, and updates inventory records and the catalog

Promotes use of library information center materials through displays and published communications

Works collaboratively with many groups within the school culture: parents, teachers, students, administrators, and community members

Instructional (Learning and Teaching)

Works with administration and curriculum leaders to ensure information literacy outcomes are a focus of instruction

Assists teachers in identifying and accessing materials to support content-area instruction as well as professional growth

Consults with teachers about students' instructional needs and learning differences

Provides leadership in the integration of technology into all areas of the curriculum and the instructional practices of the faculty

Models appropriate pedagogy, reflecting research in best practice and learning theory, and works with teachers to improve pedagogy school-wide

Develops a broad view of the entire school curriculum

Is involved with curriculum planning and assessment across disciplines and grade levels

Collaborates with classroom teachers in designing, implementing, and evaluating instruction that ensures integration of literature, information literacy skills, and technologies into student learning

Helps students develop attitudes, habits, and skills leading to lifelong learning and library use

Provides group and individual instruction in information skills, research strategies, and use of resources and equipment

Aids students in communicating the results of their research in traditional and emerging formats

Encourages and facilitates student development of independent library-information skills

Creatively and energetically promotes literacy, reading, and library use through such activities as storytelling, book talks, displays, publications, and special events

Provides reference and readers' advisory services to the general student population, including students who have special learning needs or unusual intellectual interests

Provides targeted and differentiated assistance to students with special learning needs

Provides professional development for the faculty in such areas as new information technologies and information literacy

Supports the continuing educational research of faculty and administrators

Models effective pedagogy and supports classroom teachers in improving their practice

Information Access and Delivery

Functions as the informational technology leader within the school

Understands the role of technology in instruction, student learning, and professional development

Develops policies, procedures, and criteria for selecting a balanced collection to support the curriculum, representative of diverse points of view and conscious of our pluralistic society

Systematically evaluates and weeds the collection

Encourages faculty and student input concerning suggestions for purchase

Develops and maintains information networks and services, and organizes, retrieves, and disseminates or circulates resources to support learners' needs

Provides training to students and faculty in effective use of information systems

Interprets and applies information technologies in curricular context

Promotes effective use of information resources and services both within the school and beyond

Assumes a leadership role in promoting the principles of intellectual freedom by creating and sustaining an environment promoting free inquiry and exposing students to a broad range of ideas

Ensures intellectual and physical access to materials in all formats for all learners

Promotes use of school information services for independent reading, listening, viewing

Promotes awareness of information resources beyond school facility

Functions as a district/school resource for issues regarding ethical use of information including issues of copyright and intellectual freedom

Prepares lists of topical and new materials to support class assignments and to promote interest in reading

Guides students in materials selection

Provides orientation for new students and faculty

Professional

Presents and attends workshops, in-service activities, and conferences, and takes courses to update professional skills

Reads field-related professional literature and scans materials in content-area journals for items of interest to the professional growth of colleagues

Plans for professional development relating to information technology and pedagogical methods for other staff members

Keeps aware of electronic resources (mailing lists, databases, websites) that foster professional growth

Maintains professional relationships with faculty, administrative staff, and library colleagues

Participates actively in professional associations on the local, state, and national level

Other

Performs such other duties as may be required by the principal or assistants to the superintendent

Reporting Relationships

The teacher-librarian reports to the building principal for all building concerns and to the assistants to the superintendent (or the district library coordinator) for district (curricular) concerns

Interview Questions for Teacher-Librarians

PERSONAL/TEACHING STYLE

Tell us a little about yourself. (Classroom teaching and library information center experience)

If I were to visit your last school, how would the students describe you?

How would the classroom teachers with whom you worked describe you?

What kind of atmosphere would you like to create in your library information center?

Please describe a project or program that you implemented about which you feel proud.

How would you coordinate your lessons with our language arts program?

How would you work to integrate information skills into the various grade levels or content areas?

How would you encourage collaboration with more reluctant classroom teachers?

How does block scheduling affect student learning in the library?

Describe the process you use to select library materials, and in the larger sense, develop a library collection.

How would you handle discipline issues in the library?

How can the library program improve student achievement?

Please describe one of your most successful lessons.

Do you have a teaching portfolio? Website?

PHILOSOPHY/PROFESSIONALISM

What do you consider the most important role(s) of the teacher-librarian?

How do you balance the three roles for teacher-librarians outlined in *Information Power* (learning and teaching, program administration, information access and delivery)?

What is your view on the importance of information literacy?

Which model of information literacy do you prefer?

How would you work with our staff to ensure that information skills are integrated into teaching or learning programs in classrooms?

How would you handle issues relating to plagiarism? Challenged materials?

How active are you in professional organizations?

Which conferences do you regularly attend?

TECHNOLOGY

What are some of your favorite subscription databases?

Which electronic encyclopedia or journal index might you recommend to a third grade child? To a ninth grade child?

How would you help apprehensive staff members overcome their reluctance about using technology in instruction?

With which computer platforms/programs are you comfortable?

What examples can you give of incorporating information technologies in your lessons?

How would you rate your searching abilities? What are your favorite search tools? Online databases?

What role would the Internet play in your program?

What skills do you feel are most important for students and teachers to master as they use the Internet in learning and teaching?

We are about to automate/reevaluate our automation system. What experience have you had with circulation or catalog systems?

What is the most-recent technology skill you have developed or application you have mastered?

What recent piece of reference software have you seen recently that impressed you?

What experience have you had in Web page development?

How do you keep up with rapid changes in information technology?

LITERATURE/READING PROMOTION

What was the best children's or young adult book you read this year?

What review journals do you rely on to help you select materials?

How would you encourage recreational reading among our students?

Do you support the use of any reading promotion initiatives or commercial reading programs with students? (Like Accelerated Reader, Battle of the Books, Read Across America, Teen Read Week)

RELATIONS WITH COMMUNITY AND STAFF

How would you convince a teacher used to a regularly scheduled library period that flexible scheduling could help him or her deliver curriculum?

Parents in this school like to be very involved. What opportunities would you provide for parent involvement in your program?

What would you do if a parent challenged a book in your collection?

How might you involve the broader community in your program?

CONCLUSION/FEEDBACK

If you were responsible for selecting a teacher-librarian, what professional and personal qualities would you look for?

You've had a chance to look around a bit. What do you like about this facility? What changes do you think you'd make?

What questions do you have for us?

Library Assistant/Paraprofessional Job Description

This list is intended to be illustrative rather than complete, and serves to show major duties and responsibilities and differentiates the position from others in the district.

SUMMARY

The library paraprofessional is a person trained and skilled in the areas of technical services who provides support to the teacher-librarian in maintaining the efficient operation of the library media center. Under the supervision of the teacher-librarian, the paraprofessional is the responsible for:

- administration of the circulation desk
- supervision of library shelves and reserve collections
- preparation and processing of materials
- preparation of purchase orders
- direction and supervision of student volunteers

The paraprofessional offers *basic* guidance for students and faculty in the use of the library media center including the online catalog, location of items in the collection, subscription databases, library website, applications on library workstations, and multimedia equipment

The paraprofessional has the ability to work independently and manage continual interruptions and shifting job priorities. He or she should possess excellent word processing and database skills, as well as a strong interest in working with young people.

EDUCATIONAL REQUIREMENTS

The position requires post-high school experience or education in the fields of libraries, computers, books, and audiovisual material.

The library paraprofessional must possess an interest in and affinity for direct work with young people. The position requires strong public-relations skills.

DUTIES AND RESPONSIBILITIES

- Prepares materials for circulation.
- Supervises circulation desk and circulation procedures.
- Prepares and distributes overdue notices, letters to parents, and lists of overdues for the main office.
- Sets up reserve collections.
- Helps students and faculty access materials through the use of the online catalog, the library website, and other databases.
- Has familiarity with the library's print and online resources and assists members of the learning community in accessing print, electronic, and audiovisual services and materials.
- Assists students and faculty in setting up and using media in all formats.

- Searches for and verifies bibliographic information.
- Shelves and retrieves materials.
- Performs preliminary automated cataloging and manages processing and preparation of newly acquired materials.
- Arranges for interlibrary loans and maintains appropriate interlibrary loan records and reports.
- Prepares purchase orders. Maintains and updates databases of purchase orders, as well as video, periodical, and other special collections.
- Verifies invoices against shipments and orders.
- Aids in the preparation of library publications.
- Keeps statistical records on usage, circulation, etc.
- Notifies students when reserved materials are available.
- Assists in preparing bibliographies and updating links for websites and pathfinders.
- Assists with displays and other special projects.
- Supervises and executes automated inventory.
- Assists teacher-librarian in monitoring student behavior in the library and helps to maintain a friendly, cooperative, and productive atmosphere for students, faculty, and parents.
- Performs any other related duties that may be assigned by the teacher-librarian.

REPORTING RELATIONS

The library paraprofessional is responsible through the teacher-librarian to the school principal.

Interviewing the Library Assistant/Paraprofessional

1. Do you have any experience working in libraries?   ❏ Yes   ❏ No

2. Can you tell us a little about your experience working with children/young adults? _____
   _____

3. What do you enjoy most about working with children/young adults? _____
   _____

4. Can you remember a children's or young adult book you read and enjoyed? _____
   _____

5. How would you describe your clerical skills?   ❏ Fair   ❏ Good   ❏ Excellent

6. Do you mind doing physical work like shelving books?   ❏ Yes   ❏ No

7. How familiar are you with the Dewey Decimal Classification System? _____
   _____

8. What computer applications are you comfortable working with? _____
   _____

9. Have you had any experiences working with databases?   ❏ Yes   ❏ No

10. This is a very busy facility. How well do you work under stress? Can you work well with continual
    interruption? _____

2-6A

11. This job involves a great deal of detail and requires someone who is extremely organized. How well do you

    work with detail? How organized are you? _____

    _____

12. This job is constantly changing as new information and communications technologies emerge.

    Do you like to learn new skills?   ❑ Yes   ❑ No

13. How would you handle a group of students behaving inappropriately in our library?_____

    _____

14. What do you view as your most positive work traits? _____

    _____

15. How would you describe your work ethic?_____

    _____

16. In what ways do you feel you could contribute to our library? _____

    _____

17. Do you have any questions of us regarding this position?   ❑ Yes   ❑ No

Dear
Teacher-Librarian
Substitute,

Thanks for coming in for me. A list of today's visiting classes is on the clipboard. My planning forms and any student handouts and rubrics are attached.

Our library information center staff members are _____

_____.

They will be happy to help you locate materials and answer any procedural questions.

The URL for our library website is:

It provides access to many of the resources our students use on a regular basis.

Our students and staff are our first priority. Even if there is no "official" class here, please circulate around the floor to see if anyone needs help with our print resources or at the workstations. During the slow periods, please help us continue the level of service our students and staff expect of us. There are many day-to-day tasks that require attention.

Some tasks you might help with include

- processing books, magazines, software, and other materials
- bookmarking promising websites for upcoming classes or updating a page on the library website
- preparing bibliographies, pathfinders, and reading lists for upcoming assignments
- reading our shelves for misshelved items
- cataloging new materials and gifts
- creating a bulletin board or display
- gathering materials onto a cart for an upcoming student project
- sorting books for shelving
- shelving books
- helping prepare overdue lists or checking to see if "lost" materials wandered back to our shelves
- laminating display material
- repairing materials
- pulling items for the bindery
- troubleshooting any computer problems

It would be best if you could arrange to take lunch during the slowest lunch period. Stagger your lunch with the other staff members.

Please leave a note describing any problems you may have had today.

If there is an emergency you can reach me by phone or e-mail at:

Good luck and thank you again for your help,

Teacher-Librarian

Academic Integrity Policy
for Student Research

RATIONALE

We in the School District of _____ understand and value the concept of intellectual property. Therefore, we strive to teach students the ethic of responsibly documenting the ideas of others in all formats. To do so, we believe that we must not only teach the ethics and mechanics of documentation, but we must also hold students accountable for the ethical use of the ideas and words of others.

Therefore, all teachers provide the instruction and scaffolding necessary for students to research ethically, and all students are expected to exercise good faith in the submission of research-based work and to document accurately regardless of how the information is used (summary, paraphrase, and quotation) or regardless of the format used (written, oral, or visual). Plagiarism, in any form, is unethical and unacceptable.

Specifically,

It is the **teacher's responsibility** to provide:

- an assignment sheet with explicit requirements and directions
- a specific rubric for assessment of the process and the product
- checkpoints to facilitate the research process, to assist students in time management, and to provide opportunities to help students during the process
- availability for students who are having difficulty with note-taking, documenting, or formatting procedures
- clear guidelines for acceptable help from human sources (peers, adults)

It is the **student's responsibility** to:

- meet checkpoint deadlines
- ask questions and to seek help from teachers and librarians
- follow our school's Research Guide and documentation guidelines
- submit an Acknowledgments page to credit help given by others (help that has been approved by the teacher giving the assignment)
- use in-text or in-project documentation accurately and appropriately use Works Cited and Works Consulted pages accurately and appropriately
- submit only his/her own work

Plagiarism includes:

- Direct copying of the work of another submitted as the student's own (from that of another student or other person, from an Internet source, from a print source)
- Lack of in-text or in-project documentation
- Documentation that does not check out or does not match Works Cited/Works Consulted.
- Work that suddenly appears on final due date without a clear provenance (does not include checkpoint process requirements)

CONSEQUENCES AND OPPORTUNITY FOR LEARNING

1. The Academic Standards Committee (which includes the principal, teacher-librarian, Language Arts department coordinator, department coordinator, and classroom teacher involved in referring issue) will confer to confirm the teacher's suspicion of plagiarism and to determine the options for the student to learn from his/her error in judgment. Upon confirmation of plagiarism, the student earns a zero for the plagiarism, the teacher files a disciplinary referral, and a member of the committee writes a letter to the student and parents to explain the decision and its ramifications, etc. Options include but are not limited to:

   - No second opportunity (Ex. A senior who is not new to the high school or any student who has blatantly copied a paper from another source, i.e., Internet source or another student)
   - Redoing the project (Ex. A senior who is new to the high school)
   - Redoing the project from an earlier checkpoint that was satisfactorily met (Ex. An underclassman who, as determined by the committee, will benefit from the opportunity to complete the process correctly)
   - Adding the appropriate documentation that is missing (Ex. An underclassman who has used a variety of sources and will benefit from the opportunity to add the necessary documentation)

     Notes:
     - The student may choose not to take advantage of the second opportunity. If so, the zero stands.
     - A student may have only one "second opportunity" offer in his/her high school career.
     - A second offense automatically earns a zero without redress.

2. The teacher will assess the "second opportunity" work. If satisfactory, the zero will be replaced by the lowest passing grade. If the work is unsatisfactory, the zero stands.

3. It is possible that a student will fail a course if s/he plagiarizes a project of sufficient weight. In this case, the student repeats the course or attends summer school. The student's summer school experience must include satisfactory completion of a similar research-based project in order to earn course credit; otherwise, the student must repeat the course.

SOURCE: Developed by Carol H. Rohrbach, K–12 Language Arts Coordinator, School District of Springfield Township, Erdenheim, PA. With revisions by Joyce Kasman Valenza.

Material Selection Policy

It is the policy of the Board of the _____ School District to provide a broad range of educational materials to enrich and support the curriculum and to meet the needs of the individual students and teachers. The professional staff should provide students with a wide range of materials of diverse appeal. Materials should be available in a variety of formats and represent varying levels of difficulty and varying points of view. In selecting materials, principles outweigh personal opinion. Materials are considered for their quality and appropriateness.

RESPONSIBILITY

1. The board of school directors assumes legal responsibility for the selection of materials in the district's library information centers.

2. Responsibility for the selection of all library materials is delegated to the professional library staff through the building principal. The selection process involves open opportunity for consultation with administrators, faculty, supervisors, and students. Selection is based upon evaluation

   a. by the professional library staff

   b. in professional library tools and other review media

   c. by other responsible professionals

3. In selecting materials, library staff, administrators, and faculty are guided by the principles incorporated in the School Library Bill of Rights, the Freedom to Read Statement, standards adopted by the American Association of School Librarians, and the School Library Standards of the _____ State Department of Education.

4. The collection will be developed systematically ensuring global perspective, recognizing diversity, representing differing viewpoints, and presenting a well-balanced coverage of subjects and opinions. The collection will include a variety of formats (print, electronic, multimedia, etc.) and a wide range of current materials on various levels of difficulty supporting the diverse interests, learning styles, and viewpoints of the learning community.

CRITERIA FOR SELECTION

1. Materials should support and be consistent with the district's general educational goals and the educational goals and objectives of our individual schools and specific courses.

2. Materials should be selected to enrich and support both the curriculum and the personal needs of our students and faculty, taking into consideration diverse interests, abilities, socioeconomic backgrounds, maturity levels, and students' extracurricular interests. Materials selected should encourage an appreciation for both informational and recreational reading, viewing, or listening.

3. Care will be taken to select materials of educational significance meeting standards of high quality in presentation, educational significance, aesthetic character, artistic quality, literary style, factual content, authenticity, readability, accuracy, durability, and technical production.

4. Materials should be free of stereotype and sexual bias.

5. Materials should be considered relating to their overall purpose and their direct relationship to instructional objectives and/or the curriculum. Selected materials should support needs in the content areas and be appropriate to the variety of ages, developmental stages, ability levels, and learning styles represented by the particular facility for which they are chosen.

2-9A

6. Materials should be selected representing opposing points of view on controversial issues, encouraging individual analysis. Library materials concerning controversial political, social, and religious issues should inform rather than indoctrinate.

7. The literary style of a work should be appropriate and effective for the subject matter and its intended readers or viewers.

8. The value of any work must be examined as a whole. The impact of an entire work will be considered, transcending individual words, phrases, and incidents.

9. Resource sharing will be considered in purchasing decisions. Materials may be purchased or not purchased based on networking and collaborative relationships with other area collections and depending upon extent of need.

10. Materials will be purchased in a variety of formats with efforts made to incorporate emerging technology when they meet the criteria outlined above.

11. Gift materials will be evaluated by the criteria outlined above and shall be accepted or rejected in accordance with those criteria.

PROCEDURES FOR SELECTION

The teacher-librarian, in conjunction with teachers, administrators, and the school library media advisory committee, will be responsible for the selection of materials. In coordinating this process, the teacher-librarian will do the following:

1. Arrange, when possible, for firsthand examination of items to be purchased.

2. Use reputable, unbiased, professionally prepared selection aids when firsthand examination of materials is not possible. Among the sources to be consulted are:

AASA Science Books and Films

ALA's Award Winning book lists: Newberry, Prinz, Coretta Scott King, etc.

ALAN Review

American Film & Video Association Evaluations

Basic Book Collection for Elementary Grades

Basic Book Collection for Junior High Schools

The Best in Children's Books

Booklist

Bulletin of the Center for Children's Books

Children's Software Review

Criticas

Horn Book

Kirkus Reviews

Library Media Connection

Library Journal

Multicultural Book Reviews

Multimedia Schools

New York Times Book Review

Publishers Weekly

Reference Books for School Libraries

School Library Journal

VOYA

Such core collection tools as the Wilson Catalog series: *Children's Catalog, Junior High School Catalog, Senior High School Catalog*

other sources as appropriate

3. Strongly consider the recommendations of faculty, students, and parents.

4. Judge gift items by standard selection criteria and, upon acceptance of such items, reserve the right to incorporate into the collection only those meeting the above criteria.

5. Purchase duplicates of extensively used material.

6. Purchase replacements for worn, damaged, or missing materials basic to the collection.

7. Determine a procedure for preventative maintenance and repair of material.

WEEDING

The collection of the library information center will be continually reevaluated in relation to evolving curriculum, new material formats, new instructional methods, and the current needs of its users. Materials no longer appropriate should be removed. Lost and worn materials of lasting value should be replaced. Weeding is essential to maintaining a relevant, attractive collection. Materials considered for weeding should include items:

- in poor physical condition
- containing obsolete subject matter
- no longer needed to support the curriculum or student/faculty interests
- superseded by more current information
- containing inaccurate information

PROCEDURE FOR CHALLENGED MATERIALS

The following procedures will be followed when a citizen challenges the appropriateness of an item in the collection:

1. Complainant will be asked to complete a Citizen Request for Reconsideration of Materials. This report will be forwarded to the superintendent, who will then inform the school board of directors.

2. The Citizen Request will be forwarded to a library review committee, appointed by the superintendent, that will consist of the teacher-librarian, the reading specialist, the principal, a teacher from the school involved, and an administrator from the central office.

3. A meeting of the library review committee will be scheduled within one week of receipt of the Citizen Request.

4. Material will be judged by the committee as to its conformance with the criteria for selection listed in this selection policy.

5. The written decision of the committee will be forwarded to the superintendent, who will inform the school board of directors and complainant of the committee's decision.

6. If the complainant is dissatisfied with the decision, a request may be submitted to the superintendent for a review of all proceedings by the school board of directors, who will render a final decision as to the appropriateness of the materials in question.

7. Challenged materials will remain in circulation until the process is completed.

Citizen Request for Reconsideration of Materials

Initiated by (name) _____

Phone _____ Address _____

Group affiliation (if any) _____

Have you discussed your objections with the principal, librarian, or a teacher?   ❏ Yes   ❏ No

Please list staff members with whom you have spoken. _____
_____

Material in question

Author _____

Title _____ Copyright date _____

Format   ❏ book   ❏ periodical   ❏ CD-ROM/DVD   ❏ film
❏ other (please specify)_____

Publisher _____

Please respond to the following questions. If you need more space, please attach additional pages.

1. Did you read/hear/view/examine the entire work?   ❏ Yes   ❏ No

2. If not, which part did you read or view?

3. Specifically what part of the work did you find objectionable? (Please cite specific passages, pages, sections, etc.)

4. For what age group(s) would you recommend this material?

5. Have you read our district's Material Selection Policy? ❐ Yes ❐ No

6. What do you believe is the theme or purpose of the work?

7. Could you find any value in the work? (Please describe.)

8. Are you aware of any professional reviews of the work? (Please list.)

9. How would students be affected by exposure to this work?

10. What do you suggest the school/library information center do about this material?

11. What material of equal value would you recommend to convey a similar picture or perspective?

12. How did you come in contact with this material?

Signature: _____ Date: _____

Received by: _____ Date: _____

Weeding and the Teacher-Librarian

WHY WEED?

A quality library media center offers learners a dynamic collection of materials, materials that are carefully selected to meet student needs. Materials on a library's shelves, as well as electronic and online resources, should be continuously and systematically evaluated for relevance, timeliness, and appeal. The American Library Association recommends that 5% of a collection be weeded annually.

Weeding is an ongoing part of the collection development process. Consider it *de-selection,* a process of evaluating and sometimes withdrawing materials that are rarely used, contain inaccurate or dated information, are in poor physical condition, or are no longer relevant to curriculum or student or faculty needs. The flipside of selection, weeding is a process of equal importance. But because weeding is often subject to community controversy, your policy should be a part of your library's/district's collection development policy.

Remember: something is **not** always better than nothing!

THE RATIONALE . . .

Weeding allows a school library to

- Present a more appealing, inviting, easier to use collection
- More effectively utilize limited space
- Ensure that library users access current, accurate information
- Correct past mistakes in the selection process
- Dispel the illusion of a sizable collection when critical need exists for new resources (Numbers can mislead!)
- Identify materials in need of repair or replacement
- Eliminate outdated material or material that has been superseded

HOW TO WEED

Weeding is both a formal and informal process. It occurs informally as you and your staff check books in and out, as you shelve, and as you look for materials on the shelves. Keep an area or a book truck aside for books you may want to discard, repair, or replace.

Plan for formal weeding times during periods you are not likely to be interrupted. It is not necessary to weed the whole collection at one time. Select a focus area, perhaps one in most serious need of weeding, either because of the age of the collection or because you just cannot fit another book in the section. Don't overwhelm yourself!

Make sure your administrator understands the importance of weeding in maintaining a strong library. Let your administrator and your custodian know when you begin to weed in earnest. Your administrator will advise you about how and when to best discard materials. He or she might appreciate the heads-up in the event that *trash scavengers* question your policies.

Rely on the expertise of faculty partners in areas where your knowledge is lacking. A physics teacher might offer significant insight if science is not your bag. This activity may serve to inspire new faculty interest in the collection and involvement in your program. Hint: avoid asking pack-rats to help!

If you are new to a building, it is wise to avoid weeding until you have been through one cycle of the curriculum, in other words, probably a year. Assignments in any given school may be quirky, unique, or unpredictable. If you don't observe the cycle, you may dispose of a treasure your history teacher relies on.

WEEDING TOOLS

When you are weeding, have on hand:

- Book truck for possible weeds
- Book truck for items to be bound or repaired
- Boxes for definite discards
- Post-it notes to identify individual issues. (Should we check circulations, out-of-print status, etc?)
- Appropriate school reading lists
- Appropriate collection development tools
    - H. W. Wilson's *Children's Catalog, Middle and Junior High School Catalog, Senior High School Library Catalog*
    - Brodart's *Elementary School Library Collection*
    - Libraries Unlimited's *Recommended Reference Books for Small and Medium-Sized Libraries and Media Centers*
    - Scarecrow's *Reference Books for Children*
    - Bowker-Greenwood's *Best Books for Children, Best Books for Young Teen Readers* (John T. Gillespie)
    - Neal-Schuman's *Core Collection for Young Adults* (Patrick Jones et al.)
- Printed collection reports from your automated system for the section of books you are examining, listing latest checkout dates/circulation history
- Access to Amazon.com (to check on and note out-of-print status, replacement availabilities, alternate purchases, etc.)
- Access to state library catalogs (If many libraries own the title, there might be good reason to keep it.)
- Place marker to note where you left off on the shelves
- Note pad to list materials that need to be replaced

REMEMBER TO

Delete holdings from the automated circ/cat system and update any inventory records.

Mark or stamp the item as WEEDED or DISCARDED. Remove pockets and cards and other identifying markings.

Avoid distributing weeded items.

Dispose of items with as little publicity as possible. If it's too old and unattractive for your collection, it is not likely to be useful elsewhere.

Avoid donating items to garage sales or other organizations.

If you are weeding because you have unneeded multiple copies, you might consider distributing extra copies to teachers who could use them.

EIGHT CRITICAL Cs TO CONSIDER IN WEEDING

Condition: Is the material too beat-up, worn out, or simply too icky or ugly to borrow? Would anyone really want to borrow it? Is it worth repairing? Is it repairable?

Copyright: Is it too old to be relevant? Remember, the relevance of copyright will vary in different areas of the collection. History and folktales have far longer shelf lives than technology and health materials! Pay special note before weeding books that are out-of-print. (Amazon.com might help you determine this.)

Curriculum and Content: Does this material support your curriculum or student or faculty interests? Is it on current reading lists? Is it a primary source?

Circulation: Has the material *moved?* How recently was it borrowed, referred to, or assigned? Use your circulation statistics to seriously evaluate books that have not circulated in the past five years.

Classics: Is the book a classic, award winner, or of historic or literary significance? Does the author have unique authority? Is the illustrator noted? Is it included in standard collection development tools (*Children's Catalog, Senior High School Catalog,* etc.)? Nonfiction books can be classics too! Be careful about avoiding such titles as Rachel Carson's *Silent Spring* if they are in good condition and relevant to curriculum and research.

Confusing: Is the item culturally or factually "dated," inaccurate, or obsolete? Does it contain gender or ethnic stereotyping?

Community: Does the item have special relevance to the community? Does it deal with local history? Is it a memorial gift?

Copies: Do you have far too many copies of an item no longer in great demand, perhaps no longer required reading? Is it redundant?

COPYRIGHT SUGGESTIONS TO CONSIDER

(Remember to examine each item individually, applying multiple criteria! Every library has different needs. Understand your curriculum and students interest before attempting any major weed!)

Dewey Class or Type	Number of years	Special Considerations
000	2–10	Books on technology age quickly! Books on computers, unless historical, date after three years. Circulating encyclopedia should be no older than eight years.
100	10–15	Look for and avoid weeding classics and famous names in the areas of philosophy and psychology, which may have long shelf lives! The history of witchcraft is likely to be both in demand and on assignment lists. Popular psychology may date quickly.
200	5–10	Titles on the history of religion and mythology may have long shelf lives. Check to ensure your collection represents the religious diversity of the community.
300	3–10	Titles relating to social and controversial issues and careers will date quickly. Keep these very current and balanced! Materials on education, government, holidays, folklore, fashion history, and the law may have lasting value. Weed old versions of test prep books when new versions of tests are in place. Circulating almanacs should be no older than three years, unless the curriculum includes work in historic statistics.
400	10	Your ESL materials should be appealing. Weed frequently. English and foreign language dictionaries and thesauri may be valuable for ten years.
500	5–10	Examine all science books for currency after five years. Natural history, botany, science history, and classic works may have longer lives. Make sure all science works reflect current discoveries. Engage science faculty in helping you with these decisions.
600	5–10	Look carefully at books on health and diseases. Information here is in constant flux. Weed books on popular culture, home-making, and crafts no longer in style.

700	Flexible: Use judgment	Art, music, film, theater, and sports history have permanent value. Weed current musical artists and athletes no longer popular. Evaluate sports for local interest.
800	Flexible: Use judgment	Literary classics and literary criticism may have permanent value. Keep poetry collections in good condition.
900	5–15	Historical resources will have longer shelf lives. (Middle Ages, Renaissance, Civil War, etc.) Carefully examine materials on travel, regions, countries, and current events for changes, especially in volatile geographic areas. Consider bookmarking or linking to web travel guides rather than holding on to guides more than five years old.
Biography	Flexible: use judgment	Keep materials on important historical and popular individuals. Keep titles of individuals of local interest. Eliminate "one-hit wonders" and biographies and memoirs of popular individuals your students have never heard of. Keep works of literary and historic value (*Death Be Not Proud, Diary of Ann Frank*).
Reference	Evaluate titles on individual basis, applying Dewey criteria when appropriate	Print encyclopedias—replace at least one set every five years and consider replacing with continually updated online editions. Weed last year's almanacs and yearbooks after new ones arrive. Be aware of any need for historical statistical research. Standard references, like *Facts About the Presidents,* should be weeded when new editions arrive. You may want to keep one or two years in the circulating collection. Evaluate atlases after five years. If space is tight and funding is regular, weed materials duplicated by subscription databases (*Wilson Biographies Online replaces Current Biography*). Dictionaries, especially unabridged versions, may have long shelf lives.
Fiction	Flexible: use judgment	Avoid weeding classics in good condition and award-winning titles. Replace if worn. Weed duplicates after titles are no longer popular. Unless it's a classic or popular, weed young adult fiction older than ten years. Consider weeding abridged and poorly bound materials. Replace shabby paperbacks with new copies.
Periodicals	3–5	Is this material available through your online databases? If it isn't, even if it is old, should you keep it for research in current history? (Woodstock, Challenger Disaster, etc.) Unindexed periodicals have little value after two years.
Multimedia materials		Use criteria listed above according to class. Weed materials in obsolete formats (phonograph albums?). Begin to migrate to emerging formats when (or before) equipment reaches *critical mass* (VHS to DVD).

MORE RESOURCES ON WEEDING

Weed It! For an Attractive and Useful Collection (Prepared by Karen Klopfer, formerly Western Massachusetts Regional Library System) http://www.wmrls.org/services/colldev/weed_it.html

Sunlink Weed of the Month http://www.sunlink.ucf.edu/weed

Introduction to Weeding, Sally Livingston Jefferson County Schools http://www.pld.fayette.k12.ky.us/lms/weed_int.htm

Weeding (Arizona Public Libraries) http://www.lib.az.us/cdt/weeding.htm

Weeding the School Library (PDF brochure) California Department of Education http://www.cde.ca.gov/library/weedingschlib.pdf

Suggestion for Library Purchase

Name _____ Date _____

Suggested item(s):

Format:

❏ Book   ❏ Database   ❏ Magazine   ❏ CD-ROM   ❏ DVD   ❏ Video   ❏ Other:

Details about the resource: (author, publisher, price, ISBN number, date)

Briefly describe how the resource will enhance our curriculum or respond to student/staff needs.

Please attach any printed information about the resource (ads, reviews, etc.) to this request form.

Itemized Budget Proposal Worksheet

Total Budget Requested: _____ **School Population:** _____ **Total Per-Learner Expenditure:** _____

Category (Budget # or Code)	Item(s)	Estimated Cost/Cost per Learner	Rationale (Connection with Goal, Curriculum, Standard, Etc.)	Priority 1–3 (1 = Critical)
Books and print materials (reference series updates, new fiction, nonfiction, new curricular needs, replacements)				
Print magazine and newspaper subscriptions				
Subscription databases				
Hardware/peripherals				

Supplies				
Maintenance/vendor agreements (OPAC, copy machine, security system, interlibrary loan delivery)				
Professional dues and conference expenses				
Bindery				
Other				

Respectfully submitted, _____

_____, Teacher-Librarian

Rules for Library Workstations

To provide access for as many students as possible, please remember:

- School assignments take priority over other activities

- Limit your time while others are waiting

- Print selectively. When possible e-mail documents home or save them as files

- Work quietly

- When there is a wait, please sign your name and wait to be called

- Please use your home computer for games and chat and large downloads

- Ask if you need help!

Library Assignment Pass

Teacher _____ Period _____

Grade _____ Class _____

Number of Students _____

Assignment _____

_____

_____

_____

_____

_____

_____

❏ Students may stay the entire period

❏ Students should return to class by _____

Please list student names
on the back of this pass

Date _____ Time _____

Library Assignment Pass

Teacher _____ Period _____

Grade _____ Class _____

Number of Students _____

Assignment _____

_____

_____

_____

_____

_____

_____

❏ Students may stay the entire period

❏ Students should return to class by _____

Please list student names
on the back of this pass

Date _____ Time _____

Library Assignment Pass

Teacher _____ Period _____

Grade _____ Class _____

Number of Students _____

Assignment _____

_____

_____

_____

_____

_____

_____

❏ Students may stay the entire period

❏ Students should return to class by _____

Please list student names
on the back of this pass

Date _____ Time _____

Library Assignment Pass

Teacher _____ Period _____

Grade _____ Class _____

Number of Students _____

Assignment _____

_____

_____

_____

_____

_____

_____

❏ Students may stay the entire period

❏ Students should return to class by _____

Please list student names
on the back of this pass

Date _____ Time _____

Library Class Time: Appointment Slip

Class:_____

Dates: _____

Block/Period: _____

Space: _____

If you need to cancel, phone extension:_____

Library Class Time: Appointment Slip

Class:_____

Dates: _____

Block/Period: _____

Space: _____

If you need to cancel, phone extension:_____

Library Class Time: Appointment Slip

Class:_____

Dates: _____

Block/Period: _____

Space: _____

If you need to cancel, phone extension:_____

Library Class Time: Appointment Slip

Class:_____

Dates: _____

Block/Period: _____

Space: _____

If you need to cancel, phone extension:_____

Library Class Time: Appointment Slip

Class:_____

Dates: _____

Block/Period: _____

Space: _____

If you need to cancel, phone extension:_____

Library Class Time: Appointment Slip

Class:_____

Dates: _____

Block/Period: _____

Space: _____

If you need to cancel, phone extension:_____

Shelving Guide

Thanks for helping us get materials back on the shelves. We are so grateful for reliable volunteers. When you shelve books and other materials it is important to remember that when an item is *mis-shelved,* it is virtually lost to our students and teachers. It is critical that we are careful when we shelve and that when we find materials that are misplaced, we move them to their proper places in the library. If you see a book that appears to have the wrong call number, show it to a member of the library staff.

Special Library Sections	How to Shelve Them

Biography	In this section, books are arranged by the subject's last name. If the library has several biographies about the same person, within that subject, shelve by author.
	
	    B
	    WAS

Fiction	Fiction books are shelved alphabetically by the last name of the author. If an author has several books, within that author's work, the books are arranged alphabetically by title.
	
	    F KIN *Carrie*
	    F KIN *Fire Starter*
	    F KIN *Pet Cemetery*
	
	If two authors have the same last name, shelve by last name, then by first:
	
	    King, Stephen
	
	    King, William
	
	We shelve Mc and Mac as if both spellings looked like Mac.
	
	Our mysteries, science fiction, and romance books have special labels, but they are interfiled in the regular fiction area.

Nonfiction	Nonfiction materials will have Dewey Decimal numbers on their spines. Shelve nonfiction books first by numbers, then by the letters under the numbers that usually stand for the author's last name or the title of the book. Nothing comes before something! Example:
	
	    973 HAR
	    973 STE
	    973.03 HAR
	    973.3 HAB
	    973.73 CAT
	    973.73 STE
	    973.734 CAT

Reference	Follow the instructions for shelving nonfiction, but make sure to shelve these materials separately in the Reference Area. A reference call number looks like this: R 973.73 ZIN
Reading list books	These are shelved by grade, then alphabetically by author in a special area. Most of these titles are fiction. Color labels note grade levels.
Videos/DVDs	Shelve videos and DVDs together on the shelves behind the desk. They are arranged by Dewey numbers just like our books. Fiction titles and nonfiction titles are arranged separately. VID or VID ALD 973.4
Magazines and newspapers	Shelve today's newspaper on the newspaper rack. Stack older issues by date in the back room. Shelve the current issue of a magazine in the spinning rack near the circulation desk. Shelve older issues by date in the boxes in the stacks.
Professional collection	The professional collection is shelved at the end of our nonfiction books. Arrange these books by Dewey numbers. These books are of special interest to teachers and administrators.

Bring back to the circulation desk, any materials that:

- Do not have spine labels
- Have spine labels that are hard to read
- Have call numbers that do not appear to be right
- Are in poor physical condition
- Have date due cards in their pockets (They may not have been checked in.)

When in doubt, ask for help!

Guidelines for Showing Films in the Classroom

Non-print materials, such as videos, have become increasingly valuable sources of information and creative expression. Our High School/Middle School supports the use of media in the instructional program. Members of our faculty are expected to use sound professional judgment in the selecting of video and other media resources used with students, and are to be aware of both the Federal Copyright Law and Fair Use practices as they apply to the use of such media in the classroom.

By law, when a teacher shows any video that does not include "public performance rights" he or she must comply with the "Fair Use" provision and Chapter 1, Section 110 of the Copyright Law. The following is a summary of the guidelines from those documents. Videos shown in school should:

- be used with students in "face to face" instruction with the teacher
- be directly related to the curriculum and the current instruction
- be correlated to instructional objectives
- be shown in the normal instructional setting, not large group settings such as the auditorium
- not be used for extra-curricular, reward, or recreational use
- not be used for fund-raising. No admission should be charged for a film showing.
- be "lawfully made." That means that the teacher has not duplicated a copy in violation of Fair Use, without the knowledge of the copyright holder, or that the teacher has not knowingly purchased an illegal copy. It is reasonable to assume that videos acquired from rental stores and libraries are lawfully made copies.

SO WHAT DOES THIS MEAN FOR MY CLASSROOM?

Videos borrowed from the High School Library:

Follow the above provisions when using videos from the library. Note that the library is careful to purchase video materials from vendors offering public performance rights. If the video is R-rated, remember to prepare a letter home for parents. A sample is attached.

Privately purchased videos:

Most privately purchased videos are sold with a "home use only" agreement, not with public performance rights. However, these videos may be used in a school if the above guidelines are met. If the video is R-rated, remember to follow procedures for showing R-rated videos in the classroom.

Rented videos:

Rented videos may be used in schools, even if they are labeled "For Home Use Only," if the above guidelines are met. If the video is R-rated, remember to follow procedures for showing R-rated videos in the classroom.

Off-air taping:

If you tape a video from a regular, commercial, or "free" network you must apply the Fair Use guidelines. You may show the video once and repeat that showing once within ten consecutive school days of the broadcast. The tape may NOT be used in school after the forty-five day period outlined in the fair-use guidelines. For the following thirty-five days, teachers may keep the tape for evaluation purposes only. The copied video must be destroyed after forty-five days. Special permission must be obtained to show any videotapes from a cable or satellite television, such as HBO or Disney. If the taped video is R-rated, remember to follow procedures for showing R-rated videos in the classroom.

It is not necessary to show off-air recordings in their entirety, but recorded programs should not be physically or electronically combined or merged to constitute teaching anthologies or compilations.

Please note: copies of videos shown in our school **should be obtained legally.** Even if you use a film for clear educational purposes, if it is a bootleg copy, it is illegal. Use of copied materials should not substitute for purchasing the work. Consider whether your continued use of the resource dilutes the market or potential sales of the copyright holder. If it does, then suggest that the school library or your department purchase a legally obtained copy.

Cable in the Classroom magazine and CIC Online (http://www.ciconline.com) offer a wealth of information about off-air copying of videos, monthly schedules of educational broadcast resources, and descriptions of the generous extended rights offered by many broadcasters.

Works Consulted

US Copyright Law, Chapter 1, Section 110
  http://www.copyright.gov/title17/92chap1.html#110

Fair Use: US Copyright Office http://www.copyright.gov/fls/fl102.html

Video and Copyright (American Library Association) http://www.ala.org/library/fact7.html

Stanford University: Copyright and Fair Use http://fairuse.stanford.edu

Cable in the Classroom Online http://www.ciconline.com

Policy for Using R-Rated Films in the Classroom

Rationale: The administration recognizes that teachers may want to use materials in instruction that may be potentially controversial or that have been rated off limits to young people despite their instructional or artistic value. Examples of video materials currently carrying an "R" rating include: *Glory, Schindler's List, Elizabeth, Hamlet,* and *The Joy Luck Club.* Despite their ratings, these materials may provide excellent opportunities for teachers to focus students on critical analysis skills, engage students in debate, present essential cultural context, or examine distinctive forms of aesthetic expression. Students may benefit substantially from viewing and discussing such carefully selected materials that directly relate to their course of study.

Teachers are responsible for assessing the maturity of their students relating to their readiness for the viewing experience, the value of the film to their curricular program, and understanding the culture of their immediate community.

Prior to showing any video in the classroom, teachers should offer sufficient introductory preparation, which includes explanation of the educational purpose of the experience. Following, or during the course of the film viewing, teachers should present appropriate discussion and follow-up learning activities.

PROCEDURE FOR USING R-RATED VIDEOS OWNED BY THE HIGH SCHOOL LIBRARY

Prepare a permission letter/form to send home to parents alerting them of your plan and the curricular value of the film. (A sample letter is attached.)

FOR USING VIDEOS NOT OWNED BY THE HIGH SCHOOL LIBRARY

Thoroughly review the film before showing it to your students, assessing its relevance to the curriculum and appropriateness for the age and the maturity level of your students.

Before showing an R-rated video to a class, submit the title to the Academic Standards Committee for approval and backing.

If the video is approved, prepare a permission letter/form to send home to parents alerting them of your plan and the curricular value of the film. (A sample letter is attached.)

(**Note:** Teachers should NOT show films rated NC-17 or X.)

FOR STUDENTS WHO WISH TO USE EXCERPTS OF R-RATED FILMS IN CLASS PRESENTATIONS

Students must obtain permission before using an excerpt of any R-rated film in the classroom. If the teacher approves, he or she should follow standard procedure (committee approval, letter home to parents) prior to allowing the class to view the excerpt.

Teacher's Request to Use R-Rated Video

. . . . **High School**

Teacher:_____ Date: _____

Title of Film: _____

Source of Video/DVD:
Note: If the video is borrowed from the library, this form is not necessary, but you will need to obtain parents' permission.

_____ Store Rental

_____ Off-Air Tape (following fair-use guidelines)

_____ Privately Owned (by teacher for classroom use only)

_____ Borrowed from source other than high school library

Source of loan: _____

Have you previewed the video in its entirety?   ❑ Yes   ❑ No

Amount of the movie/video to be shown (minutes): _____ Entire Film: _____

Film contains (check all that apply):

___ adult language

___ sexuality

___ violence

___ illicit drug or alcohol use

___ none of the above

___ other

Excerpt contains (check all that apply):

___ adult language

___ sexuality

___ violence

___ illicit drug or alcohol use

___ none of the above

___ other

Describe excerpt(s):_____

_____

Briefly describe the importance of this video to your specific curricular program and your goals for learners:

Proposed alternative assignment for students unable to obtain parent permission:

Proposed date and time of viewing:

Date(s): _____ Time(s)/Block(s): _____

_____ _____

_____ _____

Committee Comments:

_____ Approved _____ Denied

Principal's signature: _____ Date:_____

2-20B

Letter to Parents Regarding Use of R-Rated Video

The letter below is intended as a convenient template for seeking parental permission for occasions when a teacher might wish to show an R-rated video. Feel free to edit and add specifics explaining the film's value to your course of study.

Dear Parent/Guardian

Your child is currently studying _____ as part of his/her coursework in _____ class. To enhance your child's learning experience/understanding of _____, I am planning to show the film/show excerpts of the film _____ on _____ (list date or dates).

Though the film is rated R, I am convinced of its learning value. The rating is due to _____. (You might also mention how the film was reviewed.) I can assure you that the film will be shown in appropriate context, including discussion and activities before and after viewing. I sincerely believe that my students have the maturity to view this film and that _____ (Explain the learning goals this film or the specific scenes you plan to show will help you achieve in the context of your curriculum.) This film is a part of the high school library's collection/has been approved by our Academic Standards Committee.

Please complete the form below either authorizing or exempting your child from viewing _____. Unless I receive this signed permission slip, I will not permit your child to view/view scenes from the film. If you do not wish to have your son/daughter view this film, I will gladly provide a *relevant and appropriate* alternative assignment.

Feel free to phone or e-mail if you have any questions.

Sincerely,

E-mail:

Phone:

****

Please complete the following:

Name of student _____

_____ I grant permission for my son/daughter to view the film/view excerpts of the film

(film title) _____.

_____ I prefer that my son/daughter NOT view the film/NOT view excerpts of the film

(film title) _____.

Signature: _____

{School District}
Policy on District-Provided Access to Electronic Information, Services, and Networks

PURPOSE

Freedom of expression is an inalienable human right and the foundation for self-government. Freedom of expression encompasses the right to freedom of speech and the corollary right to receive information. Such rights extend to minors as well as adults. Schools facilitate the exercise of these rights by providing access to information regardless of format or technology. In a free and democratic society, access to information is a fundamental right of citizenship.

In making decisions regarding student access to the Internet, the {SCHOOL DISTRICT} considers its own stated educational mission, goals, and objectives. Electronic information research skills are now fundamental to preparation of citizens and future employees. Access to the Internet enables students to explore thousands of libraries, databases, bulletin boards, and other resources while exchanging messages with people around the world.

RESPONSIBILITIES OF TEACHERS AND PARENTS

The District expects that faculty will blend thoughtful use of the Internet throughout the curriculum and will provide guidance and instruction to students in its use. As much as possible, access from school to Internet resources should be structured in ways which point students to those which have been evaluated prior to use. While students will be able to move beyond those resources to others that have not been previewed by staff, they shall be provided with guidelines and lists of resources particularly suited to learning objectives.

Outside of school, families bear responsibility for the same guidance of Internet use as they exercise with information sources such as television, telephones, radio, movies, and other possibly offensive media.

RESPONSIBILITIES OF STUDENT USERS

Students utilizing District-provided Internet access must first have the permission of and must be supervised by the {SCHOOL DISTRICT}'s professional staff. Students utilizing school-provided Internet access are responsible for good behavior online just as they are in a classroom or other area of the school. The same general rules for behavior and communications apply.

The purpose of District-provided Internet access is to facilitate communications in support of research and education. To remain eligible as users, students' use must be in support of and consistent with the educational objectives of the {SCHOOL DISTRICT}. Access is a privilege, not a right. Access entails responsibility.

LIMITED EXPECTATION OF PRIVACY

Users should not expect that files stored on school-based computers will always be private. Electronic messages and files stored on school-based computers may be treated like school lockers. Administrators and faculty may review files and messages to maintain system integrity and ensure that users are acting responsibly.

UNACCEPTABLE USES

The following uses of school-provided Internet access are NOT permitted:
(I AM USING THE GERUND TO ENHANCE CLARITY)

- accessing, uploading, downloading, scanning, or distributing pornographic, obscene, sexually explicit, harassing, discriminatory, or defamatory material;

- transmitting obscene, abusive, sexually explicit, or threatening language;
- violating any local, state, or federal statute; or school district policies;
- vandalizing, damaging, or disabling the property of another individual or organization;
- accessing another individual's materials, information, or files without permission; sharing passwords or using the account or the identity of another user;
- violating copyright or otherwise using the intellectual property of another individual or organization without permission;
- using limited network bandwidth for downloads not related to academics;
- posting web pages for commercial purpose or political advocacy (Material posted on the school server must be reviewed and approved by a faculty member.);
- copying or downloading software without the authorization of the network administrator;
- maliciously disrupting or harming the school's workstations, network, and services through such activities as hacking, or downloading, uploading, creating, or spreading computer viruses;
- (NOTE: Consider whether or not your school will limit gaming, personal e-mail, chat, and personal blogging.)

DISCLAIMERS/ LIMITATION OF SCHOOL DISTRICT LIABILITY

The {SCHOOL DISTRICT} makes no warranties of any kind, neither expressed nor implied, for the Internet access it is providing. The District will not be responsible for any damages users suffer, including—but not limited to—loss of data resulting from delays or interruptions in service. The District will not be responsible for the accuracy, nature, or quality of information stored on District diskettes, hard drives, or servers; nor for the accuracy, nature, or quality of information gathered through District-provided Internet access. The District will not be responsible for personal property used to access District computers or networks or for District-provided Internet access. The District will not be responsible for unauthorized financial obligations resulting from District-provided access to the Internet.

SANCTIONS

Violations of this Acceptable Use Policy could result in a student's loss of access to network and Internet privileges, or other disciplinary action to be determined at the building or classroom level. When appropriate, law enforcement organizations will be involved.

WHAT PARENTS SHOULD KNOW

Parents of students in the {SCHOOL DISTRICT} shall be provided with the following information:

- The {SCHOOL DISTRICT} is pleased to offer its students access to the Internet. The Internet is an electronic highway connecting hundreds of thousands of computers and millions of individual users all over the world. This computer technology will help propel our schools through the communication age by allowing students and staff to access and use resources from distant computers, communicate and collaborate with other individuals and groups around the world, and significantly expand their available information base. The Internet is a tool for lifelong learning.
- Families should be aware that some material accessible via the Internet may contain items that are illegal, defamatory, inaccurate, or potentially offensive to some people. In addition, it is possible to purchase certain goods and services via the Internet which could result in unwanted financial obligations for which a student's parent or guardian would be liable.
- While the District's intent is to make Internet access available in order to further educational goals and objectives, students may find ways to access other materials as well. Even should the District institute

technical methods or systems to regulate students' Internet access, those methods could not guarantee compliance with the District's acceptable use policy. That notwithstanding, the District believes that the benefits to students of access to the Internet exceed any disadvantages. Ultimately, however, parents and guardians of minors are responsible for setting and conveying the standards that their children should follow when using media and information sources. Toward that end, the {SCHOOL DISTRICT} makes the District's complete Internet policy and procedures available on request for review by all parents, guardians, and other members of the community; and provides parents and guardians the option of requesting for their minor children alternative activities not requiring Internet use.

NOTICE: This policy and all its provisions are subordinate to local, state, and federal statutes.

Student and Parent /Guardian Agreements

Student User

I have read, understand, and will abide by the _____ School District Acceptable Use Policy. I realize that violations may result in my loss of my Internet and/or network access privileges, disciplinary actions per the Student Code of Conduct, and/or possible legal action

Student User Name (Print): _____

Student User Signature: _____

Date: _____ *Grade:* _____

Homeroom Teacher: _____

Parental Permission

I understand that the school district network and access to the Internet have been installed to help students develop the ability to research, evaluate, and synthesize educationally valuable information from many sources, to develop critical thinking and problem solving skills, and to enable students to work effectively with communication technologies. I expect that the school district will use its best efforts to limit student access to only those areas that have educational value. However, I understand that despite careful monitoring and supervision, there will always be the potential for a student to come into contact with offensive or illegal material on the network or the Internet. Furthermore, I understand that the school district will not be held responsible for specific Internet sites visited by students. Nonetheless, I recognize the importance of my student's use of the Internet as a tool for learning.

I hereby provide my consent for the student listed about to use the school district's network and Internet access.

Parent/Guardian Signature: _____

Date: _____

SOURCE: Adapted from the Indiana Department of Education: AUP Model http://ideanet.doe.state.in.us/olr/aup/aupmod.html. Modified by Joyce Valenza. Modified text is noted in highlighting. Agreements are modified from Springfield Township forms.

Weekly Schedule Sign-Up Form   Week of _____

	Area	A	B	C	D
M O N D A Y	CL				
	OP				
	IN/R				
T U E S D A Y	CL				
	OP				
	IN/R				
W E D N E S D A Y	CL				
	OP				
	IN/R				
T H U R S D A Y	CL				
	OP				
	IN/R				
F R I D A Y	CL				
	OP				
	IN/R				

CL = Closed Lab / IN = Instructional Area / OP = Open Lab / P = Pod / QR = Quiet Reading / R = Reference

Library Equipment Sign-Outs

Week of _____

Equipment	MONDAY Teacher/Period	TUESDAY Teacher/Period	WEDNESDAY Teacher/Period	THURSDAY Teacher/Period	FRIDAY Teacher/Period
Digital Camera 1					
Digital Camera 2					
One-Gun Projector					
TV-VCR 1					
TV-VCR 2					
TV-DVD 1					
TV-DVD 2					
Overhead Projector					

2-24

Library Weekly Schedule

You signed up for the week of _____

Block/Day	Space	A	B	C	D
Mon	CI				
16th	Op				
Day 1	I P/S				
Tue	CI				
17th	Op				
Day 2	I P/S				
Wed	CI				
18th	Op				
Day 1	I P/S				
Thur	CI				
19th	Op				
Day 2	I P/S				
Fri	CI				
20th	Op				
Day 1	I P/S				

Please remember that our periods begin at the following times:

A 8:33 a.m. **B** 10:08 a.m. **C** 11:50 a.m. **D** 1:43 p.m.

Please contact the library if you have a change in your plans;

Phone extension:

(Prepared _____)

Drop-in Students

Day _____

Please sign in when you enter the library with a pass!

Block	Students
A	
B	
C-1	
C-2	
C-3	
C-4	
D	

MARC Checklist
Essentials for Books in MARC Record

PHYSICAL DESCRIPTION

020   _a ISBN :   _c price

040   _a cataloging source code _d Modifying library code (your library code)

100   _a Main entry – name of author, _d life dates.

245   _a Title proper :

       _b subtitle /   } Directly from title page

       _c statement of responsibility.

246   _a Variant title (if applicable)

250   _a ed. (edition statement – use ordinal numbers, e.g. ,1st ed.)

260   _a Place of publication :

       _b Publisher,

       _c pub. date or © date.

300   _a number of units, e.g., pages :

       _b illustrative matter (ill.) ;

       _c dimensions (cm.) +

       _e (if accompanying materials)

440   _a Official LC series title (from LC authority list)

or   _v volume number, if applicable

490   _a Unofficial series title (Add 830 tag for Official Series title, if known)

NOTES (most useful in a school setting)

500   _a General notes (optional, put notes here that do not fit into other fields in 5XX)

504   _a Bibliographical references

505   _a Contents (parts of the work separated by - -)   } At least one of these two fields

520   _a Summary (essence of work)

521   _a Intended audience (reading, age, grade levels or special target group)

526   _a Standard reading program, if applicable (Accelerated Reader, etc.)

586   _a Awards note, date of award (Caldecott or ALA Notable Book, 2004)

590   _a Local notes (location directives, references to relative classes or teachers)

SUBJECT HEADINGS

600   _a Personal names (personal name as subject heading – e.g., biographies)

650   _a Main topics with appropriate subdivisions (usually up to 3)

651   _a Geographical emphasis, if applicable

(Most common subdivisions for 65X: _y Chronological ; _x Topical ; _z Geographical)

(Use the _v subfield for form subdivisions in 6XX – e.g., Fiction, Dictionaries, Juvenile literature . . .)

655   _a Genre headings for fiction or drama (e.g., Science fiction, Fantasy films, Love stories, Folklore, Fairy tales, Mystery fiction)

658   _a Curriculum Index term (optional)

690   _a Local subject headings (generated for local audience in your setting)

ADDITIONAL ADDED ENTRIES

7XX   _a Added entries for joint author, editor, illustrator

856   _u URL (Uniform Resource Identifier, a.k.a. Web address)

       _y hyperlink text (will display instead of URL if added)

NON-PRINT ITEMS (VIDEOS, ELECTRONIC RESOURCES, ETC.)

Use all of the above, plus the following fields:

028   _a publisher number _b source of number
245   _h [GMD]* immediately following title proper
300   _a (# min.) length of production (immediately after SMD*)
500   _a source of title (required for electronic resources only)
508   _a creators and producers of work ⎤
511   _a Performers and participants   ⎦ Credits
538   _a System requirements (VHS, PC, MAC, etc.)

* Indicators are not included in this checklist. Non-filing indicators are set automatically in MARC Magician. See the Cataloger's Reference <u>or Follett Tag of the Month</u> site for clarification of indicators for particular fields (e.g., 521 target audience – first indicator).

HOLDINGS RECORD (852 field expanded)

Add the following information for electronic shelf list copy-level records (also called Holdings record).

Barcode #
Call #
Acquisition date
Vendor
Funding source
Price
Circulation type
Category (new materials for budget year + others if applicable)
Add volume #, copy #, or part #, as needed

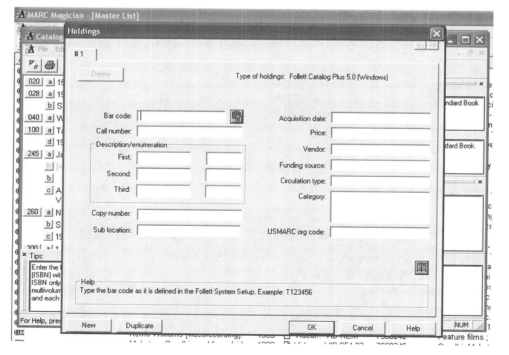

Holding record of the expanded 852 field as viewed in MARC Magician software. The field replicates the local holding record in many library automation systems according to the software set up. In this example the Follett Catalog Plus 5.0 software is used.

Image used with the permission of Information Transform, Inc.

SOURCE: Created by Candy Blessing for LSC5520 Cataloging and Classification in an Electronic Environment, Mansfield University. © 2003.

[Library Name] Vendor Barcode Log

Use this log to track the barcode ranges assigned to vendors who supply MARC records or bulk barcodes for materials.

Date	Barcode Range	Vendor

[Library Name] Import/Export Log

Track MARC records that are imported into the electronic cataloging system. Also log records that are (1) exported into a bibliographic utility for editing and enhancing records and re-imported into the system, (2) exported to be shared with other libraries, or (3) deleted from the system.

Date	Company	No. of records	Barcode Range (if applicable)	Notes

SOURCE: Created by Candy Blessing for LSC5520 Cataloging and Classification in an Electronic Environment, Mansfield University © 2003.

Library Fax Cover Sheet

Information Happy School Library
123 Literacy Road
Anywhere, USA 12345

Phone: _____

Fax: _____

E-mail: _____

Teacher-Librarian: _____

From: _____

Send to:	Date:
Attention:	Phone number:
Fax number:	

Total pages (including this cover): _____

Message:

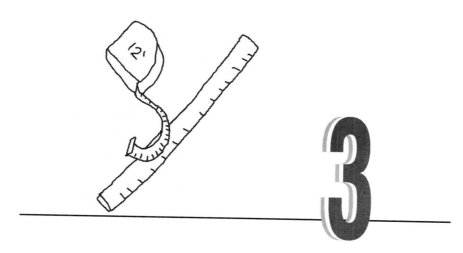

Measuring the Impact of Our Programs

If you keep doing what you've always done, you'll keep getting what you've always gotten.

—Jim Rohn

If a tree falls in the forest and no one is there to hear it . . . Most professionals measure and document their accomplishments. They reflect on and strive to improve their performance. In schools we assess to ensure that learners are learning and to improve our practice.

But aside from the importance of reflection and assessment for professional growth and increased effectiveness, the truth is: no one will really know what you are doing unless you report it. As teacher-librarians, our budgets are less likely to be cut, our positions are less likely to be eliminated, if the people in positions of power understand our direct connection in the learning process, if they know what a typical day looks like in our active facilities.

Instead of library advocacy, our real thrust must be advocacy for learners. We need to craft reporting forms that show us at our best, demonstrate how our efforts enable teachers to teach more effectively, and demonstrate the effect of our work on student achievement.

So, even if it is not a required part of our jobs, we can do our programs, and more importantly our students, a great service by documenting our contribution to the learning process. We can accomplish this by collecting evidence of use and learning. Evidence-based practice helps us to focus on goals, plan, and improve our program and improve student learning. Evidence-based practice moves us beyond the hunch to a more scientific and reflective practice. This approach also demonstrates our commitment to learning and convinces the "pie slicers" of the worth of funding school library programs.

How can we collect evidence? We can survey our customers. Surveys capture important feedback and evidence in the forms of attitudes, confidence level, needs, and growth. We can collect baseline and exit evidence—before and after units, before and during initiatives, at the beginning and end of semesters, in freshman and senior years.

Consider reporting the little things. How many book talks did you do this week? What types of books are your students reading? What kind of lessons did you teach and what was their impact?

But remember: on their own, statistics do not necessarily tell stories. When you report, it is important to give examples, share anecdotes, to use real kids and real classroom teachers to explain what those numbers mean and to make the meaning of your evidence more memorable and more tangible to your audience.

3-1
Assessment Tool for the School Library Media Program

This checklist uses categories and indicators from *Information Power* and should help you and your principal or coordinator set a focused course for program improvement.

3-2
13 Point Library/Media Program Checklist for Building Administrators

Doug Johnson's evaluation form will help you work with your administrators to improve the program. The comprehensive criteria are perfect to begin a process of long-range goal setting.

3-3
Teacher-Librarian Annual Goals

Whether or not you are asked for them, develop and prioritize your goals each year and share them with your administrators. Long or short term, goals are the steps that help you achieve your mission. Without goals, your program is not likely to breathe and grow. Address your progress toward reaching these goals in a midterm goal report and in your annual report. Goals are a strategy by which you can assess your achievements and by which you can present your achievements to stakeholders. You goals should be SMART. A popular business acronym, with uncertain attribution, SMART stands for:

- Specific
- Measurable
- Attainable
- Realistic
- Tangible

For example instead of selecting "improving student reading scores" as a goal, a SMARTer goal might be: "Over the next school year, I will work with Language Arts chair Juan Rivera to design three units addressing the skill of critical reading among eighth-graders, a skill identified as *in need of improvement* in our state assessment scores."

3-4
Annual Report Planning Sheet

Keep track of your accomplishments during the course of the year, and that important year-end report will not seem nearly as daunting.

3-5/3-6
Student/Faculty Surveys

Once a year, ask your school community how you are doing. Not only do these surveys suggest changes you might make, they also offer evidence to present to administrators. (One survey we conducted pointed to a clear need for a second copy machine. Documentation helped us get it.)

3-7
Research Unit Teacher's Assessment Form

Many of us go through our days not really considering how we might have improved our instructional activities. Since most of our work is cooperatively planned and implemented, it is critical that we seek feedback from our instructional partners. There's no sense in repeating the same activities year after year without reflection or opportunities to improve them.

3-8
Cheating and Plagiarism Survey

What is the level of academic integrity in your building? You may be surprised by the evidence you collect in this survey, developed by Education Communications, Inc., publishers of *Who's Who among American High School Students*. The key to conducting this type of survey is assuring students that answers are confidential, that you are truly interested in assessing the climate of the school and understanding student culture. You are not out to catch plagiarizers.

3-9
Reading Interest Survey

Do you ever wonder what your students are really reading? What do they really want to read? What titles and authors they'd like to see added to the collection? Results of this survey will inform your collection-building strategies.

3-10
Curriculum Map

The teacher-librarian is among a few people in the school with knowledge of the entire curriculum—crucial knowledge if he or she is to be a consultant for teachers. This chart can be used to gear up for regular units, offer teachers materials (new and old) in a timely way, plan for purchases, and plan for the integration of skills. You may consider sending a copy of this chart to the public librarian. Consider plotting the major units on a large wall calendar to get a good view of the entire program of the school.

3-11
Curriculum Tracking by Department/Grade

You may want to use this table to track curriculum for the middle or high school program. Complete one form for each department and each grade. After collecting this information through a cycle of one semester or one year, you will be able to tell where you might want to promote new student research efforts and, perhaps, where students may be overwhelmed by assigned research.

3-12
Information Literacy Log: Data Collection Form

Our school recently initiated use of this form to determine how and when the various information literacy skills are taught across grade level and discipline and to determine where the "holes" are. Our teachers will complete a form like this for each major research project. The forms are to be collected and analyzed by the teacher-librarian and department chairs. Information collected could easily be entered into a database for a clearer view of the big picture.

3-13
Snapshot of School Library Use during Typical Week

To get a better feel for how your facility is used, or to share information about its use with others, pick a typical week (perhaps at several points in the school year) and count! These snapshots can be particularly valuable around annual report time.

3-14
Library Usage by Department (Staff Library Usage Spreadsheet)

One way to document the action taking place in your library is to keep track of class visits. Lists may be sorted by department or teacher. Your annual report could note months of greatest activity, the departments who use the library most heavily, and so forth. Reports might suggest where you would want to focus outreach efforts.

Assessment Tool for the School Library Media Program

1. Learning and Teaching: The library media program (the teacher-librarian):

Indicator	Basic	Proficient	Exemplary	COMMENTS/EVIDENCE	
				Self	Administrator
a. Integrates information literacy standards into the curriculum across grade level and content area					
b. Models and promotes collaborative planning					
c. Models and promotes curricular development					
d. Models and promotes creative, facilitative, effective, and collaborative teaching					
e. Promotes access to the full range of information resources and services					
f. Encourages and engages students in reading, viewing, and listening for enjoyment, enrichment, and understanding					
g. Supports diverse learning abilities, styles, and needs					
h. Fosters individual and collaborative inquiry					
i. Assesses student learning using rubrics					
j. Integrates uses of technology for learning and teaching					
k. Functions as a link to the larger learning community					

3-1A

2. Information Access and Delivery: The library media program (the teacher-librarian):

Indicator	Basic	Proficient	Exemplary	COMMENTS/EVIDENCE Self	COMMENTS/EVIDENCE Administrator
a. Provides intellectual access to information and ideas for learning					
b. Provides physical access to information and resources for learning					
c. Provides a climate conducive to learning					
d. Provides flexible and equitable access to information, ideas, and resources for learning during and beyond school day					
e. Collaboratively develops and evaluates well-balanced collections to support curriculum and meet diverse needs of learners, with resources in all formats, extending into the classroom					
f. Is founded on a commitment to the right of intellectual freedom					
g. Develops and maintains written policies and procedures on information issues (selection, challenges, intellectual freedom, acceptable use, confidentiality) reflecting legal guidelines and professional ethics					

3. Program Administration: The library media program (the teacher-librarian):

Indicator	Basic	Proficient	Exemplary	COMMENTS/EVIDENCE Self	COMMENTS/EVIDENCE Administrator
a. Supports the mission, goals, objectives, and continuous improvement of the school					
b. Is staffed by a minimum of one full-time, certified/licensed library media specialist supported by qualified staff					
c. Is engaged in comprehensive and collaborative long-range strategic planning					
d. Is engaged in ongoing assessment for improvement					
e. Is funded sufficiently to support a large, diverse, in-depth school-wide collection, supplemented by bond issues, fund-raising, and community partnerships					
f. Collaboratively develops and evaluates collections to support curriculum and meet diverse needs of learners					
g. Is engaged in ongoing staff development to enhance professional knowledge; provides instruction in information literacy for teachers, administrators, other members of learning community					
h. Clearly communicates its missions, goals and functions through publications, reports, newsletters, e-mail, websites. Meets with other teacher-librarians for professional sharing opportunities					
i. Is managed effectively—human, financial, and physical resources					

Evidence of exemplary practice (use back of form if more room is needed):

Indicator(s)	Examples

Plan for improvement of program (use back of form if more room is needed):

Indicator(s)	Specific strategies for improvement / achievement

Teacher-Librarian _____   Administrator _____   Date _____

SOURCE: Indicators are based on the principles outlined in "Part Two: Building Partnerships for Learning." *Information Power: Building Partnerships for Learning.* Chicago: American Library Association, 1998.

A 13 Point Library/Media Program Checklist for Building Administrators

Rank each of the following items as:
3 = Doing great   2 = Making progress   1 = Needs work

Pick out all the "ones" and write down a single, short-term objective to work on within the next 6 months.

1. Professional staff and duties

_____ Does your media center have the services of a fully licensed school library media specialist (SLMS)?

_____ Is that person fully engaged in professional duties? Is there a written job description for all media personnel: clerical, technical, and professional?

_____ Does the SLMS understand and practice the roles of the SLMS as defined in *Information Power II*?

_____ Is the media specialist an active member of a professional organization?

_____ Is the SLMS considered a full member of the teaching faculty?

2. Professional support

_____ Is sufficient clerical help available to the SLMS so that she/he can perform professional duties rather than clerical tasks?

_____ Is sufficient technical help available to the SLMS so that she/he can perform professional duties rather than technical tasks?

_____ Is there a district media supervisor, director, or department chair who is responsible for planning and leadership?

_____ Does the building principal and staff development team encourage the library media personnel to attend workshops, professional meetings, and conferences which will update their skills and knowledge?

3. Collection size and development

_____ Does the library media center's book and audio visual collection meet the needs of the curriculum? Has a baseline print collection size been established? Is the collection well weeded?

_____ Are new materials chosen from professional selection sources and tied to the curriculum through collection mapping?

_____ Is a variety of media available that will address different learning styles?

_____ Have electronic and online resources been added to the collection when appropriate? Is there sufficient hardware for groups of students to take advantage of these resources?

4. Facilities

_____ Is the library media center located so it is readily accessible from all classrooms? Does it have an outside entrance so it can be used for community functions evenings and weekends?

_____ Does the library media center have an atmosphere conducive to learning with serviceable furnishings, instructional displays, and informational posters? Is the library media center carpeted with static-free carpet to reduce noise and protect electronic devices? Is the library media center climate-controlled so that materials and equipment will not be damaged by high heat and humidity, and so that it can be used for activities during the summer?

_____ Is the library media center fully networked with voice, video, and data lines in adequate quantities? Does the library media center serve as the "hub" of these information networks with routers, file servers, video head ends, etc. housed there?

5. **Curriculum and integration**

_____ Is the SLMS an active member of grade level and/or team planning groups?

_____ Is the SLMS an active member of content curriculum writing committees?

_____ Are library media center resources examined as a part of the content areas' curriculum review cycle?

_____ Are library media and information technology skills taught as part of content areas rather than in isolation? Are the information literacy skills of evaluating, processing, and communicating information being taught as well as accessing skills?

6. **Resource-based teaching**

_____ Does the SLMS with assistance from building and district administration promote teaching activities that go beyond the textbook?

_____ Is the SLMS used by teachers as an instructional design and authentic assessment resource?

_____ Does flexible scheduling in the building permit the SLMS to be a part of teaching teams with classroom teachers, rather than only covering teacher preparation time?

_____ Is there a clear set of information literacy and technology benchmarks written for all grade levels? Are these benchmarks assessed in a joint effort of the SLMS and classroom teacher? Are the results of these assessments shared with the student and parents?

7. **Information technology**

_____ Does the library media center give its users access to recent information technologies such as:

_____ computerized library catalogs and circulation systems

_____ access to a computerized union catalog of district holdings as well as access to the catalogs of public, academic, and special libraries from which interlibrary loans can be made

_____ full online access to the Internet

_____ a wide variety of computerized reference tools like full text periodical indexes, electronic encyclopedias, magazine indexes, electronic atlases, concordances, dictionaries, thesauruses, reader's advisors and almanacs

_____ a wide variety of computerized productivity programs appropriate to student ability level such as word processors, multi-media and presentation programs, spreadsheets, databases, desktop publishing programs, graphic creation programs, still and motion digital image editing software

_____ a wide range of educational computer programs including practices, simulations and tutorials, and production hardware such as multi-media computers, still and video digital cameras, scanners, and LCD projection devices

_____ educational television programming and services

_____ access to desktop conferencing equipment opportunities

_____ Are the skills needed to use these resources being taught to and with teachers by the SLMS?

8. **Telecommunications**

_____ Is the school linked by a telecommunications network for distance learning opportunities for students? Are there interactive classrooms in the building?

_____ Does the library media program coordinate programming which can be aired on the local public access channel?

9. Networking & interlibrary loan

_____ Is your school a member of a regional multi-type system or library consortium?

_____ Does the SLMS use interlibrary loan to fill student and staff requests which cannot be met by building collections?

_____ Does the SLMS participate in cooperative planning opportunities with other schools, both locally and distant?

10. Planning/yearly goals

_____ Does the library media program have a district-wide set of long-range goals?

_____ Does the SLMS set yearly goals based on the long-term goals that are tied directly to building and curriculum goals?

_____ Is a portion of the SLMS's evaluation based on the achievement of the yearly goals?

_____ Is the library media program represented on the building technology planning committee? The district technology planning committee?

11. Budgeting

_____ Is the library media program budget zero or objective based? Is the budget tied to program goals?

_____ Does the SLMS write clear rationales for the materials, equipment, and supplies requested?

_____ Does the budget reflect both a maintenance and growth component for the program?

_____ Does the SLMS keep clear and accurate records of expenditures?

12. Policies/communications

_____ Are board policies concerning selection and reconsideration current and enforced? Is the staff aware of the doctrines of intellectual freedom and library user privacy?

_____ Does the district have a safe and acceptable use policy for Internet and technology use?

_____ Does the SLMS serve as an interpreter and advocate of copyright laws?

_____ Does the SLMS have a formal means of communicating the goals and services of the program to the students, staff, administration, and community?

13. Evaluation

_____ Does the district regularly evaluate the library media program using external teams of evaluators as part of any accreditation process?

_____ Does the SLMS determine and report ways which show the goals and objectives of the program are being met and are helping meet the building and district goals?

_____ Do all new initiatives involving the library media and technology program have an evaluation component?

_____ Do the SLMS and school participate in formal studies conducted by academic researchers when requested?

SOURCE: Reprinted by permission from _The Indispensible Librarian_ by Doug Johnson. Copyright 1997 by Linworth Publishing, Inc. All rights reserved.

WORKSHEET FOR THE 13 POINT CHECKLIST

Pick the top seven areas you identified as needing improvement on previous pages. Write one or more objectives you can realistically accomplish to improve in each area of weakness.

1.

2.

3.

4.

5.

6.

7.

Handout available in: The New Improved School Library, http://doug-johnson.com

SOURCE: Reprinted by permission from *The Indispensable Librarian* by Doug Johnson. Copyright © 1997 by Linworth Publishing, Inc. All rights reserved.

Teacher-Librarian Annual Goals

Teacher-Librarian _____ School _____ School Year _____

Mission/Philosophy of the Library Information Center:

GOAL SMART: Specific, Measurable, Attainable/Action Oriented, Realistic, Timely	Connection to Mission/Comments	Assessment Plan	Time Range	Priority 1, 2, 3
Program Administration				
Learning, Teaching, Collaborating				

GOAL SMART: Specific, Measurable, Attainable/Action Oriented, Realistic, Timely	Connection to Mission/Comments	Assessment Plan	Time Range	Priority 1, 2, 3
Information Access and Delivery				
Building-Specific Goals				
District Level Goals				
Professional Development Goals				

Annual Report Planning Sheet

Bulleted summary of accomplishments (in areas of teaching and learning, information access, program administration). Can you open with a story? What did a typical day look like?

Trends over the course of the past year (discussion of circulation and use statistics, changes/trends in teacher use, student use, and learning issues)

Student achievement/activities (notable lessons, collaborations, programs. Connect to standards.)

Major new purchases/acquisitions and their impact on learners

Technology update (hardware, software, databases. Connect to ISTE's NETS standards)

Displays

Gifts/fund-raising

Out in the community (include presentations to outside groups)

Volunteers and their contributions to the program

Professional activities (professional development/in-services presented/conferences, committees, courses)

Publications (bibliographies, reviews, pathfinders, Web publications)

Needs/Issues and suggested solutions (If purchases are requested, how will they impact student achievement or teacher effectiveness?)

Goals for next year(s)

Appendix (Attach collection and use statistics, statistical reports relating to student learning, survey results, and any published articles or public relations materials. Ideally the importance of these statistics will have been discussed in the narrative.)

Student Library Survey

Dear Students,

Our purpose is to help you as you learn to become more effective users of ideas and information. Please help us better understand how you use our library by participating in this survey. We will carefully consider all responses.

Please return this form to the library information center.

When do you visit the library? (Check all that apply.)

___ before school   ___ with a class   ___ during lunch   ___ study hall   ___ after school

How many times do you visit the library each month? _____

Please check all the reasons you visit the library.

___ use the Internet
___ use subscription databases
___ find materials for assignments
___ get the teacher-librarian's advice for a project
___ find materials for my own interests
___ do homework
___ meet friends
___ socialize before school starts
___ study or do homework before school starts

___ study or do homework after school
___ word process
___ prepare a multimedia presentation
___ read magazines or newspapers
___ work on a web page
___ check e-mail
___ _____
___ other (please specify) _____

_____

Do you have enough time to visit the library?   ___ Yes   ___ No

Comments _____

_____

When you visit, do you usually find the materials you are looking for?   ___ Yes   ___ No

Comments _____

_____

Do you find the library staff approachable and helpful?   ___ Yes   ___ No

Comments _____

_____

Does the teacher-librarian offer guidance with your research?   ___ Yes   ___ No

Comments _____

Do you feel confident using the library's resources?   ___ Yes   ___ No

Comments _____

_____

Do you feel confident using online subscription databases? ___ Yes ___ No

Comments _____

_____

Which of our subscription databases do you use?

(List all your major databases for more accurate results.)

EBSCOhost	___ Yes	___ No
Biography Resource Center	___ Yes	___ No
Literature Resource Center	___ Yes	___ No
bigchalk	___ Yes	___ No
Facts.com	___ Yes	___ No
ProQuest Historical Newspapers	___ Yes	___ No
Grolier Online	___ Yes	___ No

Do you use our databases from home? ___ Yes ___ No

Which ones _____

Do you find the library's website useful? ___ Yes ___ No

Comments _____

Do you feel confident searching the Web? ___ Yes ___ No

Comments _____

_____

Do you feel you have adequate information technology skills? ___ Yes ___ No
What skills would you like to improve?

_____

Are there materials you have looked for that are not in the library's collection? ___ Yes ___ No

Please list specific materials you would like us to add. _____

_____

Do you use other libraries? ___ Yes ___ No If so, which other libraries do you use?

___ local public library ___ college library ___ other (please list)_____

Is the library a pleasant and comfortable place to visit? ___ Yes ___ No

Comments _____

_____

What is the best thing about our school library? _____

_____

List three things you have learned in the library information center:

1. _____

2. _____

3. _____

List up to three ways we could improve the school library: _____

_____

_____

Are the rules of the media center fair?   ___ Yes   ___ No

Comments _____

_____

_____

When you read for pleasure, which authors or types of books do you most often choose?

_____

Please rate the following:

	Poor ←——————→ Excellent				
facility (tables, chairs, climate, noise level, attractiveness)	1	2	3	4	5
accessibility (hours, pass system)	1	2	3	4	5
assistance/guidance provided by library staff	1	2	3	4	5
collection (books, periodicals)	1	2	3	4	5
collection (online, electronic)	1	2	3	4	5
library website	1	2	3	4	5
access to technology	1	2	3	4	5
helpfulness of the library staff	1	2	3	4	5
helpfulness of the teacher-librarian	1	2	3	4	5

Comments about any of the above: _____

_____

_____

What overall grade would you give our library information center? _____

What grade are you in? _____

Male ___   Female___

Other comments _____

_____

_____

Faculty Library Survey

Dear Faculty Member,

This survey will give us the information we need to help serve you and your students better. We appreciate your time and support. Please return this form to the library information center.

Please note your degree of disagreement or agreement with the following statements.

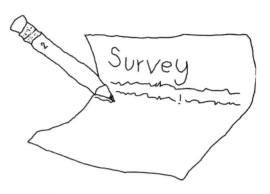

	Strongly disagree				Strongly agree
	1	2	3	4	5
The library information center is important to my program.	1	2	3	4	5
The library information center has adequate material to support my curriculum.	1	2	3	4	5
The library information specialist helps me find material I need for instruction.	1	2	3	4	5
The library information specialist helps me design instructional units.	1	2	3	4	5
The library information specialist helps me design assessments for my instructional units.	1	2	3	4	5
The library information specialist assists my students in developing information literacy skills.	1	2	3	4	5
The library information specialist understands my curricular needs	1	2	3	4	5
I feel comfortable using the electronic resources and subscription databases provided by the library information center.	1	2	3	4	5
I use the subscription services provided by the library information center in planning instruction.	1	2	3	4	5
I find the library information center support staff helpful and friendly.	1	2	3	4	5
My students find the library information center support staff helpful and friendly.	1	2	3	4	5
The library information center has or acquires materials to support my professional development and research.	1	2	3	4	5
The library information specialist offers relevant, useful professional development (in-services).	1	2	3	4	5
The library media specialist responds to my suggestions for purchase.	1	2	3	4	5
The climate of the library information center is appropriate for learning.	1	2	3	4	5
The library information specialist informs me of new published material in my field and when new material arrives.	1	2	3	4	5
The library information center is critical to learning in our school.	1	2	3	4	5

How do your students use the library information center? (Check all that apply.)

___ bring the whole class in

___ send students in small groups

___ send individual students

___ students visit before or after school

___ students visit during study halls

Directions: Please complete the following.

1. I do not choose to use the library information center because _____

_____

_____

_____

2. The best thing about our library information center program is _____

_____

_____

_____

3. Our library information center program could be improved by _____

_____

_____

_____

4. I have noticed that the collection is weak in the area(s) of _____

_____

_____

_____

5. I would like to see the following specific materials (books, magazines, online resources) added to our collection:

6. I would like assistance from the library staff in learning how to use/do _____

Subject Area/Grade _____

Name (Optional)_____ Date _____

Research Unit Teacher's Assessment Form

Classroom Teacher _____ Unit/Lesson _____ Date _____

	Poor ←————→ **Excellent**
How would you rate the success of the unit?	1 2 3 4 5
How would you rate the quality of student products?	1 2 3 4 5

Should we attempt this project again next semester/year? ___ Yes ___ No

Comments:

What recommendations do you have for improving the assignment for the next time? Should we change the student product? Our instructional strategies? Should we add an online component (Web page? Pathfinder?) Other?

Were your subject area and information skills goals reached? ___ Yes ___ No

Comments:

What materials would you like the library to add to better support this project?

I would like to make an appointment to revise or refine or rework this assignment: ___ Yes ___ No

Please return this form to the library.

Cheating and Plagiarism Survey

Please help us assess the level of academic integrity in our school culture.
Your answers will be **completely anonymous.**

1. What is your "take" on the level of cheating and plagiarism in our school? (choose one)

   ☐ Students rarely cheat

   ☐ It's very difficult

   ☐ It's somewhat difficult

   ☐ It's not very difficult

   ☐ It's fairly common

   ☐ Almost everyone does it

2. Which of the following have you done? (choose all the apply)

   ☐ Cheated on a test or quiz

   ☐ Copied someone else's homework

   ☐ Downloaded a complete paper

   ☐ Cut and pasted a paper together using online materials without appropriate documentation

   ☐ Submitted another student's work as my own with or without his/her knowledge

   ☐ Plagiarized just part of an essay

   ☐ Used Cliff's or Spark Notes to avoid reading a book

   ☐ None of the above

3. **If you have cheated,** why did you do so? (choose all that apply)

   ☐ Competition for good grades

   ☐ Didn't seem like a big deal

   ☐ Didn't think I'd get caught

   ☐ Not interested in the subject or assignment

   ☐ Parents expect good grades

   ☐ To keep grades up for college admission, sports eligibility, etc.

4. **If you have cheated,** what happened?

   ☐ I was caught and punished

   ☐ I was caught and not punished

   ☐ I was not caught

5. Have your parents talked with you about cheating?

  ☐ Never talked about it

  ☐ They encourage it

  ☐ They don't care if I do it or not

  ☐ They tell me I should not do it

  ☐ They forbid me to do it

6. Do your parents know if you cheat in school?

  ☐ Yes

  ☐ No

  ☐ I don't cheat

7. How easy would it be for you to obtain test questions or answers for a test or quiz?

  ☐ Very difficult

  ☐ Somewhat difficult

  ☐ Not very difficult

  ☐ Easy

8. How easy would it be for you plagiarize a paper without your teachers knowing?

  ☐ Very difficult

  ☐ Somewhat difficult

  ☐ Not very difficult

  ☐ Easy

9. Which of the following do you consider plagiarism?

  ☐ Changing the words around in a quote and then using them without documentation

  ☐ Using information that you consider common knowledge without citation

  ☐ Taking ideas from several of one person's writings and citing it every time, not just once.

  ☐ Paraphrasing the ideas of others without documentation

  ☐ Using information found on a Web site. Citing the source is not necessary.

10. How would you define plagiarism?

SOURCE: Adapted from a survey developed by Education Communications, Inc.

Reading Interest Survey

Our library is interested in trying harder to meet your reading interests. You can help us by answering a few brief questions.

How many books have you read (for pleasure) in the last year ____ last month ___

In the area of fiction, how interested are you in the following?

Fiction

	Very interested ◄——► Not interested					
Adventure	5	4	3	2	1	0
Graphic Novels/Anime (comic format)	5	4	3	2	1	0
Humor	5	4	3	2	1	0
Romance	5	4	3	2	1	0
Fantasy/Supernatural	5	4	3	2	1	0
Science Fiction	5	4	3	2	1	0
Mystery	5	4	3	2	1	0
Romance	5	4	3	2	1	0
Suspense	5	4	3	2	1	0
Historical Fiction	5	4	3	2	1	0

Which place and period of history interests you most? _____

Realistic Fiction	5	4	3	2	1	0
Sports Fiction	5	4	3	2	1	0
Other _____	5	4	3	2	1	0

Please list two or three of your favorite fiction authors.

_____

Please list two or three of your favorite book series.

_____

Nonfiction

When you read nonfiction for pleasure, what topics most interest you?

_____

If you read biographies, what type of people do you like to read about?

_____

Do you have any favorite nonfiction authors?

_____

General Interest

What specific titles do you wish our library had?

_____

For which areas in the library should we buy more books?

_____

What is the best book you ever read?

_____

What is the best movie you've ever seen?

_____

What is your favorite magazine?

_____

What type of music do you most like to listen to? Who are your favorite artists?

_____

Do you have any hobbies? Please list them!

_____

Thanks for helping us improve your library!

Curriculum Map

Use this form to help develop a visual snapshot of major research and content area skill instruction in your school. Look for overlap, opportunities for cross-discipline connections and class or grade-level "holes."

Month	Major Research Projects/Content and Information Skills	Class/Grade
September		
October		
November		
December		
January		
February		
March		
April		
May		
June		

Teacher _____

Grade/Department _____ Date _____

3-10

Curriculum Tracking by Department/Grade

Department _____

Department/Grade _____

MAJOR RESEARCH UNITS

CLASS/TEACHER	Sept.	Oct.	Nov.	Dec.	Jan.	Feb.	Mar.	Apr.	May	June

Information Literacy Log:
Data Collection Form

Teacher: _____ Department: _____

Class: _____ Group ____ or Individual ____

Research Assignment/Activity:

Description of Assignment/Activity:

Type of Student Product:

_____ Formal paper   _____ Webpage

_____ Video   _____ Debate

_____ Essay   _____ Performance (skit, role-play, etc.)

_____ Speech   _____ Oral/Multimedia Presentation (PowerPoint, other)

_____ Visual/Artistic (Poster, art, model, other)

_____ Other_____

Month(s) assigned: Sept. Oct. Nov. Dec. Jan. Feb. Mar. April May June

Research Process Skill Assessed (check any that apply):

_____ **Problem/Question/Thesis/Hypothesis:** Researcher(s) formulated a thoughtful hypothesis, question, or tentative thesis.

_____ **Information Seeking and Gathering:** Researcher(s) gathered information from a full range of quality electronic and print sources, including appropriate licensed databases and primary sources.

_____ **Evaluation of Resources:** Researchers carefully evaluated the resources they selected for their works consulted and/or works cited pages

_____ **Synthesis:** Researcher(s) processed and synthesized ideas and information from various sources to answer question or prove thesis.

_____ **Documentation/Information Ethics:** Researcher(s) used information ethically

_____ **Reflection/Process Conclusion:** Researcher(s) reflected thoughtfully and specifically on the research process.

_____ Other

Were these skills assessed through a rubric?   ____ Yes   ____ No

(Please attach your rubric.)

3-12

Snapshot of School Library Use during Typical Week

School: _____

Week of: _____

Teacher/Librarian: _____

Student population: _____

In-Person Visitors

Number of scheduled classes (break out by grade or department?): _____

Total number of students: _____

Number of drop-in visitors: _____

Number of faculty members visiting to plan or revise instruction: _____

Number of other group visits (faculty meetings, parent groups, school visitors, administrators, department meetings): _____

Total number of visitors: _____   Percentage of school population visiting: _____

Online Use

Database use (use administrative function of database, tally, or survey):

   1. Database: _____

   2. Database: _____

   3. Database: _____ _____

   4. Database: _____

Website visits (from online counter, tally, or survey): _____

Circulation

Statistics from online circulation system:

   Fiction: _____   Nonfiction: _____   Nonprint (video, audio, DVD, etc.): _____

Items circulated within the library (based on tallies of items left on tables for reshelving):

   Fiction: _____   Nonfiction: _____   Nonprint (video, audio, DVD, etc.): _____

Percentage of school population borrowing/using materials: _____

Interlibrary loans: requested by library: _____   requested of library: _____

LIBRARY USAGE 200X–200X BY DEPARTMENT

LAST	FIRST	SUBJECT	SEPT	OCT	NOV	DEC	JAN	FEB	MARCH	APRIL	MAY	JUNE	Total
ART		Art			4		2				1		
		Art											
		Art											
SUB TOTAL	*ART*		**0**		**4**	**0**	**2**	**0**	**0**	**0**	**1**	**0**	**7**
MUSIC/THTR		Msc/Thtr	2		3	6	3		3	3	2	1	
		Msc/Thtr		7	7		1				1		
		Msc/Thtr				10							
SUB TOTAL	*Msc/Thtr*		**2**	**10**	**10**	**6**	**4**	**0**	**0**	**3**	**3**	**1**	**39**
ENGLISH		English	4	9				1	5		2		
		English			1	3	17	20	7	20		1	
		English	12	3	3	3	9	11	5	7	14	16	
		English	5	3	4	4	4	6	9	6	3	4	
		English				9					9		
		English	5	1	3	8	8	2	3	2	10		
		English	7		4	9	6	7	3	2	12	12	
		English	13	13	8	1	9	17	14	10	13	8	
		English		1					2	1	1		
		English	1	6	4	12	2	2	1	4	7		
		English	2	2	2	4	4	2			3		
Sub Total	*English*		**47**	**38**	**31**	**53**	**54**	**68**	**49**	**52**	**74**	**41**	**507**
CONSUMER		Fmly/Consmr Sci											
Sub Total	*Fmly/Consmr Sci*		**0**	**0**	**0**	**0**	**0**	**0**	**0**	**0**	**0**	**0**	**0**
LANGUAGE		World Lang		6			4	3	4		6		
		World Lang		1	2								
		World Lang	1	4	6	6	2		3	1	5		
		World Lang				7	9	11	12	9	9		
		World Lang							3		3		
		World Lang	2		2	1							
Sub Total	*World Lang*		**3**	**11**	**10**	**12**	**15**	**14**	**18**	**10**	**23**	**0**	**116**
GUIDANCE		Guidance							1				
		Guidance											
		Guidance											
Sub Total	*Guidance*		**0**	**0**	**0**	**0**	**0**	**0**	**1**	**0**	**0**	**0**	**0**
HEALTH/PE		Health/PE		1									
		Health/PE				1							
		Health/PE					1		1	1			
		Health/PE											
Sub Total	*Health/PE*		**0**	**1**	**0**	**1**	**1**	**0**	**1**	**1**	**0**	**0**	**5**
INDUSTRIAL		Industrial Arts	1		2	3			3	2		3	
Sub Total	*Industrial Arts*		**1**	**0**	**2**	**3**	**0**	**0**	**3**	**2**	**0**	**3**	**14**

3-14A

		10	14	6		5	12	11	9	12	2	Total
MATH	Math						5	5	8	4		
	Math	1	4	1		2			2	1	2	
	Math	4	3	3		5		4	4	4		
	Math					1	3	3	3	5		
	Math				1							
	Math		5		6	2	3					
	Math	4		3								
	Math											
Sub Total	**Math**	**19**	**26**	**13**	**7**	**15**	**23**	**23**	**26**	**26**	**4**	**182**
NURSE	Nurse											
	Nurse											
Sub Total	**Nurse**	**0**	**0**	**0**	**0**	**0**	**0**	**0**	**0**	**0**	**0**	**0**
SCIENCE	Science		6	2			1	2			1	
	Science	2	6	4	2	2	3	4	3	3		
	Science		7	7	1	2	1	3	1	1		
	Science		5	5	5	2	3	6	2			
	Science		2	2			4		2			
	Science	2	11	12	3		12	11	9	3	10	
	Science		2		2		2	2	3			
Sub Total	**Science**	**4**	**39**	**32**	**13**	**6**	**26**	**28**	**20**	**7**	**11**	**186**
SPEC ED	Spec Ed	2	1		2				2			
	Spec Ed	4	1	1				2		1		
	Spec Ed			2	6		3	2				
	Spec Ed	1	4	4	2	7	25	21	20	22	2	
	Spec Ed											
	Spec Ed		5	4								
	Spec Ed	3		2			1					
	Spec Ed	4	2	3		1						
	Spec Ed	2		2			1	1		1		
Sub Total	**Spec Ed**	**16**	**12**	**18**	**10**	**8**	**30**	**26**	**22**	**24**	**2**	**168**
SS	SS	3	5	6	7	3	3	2	6	7		
	SS	12	16	9	9	7	6	9	10	9	6	
	SS	2	5	4	7	5	5		6	13		
	SS	22	11	4	10	26	20		13	43	4	
	SS											
	SS	3	6		3	3	7	3		5	11	
	SS	3	4	4	1	7	2	8	5	5		
	SS	2	14	6	4	12	11	15	11	20	5	
	SS	30	17	15	24	5	10	6	8	5	5	
	SS	5	5	2	2		4			2		
	SS	3		4	2	2		3	1	3		
Sub Total	**SS**	**85**	**83**	**54**	**67**	**63**	**68**	**46**	**60**	**112**	**31**	**669**

LIBRARY USAGE 200X–200X BY DEPARTMENT

TEC													1994
Sub Total	Tech	0	0	0	0	0	0	0	0	0	0	0	1994
GUIDANCE													
Sub Total	Guidance	0	3	1	4	1	6	1	1	0	0	17	
MISC													
				1	1	1	1	1					
Misc Mtgs		18	7	21			3	7	13	7		84	
Sub Total		18	8	22	1	3	4	8	13	7	0	84	
TOTAL		195	235	193	179	170	239	203	210	277	93	1994	

Instructional Tools for Information Literacy

> The mission of the library media program is to ensure that students and staff are effective users of ideas and information.
>
> —American Association for School Librarians and Association for Educational Communication and Technology, *Information Power,* 1998

Our mission is to teach and to integrate information skills into the school curriculum. The transferable skills of problem identification, and information location, analysis, evaluation, and communication, will stay with our students for a lifetime, long after they forget memorized facts. Whether they choose the world of academia or go directly into the world of work, these are the skills that will prepare our students to thrive in an information-rich society.

Most of the tools presented in this section will help us as we partner with classroom teachers to teach, integrate, and assess these essential process skills, the same process skills that are likely woven through the content area standards. I have also included a few orientation activities for use early in the school year to create an awareness of the richness of library resources.

4-1

Information Power: Building Partnerships for Learning: The Nine Information Literacy Standards for Student Learning

This summary of the AASL/AECT Standards, from the 1998 document, should fuel our teaching and leadership efforts.

4-2

A Big6 Skills Overview

Developed by Mike Eisenberg and Bob Berkowitz, the Big6 model is one of the most widely used approaches to teaching information skills. The model provides students a "systematic process to find, use, apply, and evaluate information for specific needs and tasks."

4-3
Best Practice for Research-Based Instruction: A Checklist for Teacher Reflection

This guide, developed by Springfield Township (PA) Language Arts Coordinator Carol Rohrbach, offers a checklist for teachers as they develop assignments and assessments. It illustrates the importance of a teacher's investment and preparation in the success of students' research efforts.

4-4
Fifty Ways to Leave Your . . . Term Paper or Book Report

As we move beyond reporting, teachers may need to develop a new "bag of tricks." Even the best and most experienced teachers could use a bit of inspiration. Share this list of alternate ideas with classroom teachers when you sense your faculty may be in a rut and suggest thoughtful ways to motivate student research. Be sure to add your own unique ideas and your suggestions for fleshing out these basic ideas.

4-5
MLA Bibliographic Style: A Brief Guide

MLA (Modern Language Association) style is perhaps the most prevalent bibliographic form in the K–12 arena. The style sheet here follows the 6th edition of Joseph Gibaldi's *MLA Handbook for Writers of Research Papers*. Many of the sample entries refer to specific sources in our high school though the materials were never actually published. We try to "change our sheets" every year, incorporating names of our teachers with books they might have written. The inside jokes keep folks reading style sheets and amuse our students. Feel free to use these examples, but you may choose instead to entertain your staff by customizing the document to include your own local celebrity authors and your own databases.

4-6
Guidelines for Documentation Formats: Rationale

Students may be comfortable documenting when preparing traditional print products, but they are often confused when the product shifts to a less traditional format. This document explains expectations for ethical work when students document the ideas of others in all types of research-based projects—papers, presentations, posters, websites, etc.

4-7
Works Cited and Work Consulted Pages: What's the Difference?

The two different lists we ask students to append to their projects often confuse them. Use this handout to explain why and when they should use each.

4-8
When Should I Document Sources in My Text?

This handout explains the *hows* and *whys* of in-text/in-project documentation.

4-9
Summarizing, Paraphrasing, and Quoting

It *is* okay to borrow from the works of others, as long as you use the material responsibly. This handout, developed in collaboration with Language Arts Coordinator Carol Rohrbach, explains how and when to credit others as you summarize, paraphrase, and quote.

4-10
Weaving Quotes into Your Writing

Springfield Township (PA) High School English teacher Ken Rodoff developed this exercise to demonstrate how to effectively weave, not just paste, quotes into essays and papers. After asking students to read each writing sample, evaluate each sample as a group.

4-11
Copyright and Fair Use Guidelines for Teachers

This chart, developed by Hall Davidson, executive director of educational services and telecommunications at KOCE-TV in California, appeared in *Technology and Learning*, October 2002. It offers guidance for teachers and students struggling to understand the practical applications of fair use—when it is acceptable and when it is not acceptable to photocopy, download, share files, and duplicate.

4-12
Zippy Scenarios for Teaching Internet Ethics

Frances Jacobson Harris shares provocative scenarios for our students to explore as they learn to distinguish right from wrong online. These scenarios should inspire lots of discussion.

4-13
Use CARRDSS to Help You Evaluate Your Sources!

CARRDSS is our schoolwide acronym, developed to remind students of the criteria we expect them to consider as they evaluate sources to use in research.

4-14
Dewey Decimal Classification System and Highlighted Numbers of Interest to Students!

This chart can be customized to reflect your own students' needs and interests. Leave a few charts at the circulation desk near the OPAC for students who prefer browsing to searching.

4-15
Web Page Evaluation Checklist

Joe Barker of the Teaching Library, University of California, Berkeley, developed this form as an activity to help students thoroughly evaluate and compare the sites they visit. Barker's hints lead students to carefully analyze the aim or intent of a page.

4-16
Why Should I Take This Author Seriously?

This handout, created for upper-level high school students, should help them assess the qualifications of a web page (or any other) author. Because credentials are often hidden on web pages, students benefit from a discussion of the detective work they might need to employ to discover who an author really is.

4-17
Why Take Notes?

This skit is fun to perform with a cooperative teacher or with two students enthusiastic about playing the roles. The lesson engages student interest while proving the practical need to take notes. The idea was originally posted on the Big6 Listserv by Claire Simpson of Moorestown Upper Elementary School (NJ) and further developed by Jane Perry of Winslow Junior High School (ME).

4-18
Group Project Plan

Help your cooperative learning groups get organized by giving each of the groups a planning form. They will be better able to divide responsibility, set goals, and plan their resources. At the end of a period of planning, they should be able to submit a full plan to their teacher.

4-19
Group Project Planning Chart

After watching teachers struggle to organize group projects on a yellow pad, I developed this organizer. Teachers can see at a glance who should be doing what and with whom.

4-20
Library Scavenger Hunt

Although I am not usually a fan of library visits without subject content connection, during orientation I find it important to get students physically oriented and comfortable with our resources when they are new to the facility. For their first visit, I have students label key areas of the library on a map. They then must continue to wander the library actually using materials and talking to staff members. Our ninth-grade Communication Arts teachers count this scavenger hunt as a quiz or homework grade. Adapt this hunt to cover the resources you want your students to discover before they start their first projects.

4-21
Library Skills Game

Use these questions for a "Hollywood Squares" game during orientation. I choose nine "celebrities" from each class. Each is given a laminated sign with an *X* on one side and an *O* on the other. The remainder of each class is divided into two teams (X and O, of course), with captains who must decide whether the "celebrity" is telling the truth or bluffing. I use as many manipulatives and visuals as possible. The game allows me to review familiar concepts and introduce new concepts and vocabulary that students will be hearing from me over the next four years in integrated lessons. Don't use all the questions! Pick and choose depending on the needs and the personality of the visiting class. To update this idea, you could use any of the newer reality shows involving questions as models. Try a *Survivor* or *Amazing Race* theme and include these questions with physical challenges (like shelving?).

4-22
700 and Nancy

Some of you may remember the old Dewey story about Art (700). I use this update, developed by my daughter, Emily, and her friend Sandie Straub, to get my interns familiar with the layout of the shelves and Dewey decimal classification. Give it a try with a class.

4-23
Search Tool Species: A Field Guide

Students have a wide range of searching options. This handout helps students (and teachers) to narrow the field by understanding the various search tool *species.*

4-24
Database Worksheet

This activity is designed to familiarize students with your database resources. During orientation assign a small group to each of your databases, and let the form guide them in exploring and presenting its features to the rest of the class. Have each group share their discoveries so that the entire class learns about each database.

4-25
Mini-Documentary Assignment

This assignment and rubric was developed in collaboration with Springfield Township (PA) Media Production teacher Dan Meder. Use and adapt

pieces of Meder's exemplary rubric in planning similar multimedia projects.

4-26/4-27
Multimedia/Web Page Research Rubric and Multimedia Project Evaluation Form (Middle School)

Teachers grading multimedia presentations have new factors to evaluate. How do you get students to balance the flash with actual content? How do you get them to understand that a thesis and good spelling still "count"? Provide them with a rubric in advance, and your students will be far more likely to satisfy all the requirements of your project. Consider distributing them to the class to conduct peer evaluations.

4-28
Research CheckBric

This assessment tool, developed in collaboration with Language Arts Chair Carol Rohrbach, focuses on the research *process,* analyzes the criteria valuable in scholarly research, and communicates clearly to students the steps they should follow to create a successful product. It assumes that students submit a research package that includes a reflection and search organizer. "Quotable quotes" are quotes truly *worth* quoting, quotes that further the student writer's narrative. "Research holes" are the major sources that students might overlook.

4-29
Rubric for a Research Project

This rubric ensures students cover all the steps for a truly information literate research process.

4-30/4-31
What Is a Thesis? and Thesis Generator: Ideas for Helping Students Develop Better Thesis Statements

"Topical research" has limited value in an information-rich landscape. Students need to *use* information to persuade, analyze, compare, and make judgments. Student work should be driven by inquiry and purpose. Topical research inspires little more than printing, and students deserve more worthy challenges. *What Is a Thesis?* offers a definition and advice for developing a thesis. *Thesis Generator* offers strategies to help students think about the questions surrounding their research topics.

4-32
Visualizing the Search Process

This model attempts to illustrate the recursive process employed by good searchers—reconsidering, refining, and responding at each step.

Information Power:
Building Partnerships for Learning:
The Nine Information Literacy Standards
for Student Learning

INFORMATION LITERACY

Standard 1: The student who is information literate accesses information efficiently and effectively.

Standard 2: The student who is information literate evaluates information critically and competently.

Standard 3: The student who is information literate uses information accurately and creatively.

INDEPENDENT LEARNING

Standard 4: The student who is an independent learner is information literate and pursues information related to personal interests.

Standard 5: The student who is an independent learner is information literate and appreciates literature and other creative expressions of information.

Standard 6: The student who is an independent learner is information literate and strives for excellence in information seeking and knowledge generation.

SOCIAL RESPONSIBILITY

Standard 7: The student who contributes positively to the learning community and to society is information literate and recognizes the importance of information to a democratic society.

Standard 8: The student who contributes positively to the learning community and to society is information literate and practices ethical behavior in regard to information and information technology.

Standard 9: The student who contributes positively to the learning community and to society is information literate and participates effectively in groups to pursue and generate information.

SOURCE: Excerpted from chapter 2, "Information Literacy Standards for Student Learning," of *Information Power: Building Partnerships for Learning.* Copyright © 1998 American Library Association and Association for Educational Communications and Technology.

A Big6 Skills Overview

by Mike Eisenberg

THE BIG6

Developed by Mike Eisenberg and Bob Berkowitz, the Big6 is the most widely known and widely used approach to teaching information and technology skills in the world. Used in thousands of K–12 schools, higher education institutions, and corporate and adult training programs, the Big6 information problem-solving model is applicable whenever people need and use information. The Big6 integrates information search and use skills along with technology tools in a systematic process to find, use, apply, and evaluate information for specific needs and tasks.

WHY BIG6?

We all suffer from information overload. There's just too much "stuff" out there, and it's not easy to keep up. At the same time, there's an irony—yes, we are surrounded by information, but we can never seem to find what we want, when we want it, and in a form we want it so that we can use it effectively.

One solution to the information problem—the one that seems to be most often adopted in schools (as well as in business and society in general)—is to speed things up. We try to pack in more and more content, to work faster to get more done. But, this is a losing proposition. Speeding things up can only work for so long. Instead, we need to think about helping students to work smarter, not faster. There is an alternative to speeding things up. It's the smarter solution—one that helps students develop the skills and understandings they need to find, process, and use information effectively. This smarter solution focuses on process as well as content. Some people call this smarter solution information literacy or information skills instruction. We call it the Big6.

THE BIG6 SKILLS

The Big6 is a process model of how people of all ages solve an information problem. From practice and study, we found that successful information problem solving encompasses six stages with two sub-stages under each:

Big6 Skills

1. **Task Definition**

    1.1 Define the information problem

    1.2 Identify information needed in order to complete the task (to solve the information problem)

2. **Information Seeking Strategies**

    2.1 Determine the range of possible sources (brainstorm)

    2.2 Evaluate the different possible sources to determine priorities (select the best sources)

3. Location and Access

3.1 Locate sources (intellectually and physically)

3.2 Find information within sources

4. Use of Information

4.1 Engage (e.g., read, hear, view, touch) the information in a source

4.2 Extract relevant information from a source

5. Synthesis

5.1 Organize information from multiple sources

5.2 Present the information

6. Evaluation

6.1 Judge the product (effectiveness)

6.2 Judge the information problem-solving process (efficiency)

People go through these Big6 stages—consciously or not—when they seek or apply information to solve a problem or make a decision. It's not necessary to complete these stages in a linear order, and a given stage doesn't have to take a lot of time. We have found that in almost all successful problem-solving situations, all stages are addressed.

In addition to considering the Big6 as a process, another useful way to view the Big6 is as a set of basic, essential life skills. These skills can be applied across situations—to school, personal, and work settings. The Big6 Skills are applicable to all subject areas across the full range of grade levels. Students use the Big6 Skills whenever they need information to solve a problem, make a decision, or complete a task.

The Big6 Skills are best learned when integrated with classroom curriculum and activities. Teachers and library media specialists can begin to use the Big6 immediately by:

- Using the Big6 terminology when giving various tasks and assignments
- Talking students through the process for a particular assignment
- Asking key questions and focusing attention on specific Big6 actions to accomplish.

Various computer and information technology skills are integral parts of the Big6 Skills. For example, when students use word processing to compose a letter, that's Big6 #5, Synthesis. When they search for information on the World Wide Web, that's Big6 #3, Location and Access. When they use e-mail to discuss an assignment with another student or the teacher, that's Big6 #1, Task Definition. Using computers can "turbo-boost" students' abilities.

SOURCE: Adapted with permission from Michael B. Eisenberg and Robert E. Berkowitz, The Big6 Model. Big6 website http://www.big6.com.

Best Practice for
Research-Based Instruction:
A Checklist for Teacher Reflection

In their research-based products we want students to demonstrate ethical behavior, individual thought, evidence for assertions, accuracy in documentation, and problem-solving process. How can teachers ensure that students have both the experiences and the tools to help them develop these qualities?

_____ **PROVIDE—challenging assignments that require students to manipulate and synthesize information.**

    _____ Develop inquiry-driven (thesis-driven or hypothesis-driven) assignments for papers, projects, and presentations. Ask students to compare/contrast, evaluate, justify, conclude rather than to regurgitate or report.

    _____ Give the assignment a voice that allows and encourages students to see themselves as detectives: asking questions, evaluating and weighing evidence, making inferences.

    _____ Change the approach, format, perspective, and/or time period.

    (e.g., the "What if ?" approach—What if Othello were the protagonist in *Hamlet* and Hamlet were the protagonist in *Othello*? a thesis based on unlikely pairs; a dialogue between the mayors of the same city in different decades with a concluding piece of commentary/analysis/evaluation/prediction, etc.; a short story in which the conflict involves five different characters affected by the Alaskan oil spill; a scientist whose theory went unrecognized during his/her lifetime gets his/her say in a forum; what a specific historical figure or literary character would/should do differently; a filmmaker responds to reviews; a teenager of today time travels to 19th c. Paris; a baby in utero criticizes pre-natal care available to his/her given socio-economic situation or nation or time period; etc.).

        _____ Require primary sources (letters, maps, interviews, etc.).

        _____ Require specific primary and secondary sources or types of sources or combination of sources; vary the requirements each time you give the assignment.

        _____ Add an oral and/or in-class piece

        (Student leads a discussion based on his/her product, prepares an abstract of the work, summarizes learning, defends conclusions or aspects of the process or aspects of the product, defends sources.)

        _____ Keep the assignment fresh and meaningful.

        _____ Make regular and frequent changes to the particulars of the assignment; vary the particulars from class to class, from one year to the next.

    _____ Make the assignment "unique" to the experience of these students in this class during this year/semester. Allow assignments to grow out of the classroom activities and experiences of this particular group of students as a distinct community of learners in this time and place.

    _____ Consider individual differences in learning style, experiences, interest, readiness, etc. Give differentiated learning options and individual choice.

_____ **COMMUNICATE—explicit expectations.**

_____ Provide an explicit assignment sheet that specifies the requirements and expectations and includes a context that connects the paper/project/presentation to class work and to instructional goals.

_____ Make sure that students understand why the assignment is valuable and that research takes time and focused attention.

_____ Include a checkpoint calendar for various aspects of the process.

_____ Provide an explicit rubric that values process and product; give it to students in advance.

_____ Create a climate that values ethics—model it, talk about it regularly, monitor it, and specify what constitutes acceptable collaboration.

_____ Require documentation ("Works Cited," "Works Consulted") for all research-based work including posters, videotapes, skits, panels, debates, etc.

_____ Require an "Acknowledgments" page where students specify the help they received from others (peers, siblings, parents, etc.).

_____ Distribute an explicit policy that states the consequences of plagiarism.

_____ Encourage students to seek help from you, from the librarian, and from peers and other adults as appropriate. Provide opportunities for help.

_____ Use peer revision/edit groups, problem-solving groups, pair chores, conferences in class, adjusting checkpoint stages to accommodate individual needs/weaknesses/difficulties, phone calls to parents.

_____ **FOCUS INSTRUCTION—and provide the tools that students will need to be successful during the process and in completion of the product.**

_____ View yourself as a facilitator for students. Help them to think through the issues, problem-solve, etc. (Provide graphic organizers, structures, resources, etc. as the individual need arises.)

_____ Teach or review as necessary and require precision in the technical aspects of ethical documentation (in-text documentation format, Works Cited and Works Consulted pages, paraphrase, summary, common knowledge) particularly as they relate to your discipline and in relation to graphs, charts, maps, visuals, etc.

_____ Manage the process (require checkpoints, conferences; accomplish tasks during class).

_____ Use time management intervention (parent contact, workshop points, detention with production requirement).

_____ Require students to submit with the final product all checkpoint aspects.

_____ Help students locate materials meaningful to them and appropriate to their developmental level. With assistance from the librarian, create a "research hotlist" for students (_Guiding Readers and Writers: Grades 3–6,_ Fountas and Pinnell 433).

_____ Give students strategies and graphic organizers for note-taking, weighing ideas, looking for absences and tailor these to your content perspective (e.g., How does a historian approach these issues, this time period, this contradiction? How does a parent weigh conflicting theories about child-rearing?)

_____ Teach mini-lessons as needed and remind students to use chunking, highlighting, topic sentences, chapter heading, paraphrasing, etc. independently as reading tools.

_____ Communicate with your colleagues to establish grade level/course/cross-curricular expectations, commonality of terminology, co-teaching opportunities, etc.

4-3B

_____ **PROVIDE PRACTICE—that is content-based.**

_____ Teach/expect/assess higher level thinking on a regular basis (see Bloom's Taxonomy or Marzano's *Dimensions of Learning* 3, 4). As you develop curriculum and plan instruction in the content/process/skills of your content area, include inducting, deducting, abstracting, inferring, analyzing, synthesizing (e.g., class discussion points), applying (e.g., students write alternative scenarios as homework after reading a history text chapter rather than complete end-of-chapter questions; write entrance slip summaries of last night's reading and make one prediction; write paraphrases of conflicting opinions in class using correct documentation format, then evaluate the opinions; etc.).

_____ Create research projects that grow out of classroom activities and expectations that students will extend through:

_____ Analysis (identify the parts and their relationships; what makes it work or not; find the errors or absences. Use to study a poem, painting, music score, legal case, government policy, scientific theory, mathematical process, etc.)

_____ Synthesis (pull several sources or ideas together and "make sense" of them)

_____ Evaluation (develop criteria, weigh issue or works)

_____ Develop class activities throughout the course/grade level to give students multiple opportunities for judgment and evaluation (e.g., determine the effectiveness of . . . ; justify the . . . ; judge the performance of . . . ; develop criteria for . . . ; defend (answer questions about assumptions, facts, research, conclusions); look for bias, separate fact from opinion; compare and contrast).

_____ Work with primary documents as resources for information (letters, interviews, documents, notebooks/journals, logs).

_____ Use paraphrase, summary, and quotation as tools for learning content.

_____ Use mini-papers/projects/presentations and/or develop multi-stage, scaffolded, research-based class performance activities for curricular learning. (Debates, interview with a historical figure, create a comic strip, etc.)

_____ **REFLECT—on the efficacy of your practice.**

_____ Use your students' work (process and product) to inform you about the challenge and clarity of the assignment, the effectiveness of the communication, focused instruction, and everyday classroom practice strategies. On the basis of what students have accomplished and what they have not, determine how specific revisions to assignments, rubrics, expectations, instructional practice will improve student performance next time.

SOURCE: Developed by Carol H. Rohrbach, K–12 Language Arts Coordinator, School District of Springfield Township, Erdenheim, PA.

Fifty Ways to Leave Your . . . Term Paper or Book Report

Dear Classroom Teacher,

Although we believe that students need to develop the skills to prepare a thoughtful, well-written research paper, there are other product options. Students can acquire subject knowledge and develop transferable information literacy and technology skills through a variety of creative activities. The following is a list of some enriching assignment ideas for your class. For any research products or response to literature, consider how technologies like video, desktop publishing, web development, or multimedia presentations might enhance students' communication of the knowledge they have gained. Stop by the library information center, and together we can plan and discuss project ideas, available resources, and assessment options.

Annotated bibliography: Students search for the best materials relating to their question or thesis and evaluate them for relevance, scope, point of view, and credentials of the author. Posted on the Web, these bibliographies may be useful for future researchers.

Pathfinder: Students create a path for future researchers on a defined area of knowledge. Students carefully evaluate available resources and select and annotate the best print and online sources, offering search strategies, context for the topic, question or thesis, and concluding summaries reflecting on the issues they discover while researching.

Newsletter: Using a desktop publishing program, students set their newsletters in another time or place. They create classified ads, theater and book reviews, sports stories, and business information. This is a perfect collaborative project.

Debate: Choosing two historic figures and an issue, students "duke it out." The rest of the class is responsible for asking questions and judging the debate. Videotape the debate for later discussion.

Brochure: Using a desktop publishing program, students create flyers to advertise a product they've developed, a place they've researched, a period of time, a solution to a problem, or to offer health advice.

Résumé: Using a desktop publishing program, students create professional-looking (print, online or multimedia) résumés for a famous person and attach cover letters in the individual's voice. They might simulate interviews of the historical figure applying for a job at a university or business.

Students present the résumés and "sell" their character's qualifications.

Database: Students collect and organize facts on any topic with an eye toward comparing information for patterns. They create a chart or graph to illustrate conclusions. For example, the topic of Italian Renaissance artists could be presented through charts to compare style, training, support of patrons, colors used, and subjects of paintings.

Family tree: Students design a tree for a character in a novel. They can make the boxes large enough for illustrations and descriptions of characters and their relationships.

Press conference (with famous people of a time period): Select a group of famous people to be interviewed and have the bulk of the class prepare questions. Students being interviewed should prepare well enough to imagine how their famous person would respond to provocative questions.

Trip itinerary: Students studying countries, states, or time periods prepare a detailed itinerary listing sites of importance, what to pack, costs considering exchange rates, temperature for the

season, where to stay, how to get from place to place, special events, etc.

Detailed journal entries or online blog: For a fictional or historical character, students imagine what a real week would be like and create a series of entries in the life of a person present at a historical event or that a book character might have kept during a specific period. Include interaction and quotes from family and friends. Reveal deep feelings, thoughts about others, and respond to big events.

Mock trial for a controversial historical figure or fictional character: Bring Napoleon, Hitler, Socrates, Lee Harvey Oswald, Saddam Hussein, Galileo, or Richard Nixon in front of a well-prepared class made up of jurors, attorneys, witnesses, and a judge. Or hold a court simulation with students deciding a major issue, such as affirmative action, assisted suicide, or major constitutional controversies.

Board game: Let an event in history or a novel inspire a truly playable game. Host an hour of game playing in the classroom as your evaluation.

Web home page: Web pages can advertise fictitious businesses, invented products, or present electronic résumés for historical or fictional characters.

Visit by a person in history to the school (à la Bill and Ted's Excellent Adventure*):* Students plan an entire visiting day and record the visitor's reactions to gym, lunch, your classes, the mall, etc. Get cameras ready. Present as a skit, video, web page, or monologue.

A day in the life of plant/machine/disease/person: Students prepare an essay or speech in first person to give the class a better idea of the history and daily life of the AIDS virus, for instance.

Awards event: Students plan a science fair for famous scientists; Grammy awards for classical musicians; or Latino culture awards for a Spanish class. Students present rationale for their selected person to win; they write detailed acceptance speeches, and plan the entertainment.

Dinner party: Students invite people from a particular period and plan what to serve and who will sit next to whom. Design the invitations. And describe the entertainment. Re-create the

conversation. Or hold live and teachers may evaluate the interaction among characters.

Historic experience simulation: Try a Civil War battle or a day at Ellis Island. Assign each student a role. The teacher should assume the role of a critical player to ensure the continuation of the action.

Skit: Students represent a typical day at a job for a career project or a major historical event.

Online threaded discussion: Teacher poses questions among a group of related historical figures or characters in a play or novel. Students maintain assigned roles as they respond to each others' posts in threaded discussion.

Film treatment: For a historical event or a novel, have a critical character or the author plan the film version. Address a letter to a producer suggesting and defending choice of actors based on knowledge of characters, select locations, and describe how you would stage specific scenes. Design the movie poster. Plan the trailer. (Avoid books that have already been made into movies.)

News article: Write an authentic newspaper-style article about a historic event or event from a novel. Include quotes from the major players. (Require primary sources if this is historical.)

Dear Abby letter: Have a novel protagonist or historical figure write to an advice columnist. Present the character's problems and create a sincere, researched response from the columnist. Expect the advice columnist to use historic or book evidence and furnish serious insights.

Letter from one character or historical figure to another: Characters can share deep thoughts and reveal their personalities and rationale for their actions in personal letters. The letter should reveal something about the recipient's character, as well.

You are the president, the general, the inventor, the senator: Create two reasonable alternate scenarios for a historic event or decision. How else might Lee have responded at Gettysburg? After the student presents the three possible scenarios, have the class determine the most reasonable choice, or the choice actually made.

Write a short story about people who lived during a particular period or event or in a particular place: For instance, describe the last few minutes of the

Space Shuttle disaster from the perspectives of three of the astronauts.

You are the author, playwright, or filmmaker: Respond to newspaper and magazine reviews of your work.

What if? If you could change one aspect of an event or book, would you choose to change the setting—place or time? Would you alter a character's personality or one of his choices? What if Richard III were the protagonist in *Macbeth* and Macbeth were the protagonist in *Richard III?* What if the Pilgrims met more hostile Native Americans? How would one change affect the big picture?

Lesson plan: Have students creatively present the results of their research in a lesson of their own. The lesson should not be a lecture; it should actively engage the class.

Original song or rap: Ask students to describe an event, a person, a concept, or a character musically. A refrain goes a long way toward getting the class involved.

Oversized baseball card or wanted poster: What is the essence of the person you've studied or met through a novel? Capture those qualities economically in the form of a large baseball card (with quotes, stats, image) or wanted poster. The baseball card should include statistics and quotes, and use the border effectively.

Alternate book jacket with blurb: Ask students to create new art to advertise a book—fiction or nonfiction. A compelling blurb to draw readers in.

Advertising campaign: Ask students to create a full-blown campaign for an invention or industry or a book. Or choose an important person and run his or her campaign for a major political office.

Postage stamp for a person or event in history: Students attach a desktop-published stamp design to a three-paragraph essay describing why the subject was important enough to deserve a commemorative stamp.

Picture book: Students explain a concept or event through artistic illustration and economic language.

Phone message or telegram: Students write a lengthy message from one historic character to his

or her spouse or other contemporary about an important event.

CD or album cover with inside background pages: Students design a cover to represent an event and plan the songs with descriptions. They decide who would be the producer and musicians.

Crossword puzzle or word search: Students use related vocabulary to create a puzzle for the class to attempt.

Petition: Students lobby for or against an issue they have researched with a formal petition.

"This Is Your Life" television show: Students videotape or enact the show complete with guests, illustrations, and special surprises.

"Survivor" television show: Place teams of your students in a historic time or far off place. Provide challenges to solve to see who knows enough to "outwit, outplay, outlast."

Epitaph and obituary or eulogy: Focusing on a person in history, students write epitaphs for tombstones, write newspaper obituaries, and deliver well-researched eulogies.

Recipe: What ingredients and conditions would students need to create the French Revolution? How would they prepare and cook their recipes?

Photograph album or scrapbook: Students seek authentic historical photographs and label all the pictures in their albums, sharing "personal anecdotes" with the class, and including journal entries and letters. This assignment could be creatively extended to be the album of a character, a teen of a period in history, a disease, animal, or invention.

Political cartoon: Students satirize a political or historic person or event.

Monologue: More-dramatic students may opt to create a scene from the life of a famous person or a fictional person caught up in a real event.

Want ad: Students compose an ad requesting personnel to solve a problem in history.

Time line: Students create a wall-sized, annotated, and illustrated time line, including important quotes.

Soap opera based on a historical event: Students can add lots of drama and over-the-top characters.

MLA Bibliographic Style: A Brief Guide

For full information about the style required by the _____ High School faculty, visit our school's Research Project Guide.

This handout is designed to be a quick reference guide to the MLA style of documenting sources in research papers. Your "Works Cited" section should appear at the end of your paper and you should arrange the entries works alphabetically by author, or by title, if no author appears in the entry. In this section you should list only works you actually cited. Your teacher may also request a separate list of works consulted. For further information about types of entries not listed here, consult Joseph Gibaldi's *MLA Handbook for Writers of Research Papers,* 6th edition, which is available at the circulation desk. For further information, consult the official page of the Modern Language Association (http://www.mla.org).

Some of your teachers might suggest you use APA, an alternate style used more often in scientific research and developed by the American Psychological Association. You can find advice on using APA style at the Purdue OWL (http://owl.english.purdue.edu/handouts/research/r_apa.html) and at the APA site (http://www.apastyle.org/aboutstyle.html).

Underlining vs. italics: MLA style traditionally recommends underlining the titles of major works, but some school districts and many publications now utilize italics for this purpose. The MLA website addresses this fascinating controversy! "Most word processing programs and computer printers permit the reproduction of italic type. In material that will be graded or edited for publication, however, the type style of every letter and punctuation mark must be easily recognizable. Italic type is sometimes not distinctive enough for this purpose. . . . If you wish to use italics rather than underlining, check your instructor's or editor's preferences."

OTHER TIPS

- If no author is given, start the citation with the title.
- Abbreviate the names of all months except May, June, and July.
- Use shortened forms of publishers' names. Leave out articles—A, An, The—and words like Co., Inc., Books, House, Press, Publishers. When citing a university press, add the abbreviations *U* and *P* (Ohio State UP). If the publisher includes a person's name, cite the surname alone (instead of John Wiley, use Wiley). If the publisher's name includes the names of more than one person, cite the first surname only.
- Use familiar abbreviations in publisher's names (MLA or GPO).
- Use *hanging indentation* format. Indent the second line of an entry and all other lines half an inch or 5 spaces (if using a typewriter).
- All parts of a research paper should be double-spaced, including your list of works cited. Double space between and within entries.
- Titles of newspapers, magazines, and journals are not followed by punctuation.

PRINT SOURCES

Format for the Works Cited and Works Consulted Sections

A Book by One Author

English, Carol. The Cliffs Won't Do: Read the Book. Philadelphia: McGraw Hill, 2004.

Two or More Books by the Same Author

Small, Chris. Please, Help Me Carry My Keys! Topeka: Rand, 2002.

——— . Don't Measure a Chemist by Her Size. New York: Feminist, 2004.

A Book by Two or Three Authors

Drucker, Darla, and Amy Jones. <u>How to Survive Your Wedding</u>. New York: Simon, 2003.

A Book by a Corporate Author

Springfield Township Family and Consumer Science Department. <u>Cooking with Spice</u>.
    New York: Scribner, 2003.

A Book with an Editor

Valenza, Joyce, ed. <u>Bagels and Books: An Anthology</u>. Brooklyn, NY: Random House, 2001.

A Work in an Anthology

Smith, James. "The Physics of Sushi." <u>The Fabulous Physics Paper</u>. Ed. Samuel Klein.
    Rome: Cambridge UP, 2004. 46-59.

An Edition Other Than the First

Peters, Michael. <u>Everything You Always Wanted to Know About Keeping Your Classroom</u>
    <u>Neat and Clean</u>. 4th ed. Philadelphia: Lysol, 2005.

A Signed Article in a Reference Book

Cohen, Sandra. "Zen and Art." <u>Encyclopedia Americana</u>. 2004 ed.

An Unsigned Article in a Reference Book

"Best Beards of All Time." <u>Encyclopedia of Anatomy and Hair</u>. 15th ed. 2003.

An Article in a Journal with Continuous Pagination

Skater, Andrew. "High School Rollerblading." <u>Secondary Education</u> 54(1990): 113-25.

An Article from a Monthly or Bimonthly Periodical

Ramsey, Pamela. "Where's My Smiley Face?" <u>MacWorld</u> Sept. 1997: 86-94.

An Article from a Weekly or Biweekly Periodical

Henry, Mary Ann. "Announcing Bus Changes With Flair." <u>Time</u> 4 July 2001: 17-76.

A Signed Article from a Daily Newspaper

Goldberg, Grace. "The Inside Track: Alumni Life." <u>Trojan Times</u> 10 Oct. 2004: 17.

Smith, Bob. "Schools Losing Ground." <u>USA Today</u> 5 May 2001: 5D.

An Unsigned Article from a Daily Newspaper

"Striking a Pose with Sally Miles." <u>New York Times</u> 15 Oct. 1997, late ed. sec.6: 35+.

A Critical Analysis, Signed Excerpt

Ross, Stephan S. "Tom Wolfe." <u>Contemporary Literary Criticism</u>. Ed. Daniel G. Marowski. 35: 458-60.

Films; Radio and Television Programs

"Starring the Other Peggy Lee." <u>Slightly Off Broadway—The Series</u>. Prod. Sheldon Wang. PBS.
    WNET, New York. 6 Aug. 1995.

<u>Creative Bookbinding</u>. Dir. Tom Martin. Videocassette. Clemens, 1997.

Personal or Telephone Interview

Craig, John. Personal interview. 23 Sept. 2004.

Personal Photograph (for your scanned images!)

Begin with a description of the photo. Do not use italics or quotation marks. Indicate who took the photo and the date it was taken.

Grandpa Al at Home. Personal photograph by Susan Student. 28 May 2003.

Citing works within your text (in-text or in-project documentation)

To document your sources, cite the author's name and the page number of the source in parentheses at the end of the sentence, before the final period:

> Lowfat cream cheese can save you 300 grams of fat per year (Valenza 35).

If the author's name is used in your sentence, you may just refer to page numbers:

> Copaset argues "yellow simply does not interact well with khaki" (45).

If you are referring to the whole work rather than a specific section, you may omit any reference in parentheses:

> Through his work, Berger's main thesis is that by using motifs, organic unity is easier to achieve.

CITING ELECTRONIC SOURCES

Uniform standards continue to develop to address dramatic changes in information formats. Web sources often challenge researchers to locate missing pieces of citations. While researchers should make every effort to locate that information, what is most important in documenting electronic resources is to give the reader as much specific information as possible (e.g., author, title, publication data) to identify the source you are citing.

Parenthetical notes: The information in your parenthetical notes must match the corresponding entries in your list of works cited. One of the most frequent questions students asked is "How do I prepare a parenthetical note for a Web page if a Web page has no page numbers?"

The MLA has an answer: "nonprint sources such as films, television programs, recordings, and performances, and electronic sources with no pagination or other type of reference markers cannot be cited by page number. Such works are often cited in their entirety and often by title" (Gibaldi 239).

Do not include hyperlinks in your works cited; they are useful to online readers only. Turn off autoformatting before you begin your draft, or enter Control Z to undo automatic hyperlinking by your word processor.

World Wide Web (general Web site)

Format:

> Author (if known). "Title of Page or Document." Title of Site or Larger Work *(if applicable)*.
>> Date of electronic publication, last update, or date of posting. Name of any
>> Associated Institution. Date of download. <http://address/filename>.

Examples:

> Valenza, Joyce. "Springfield Township High School Virtual Library." 8 June 2003. Springfield
>> Township High School. 3 Oct. 2005. <http://mciu.org/~spjvweb>.

or

> Smith, George. "Graf Has Look of a Champion." ESPNET SportsZone. 29 Aug. 1996.
>> <http://www.espn.com/gen/top/0108716001.html>.

Article in an online magazine (not accessed through a subscription service)

Format:

> Author. "Title of Article." Title of Magazine Date of electronic publication. Date of access.
>> <http://address/filename>.

Example:

> Smith, Jane. "Who Really Invented the Internet?" Web Weekly 26 Feb 2001. 4 May 2001.
>> <http://webweekly.com/smithwho/>.

Article in an online encyclopedia

Format:

> Author. "Title of Article." Title of Reference Work. Edition or version (if available). Date of electronic
>> publication. Title of the Database or Online Service. Date of access. <http://address/filename>.

Example:

Cook, Sarah Gibbard. "Berlin, Germany." <u>Encyclopedia Americana Online</u>. Mar. 2003.
<u>Grolier Online</u>. 29 Feb. 1999. <http://grolier.go.com>.

Article in an online scholarly journal (available independently)

Format:

Author. "Article Title." <u>Periodical Title</u> Volume. Issue (Year): Pages (if available).
<u>Larger Site or Database Name (if any)</u>. Date of access. <http://address/filename>.

Examples:

Smith, Winston. "Life in Dystopia." <u>Journal of Utopian Literature Online</u> 23.4 (2004): 20-33.
<u>Project Future World</u>. 20 Feb. 2006. <http://projectfw.com/julo/distopia.htm>.

Entire Online Book

Twain, Mark. <u>Adventures of Huckleberry Finn</u>. New York: Harper, 1884. <u>Electronic Text Center</u>.
U of Virginia Library. 20 July 2004. <http://etext.lib.virginia
.edu/toc/modeng/public/Twa2Huc.html>.

Section of an Online Book

Frost, Robert. "Birches." <u>Mountain Interval</u>. 1920. <u>Bartelby.com: Great Books Online</u>. 25 May 2005.
<http://www.bartleby.com/119/11.html>.

Article in an online magazine (available independently)

Format:

Author. "Article Title." <u>Periodical Title</u> Date of print publication (if available): Pages (if available).
Date of access. <http://addressofarticleorjournalsearchpage>.

Example:

Oreklin, Michele. "Spending It All on the Kids." <u>Time</u> 7 July 2003: 24-25. 2 Aug. 2004.
<http://www.time.com/time/magazine/article917.html>.

Journal material accessed from a subscription service (EBSCO, elibrary, GaleNet, CQ Researcher, etc.)

Format:

Author. "Article Title." <u>Periodical Title</u> Date of print publication (if available): Pages. <u>Database
Name (if any)</u>. Name of Providing Library, Consortium or Library System. Date of access.
<http://addressofdatabasehomepage>.

Examples:

Brown, Susan. "Writing the Perfect Paper." <u>High School Weekly</u> 12 Sept. 2004: 22. <u>EBSCOhost</u>.
ACCESS PA. 25 Nov. 2004. <http://www.epnet.com/>.

or

Williams, Larry. "Speedy Internet May Spur Innovations." <u>Philadelphia Inquirer</u> 16 Aug. 1996: A03.
Montgomery County Lib. 7 Dec. 2003 <http://www.phillynews.com/archive.htm>.

or

Clark, Charles S. "The FBI Under Fire." <u>CQ Researcher</u> 11 April 1997: 315-22. Springfield Township
HS Lib. 3 Sept. 2003. <http: resource.cq.com>.

or

Brown, Charlie. "My Life in Cartoons." <u>Cartoon Week</u> 21 Nov. 1999: 7-12. <u>InfoTrac: General
Reference Center Gold</u> on <u>Student Resource Center.</u> Gale Group. Springfield
Township HS Lib.15 Dec. 1999. <http://www.galegroup.com/>.

SIRS Online Products

Format:

Author. "Article Title." <u>Original Source of Article</u> Date of original source: pages. <u>Product Name</u>. Name of Providing Library, Consortium or Library System. Date of access. <http://address/filename>.

Example:

Frick, Robert. "Investing in Medical Miracles." <u>Kiplinger's Personal Finance</u> Feb. 1999: 80-87. <u>SIRS Knowledge Source: Researcher.</u> (May substitute <u>Renaissance</u> or <u>Government Reporter</u>) Springfield Township HS Lib. 25 July 1999. <http://sks.sirs.com/>.

Facts.com

Format:

"Article Title." <u>Original Source of the Article</u>. Date of original source. <u>Product Name</u>. Publisher. Name of Providing Library, Consortium or Library System. Date of access. <http://www.2facts.com>.

Facts.com examples:

"Safe Drinking Water Act Signed." <u>Facts On File World News Digest</u> 22 Aug. 1996. <u>FACTS.com</u>. Facts On File News Services. Springfield Township HS Lib. 20 Jan. 2000. <http://www.2facts.com>.

"Issues and Controversies: Racial Disparities." <u>Issues and Controversies on File</u> 13 Jan. 1996. <u>FACTS.com</u>. Facts On File News Services. Springfield Township HS Lib. 15 Nov. 1999. <http://www.2facts.com>.

GaleNet/Student Resource Center

Format for a periodical reference:

Author. "Article Title." <u>Original Source of the Article</u> Date of original source. Pages of original source. <u>Specific Database</u> on <u>Student Resource Center</u>. Gale Group. Name of Providing Library, Consortium or Library System. Date of access. <http://www.galenet.com>.

Example:

Brown, Charlie. "My Life in Cartoons." <u>Cartoon Week</u> 21 Nov. 1999: 7-12. <u>General Reference Center Gold</u> on <u>Student Resource Center</u>. Gale Group. Springfield Township HS Lib. 15 Dec. 1999. <http://www.galenet.com>.

Format for an article that appeared in a book:

Author. "Article Title." <u>Title of Book</u>. City of Publication: Publisher, Date. Pages. <u>Specific Database</u> on <u>GaleNet</u> or <u>Larger Database</u>. Name of Providing Library, Consortium or Library System. Date of access. <http://galenet.gale.com>.

Example:

Hoffman, Baruch, Elaine. "The Golden Country: Sex and Love in <u>1984</u>." <u>1984 Reviewed in Our Century</u>. New York: Harper, 1983. 47-56. Republished in <u>Contemporary Literary Criticism Select</u> on <u>Student Resource Center</u>. Springfield Township HS Lib. 20 May 2004. <http://www.galenet.com>.

Format for a reference article (not previously published):

Author (if provided). "Article Title." <u>Specific Database</u> on <u>Student Resource Center</u>. Gale Group. Name of Providing Library, Consortium or Library System. Date of access. <http://www.galenet.com>.

Examples:

"Classical Greek Civilization, 2000 B.C.-300 B.C." <u>DISCovering World History</u> on <u>Student Resource Center</u>. Gale Group. Springfield Township HS Lib. 12 Oct. 1999. <http://www.galenet.com>.

or

"Dean Koontz." <u>DISCovering Authors Modules</u> on <u>Student Resource Center</u>. Gale Group. Springfield Township HS Lib. 3 Dec. 2000. <http://www.galenet.com>.

Format for a republished journal essay:

Author (if provided). "Article Title." <u>Original Source of Article</u>. Date of original source: Pages of original source. <u>Specific Gale Database</u> on <u>Larger Database</u>. Gale Group. Name of Providing Library, Consortium or Library System. Date of access. <http://www.galenet.com>.

Examples:

Levin, Harry. "Wonderland Revisited." <u>The Kenyon Review</u> Autumn, 1965: 591-93. <u>Contemporary Literary Criticism Select</u> on <u>Literature Resource Center</u>. Gale Group. Springfield Township HS Lib. 13 Oct. 1999. <http://www.galenet.com>.

or

Berger, Carol. "Profile of a Basketball Great." <u>Sports in Philadelphia</u> 12 Nov. 1999. <u>Biography Resource Center</u>. Gale Group. Springfield Township HS Lib. 20 Dec. 2004. <http://www.galenet.com>.

Format for an article republished from a multi-volume reference series:

Author (if provided). "Article Title." <u>Original Source of Article</u>. Editor. Volume: Pages of original source. <u>Specific Gale Database</u> (if noted) on <u>Larger Database</u>. Gale Group. Name of Providing Library, Consortium or Library System. Date of access. <http://www.galenet.com>.

Example:

Sturber, Robert. "Imagery in Great Expectations." <u>Nineteenth-Century Literary Criticism</u>. Ed. Carol Packard. 26: 235-50. <u>Literature Resource Center</u>. Gale Group. Springfield Township HS Lib. 23 Jan. 2003. <http://www.galenet.com>.

Wilson Biographies

Format:

Author (if provided). "Article Title." <u>Original Source of Article</u>. Date of original source. Pages of original source (if available). <u>Specific database</u> on WilsonWeb. Name of Providing Library, Consortium or Library System. Date of access. <http://vweb.hwwilsonweb.com/>.

Example:

"Edward Albee." <u>Current Biography</u>. 1996. <u>Wilson Biographies Illustrated Plus</u> on WilsonWeb. Springfield Township HS Lib. 15 Dec. 1999. <http://vweb.hwwilsonweb.com/>.

Beyond Books

Format:

Corporate Author. "Book: Section: Article Title." Date of Original Source. <u>Name of Database</u>. Name of Providing Library, Consortium or Library System. Date of access. <http://www.beyondbooks.com/>.

Example:

Beyond Books, New Forum Publishing. "Shakespeare: Shakespeare's London: Women." 13 March 2003. <u>Beyond Books.com</u>. Springfield Township HS Lib. 31 March 2003. <http://www.beyondbooks.com/sha91/1f.asp>.

CD-ROMs, Diskettes, DVDs

Non-periodical (encyclopedias, etc.)

Format:

Name of Author (if given). "Title of Part of Work." <u>Title of Publication</u>. Name of Editor, Compiler, or Translator (if relevant). Edition or release, if relevant. Publication medium (CD-ROM, diskette, etc.). City of Publication: Publisher, Year of publication.

Example:

Wallechinsky, David. "Olympic Games." <u>Encyclopedia Encarta</u>. CD-ROM. Redmond, WA: Microsoft, 2003.

Personal Subscription Service (one you might subscribe to at home)

Format:

Author (if available). "Title of Article." <u>Title of Larger Work</u>. Version (if available). Date of source. Name of Service. Date of access. Keyword: Word.

Example:

Jones, Charles O. "Political Party." <u>World Book Online</u>. 2003. America Online. 12 Jan. 2004. Keyword: Worldbook.

CD-ROM (periodical)

Format:

Name of Author (if available). "Title of article." <u>Title of Journal or Newspaper</u> Publication information for printed source. <u>Title of Database</u>. Publication medium (CD-ROM, diskette, DVD). Name of Vendor (if relevant). Electronic publication date.

Example:

Nethead, Jane. "Email Rules." <u>New York Times</u> 15 Nov. 1995, late ed.: B3. <u>New York Times Ondisc</u>. CD-ROM. UMI-Proquest. Jan. 2004.

E-mail

Format:

Author's Name. "Subject Line from Posting." Personal e-mail. (or E-mail to recipient's name.) Date of message.

Example:

Smith, William. "Trial results." E-mail to John Henry. 29 May 1999.

Online mailing list posting

Format:

Author (if given). "Subject of Message." Date of posting. Online posting.
Name of Forum. Date of access. <URL or e-mail address of the list>.

Example:

Williams, Jim. "Computer to T.V. Screen." 6 Aug. 1999. Online posting. Global Technology
Discussion Group. 21 Nov. 2003. <http://www.gtdg.org> or <listserv@citation.edu>.

Online Chat or synchronous communication

Format:

Name of Speaker. (if available). "Description of the event." Date of session or event.
Forum for the Communication. Date of access. <Web or network address>.

Example:

Yente, Ima. "Online discussion of future fuels." 24 Oct. 2002. EnvironMOO. 28 June 2004.
<http://IRC@envirosite.edu>.

Images/Sound/Video Clips/AP Photo Archive

Online images (Photographs, Sculpture, Paintings)

Format:

Artist if Available. Description or Title of Image. Date of image. Physical Source of Image/
Collection (if available). Title of Database or Larger Site. Date of access.
<http://address.website.org>.

Examples:

Mars Landing. 3 Nov. 1999. NASA. 4 Oct. 2002. <http://www.nasa.org>.

or

Weaver, Bruce. Challenger Explosion. 28 Jan 1986. AP Photo Archive. 30 Jan. 2004.
<http://accuweather.ap.org/cgi-bin/aplaunch.pl>.

or

Van Gogh, Vincent. Irises. 1889. Getty Museum. 20 July 2003. <http://www.getty.edu/art/
collections/objects/o947.html>.

Online Map

Format:

"Title of Map." Map. Date of Map (if available). Title of Larger Site. Organization or Institution.
Date of access. <http://address.website.org>.

Example:

"Israel and Neighboring States." Map. 1990. Perry-Castañeda Library Map Collection. U Texas.
8 May 2004. <http://www.lib.utexas.edu/maps/israel_nbr90.jpg>.

Online sound

Format:

Creator (if available). "Description or Title of Sound." Date of Sound. Title of Larger Site.
Associated Organization or Institution. Date of access. <http://address.website.org>.

Examples:

"Weekly Saturday Radio Address." 25 Oct. 1998. <u>Whitehouse Briefing Room</u>. 23 Oct. 2003.
<http://www.whitehouse.gov/WH/html/briefroom.html>.

or

"Conversation 9326 with Defense Secretary Robert McNamara." 20 Dec. 1965. <u>LBJ Whitehouse
Tapes Archives</u>. C-SPAN. 20 May 2004. <http://www.c-span.org/lbj/>.

Online video clip

Format:

Director (if available). <u>Description or Title of Video Clip</u>. Date of clip. <u>Title of Larger Work
or Site</u>. Date of download. <http://address.website.org>.

Examples:

<u>Hindenburg Broadcast</u>. 6 May 1937. <u>Encarta Online Deluxe</u>. 4 Nov. 2000. <http://encarta.msn.com/>.

Online Television or Radio Program

Silberner, Joanne. "Food Labels." <u>All Things Considered</u>. 11 July 2003. National Public Radio.
12 Aug. 2004. <http://discover.npr.org/features/feature.jhtml?wfld=1331099>.

SOURCE: Style information based on: Gibaldi, Joseph. *MLA Handbook for Writers of Research Papers.* 6th ed. New York: Modern
Language Association, 2003.

Guidelines for
Documentation Formats: Rationale

We in the _____ School District understand and value the concept of intellectual property. Therefore, we strive to teach students the ethic of responsibly documenting the ideas of others regardless of the format in which they choose to communicate their knowledge or express their creativity.

POLICY

All research-based projects/papers/presentations/posters must include documentation of sources in the forms of Works Consulted, Works Cited, and in-project documentation, as required by the content.

VISUAL WORK

Examples: triptych, poster, PowerPoint, videotape

Students must submit a Works Consulted page attached to the product (or submitted per teacher direction) as in triptych or poster, or as the last frame of the presentation (as in PowerPoint or videotape). Annotation of Works Consulted entries may or may not be required.

In all visual work that employs copyrighted visual material (such as drawings and photographs) students must also use in-project documentation with an accompanying Works Cited page.

WRITTEN WORK

Examples: expository essay (including informative, persuasive modes), narrative (memoir, story), poem, play, formal research paper, biography, booklet, brochure

Students must submit a Works Consulted page (as in booklet, brochure, narrative, poem, play). Annotation of Works Consulted entries may or may not be required.

In all written work that employs summary, paraphrase, or quotation, students must also use in-text documentation with an accompanying Works Cited page.

In all written work that employs copyrighted visual material, students must also use in-text documentation in conjunction with the Works Cited page.

ORAL WORK

Examples: speech, debate, group or individual presentation, role play, simulation

Students must submit a Works Consulted page. Annotation of Works Consulted entries may or may not be required.

Note: Teachers may also wish to require an Acknowledgments page. The purpose is to document the help that students received in the development of the product during the process. Help may range from peer input and parent editing to the teacher/librarian locating resources and mentor input. Students learn intellectual integrity not only by citing sources in the Works Consulted/Works Cited, but also by using the Acknowledgments page to document all sources of help that contributed to the final product.

SOURCE: Adapted from a teacher handout developed by Carol H. Rohrbach, K–12 Language Arts Coordinator, School District of Springfield Township, Erdenheim, PA.

Works Cited and Works Consulted Pages: What's the Difference?

Works Consulted is the term used for the list of sources used in the preparation of a research project. It is used to list background reading, summarized sources, or any sources used for informational purposes but not paraphrased or quoted. It is used to document those sources referred to, but not cited in your project.

research project

Cite those sites!

Works Cited is the term for the list of sources actually documented (paraphrased or quoted) in your project, generally through parenthetical citation. All of the parenthetical references in the paper or project should lead the reader to this list of sources.

SHOULD I USE ONE OR BOTH?

A student might prepare only a Works Consulted page if he or she did not quote or paraphrase at all in the project.

A student might prepare only a Works Cited page if he or she paraphrased or quoted from and therefore cited all sources used.

A student might prepare both Works Consulted and Works Cited pages if, in addition to the sources cited in the project or paper, he or she also consulted other sources that were not paraphrased or quoted.

PREPARING THE WORKS CITED AND WORKS CONSULTED PAGES

- Head a new sheet of paper "Works Cited" or "Works Consulted" (Do not use quotation marks around your title.)
- Alphabetize your sources by author, or first entry, which may be an association or a title, if no author is noted. This should be easy if you have collected source cards.
- Place the "Works Cited" page(s) immediately after the last page of the text.
- If your paper includes both Works Cited and Works Consulted, the Works Consulted page should follow the Works Cited page.

SOURCE: Developed by Carol H. Rohrbach, K–12 Language Arts Coordinator, School District of Springfield Township, Erdenheim, PA.

When Should I Document Sources in My Text?

In-text (or in-project) documentation is the accepted format for acknowledging borrowed information within your original text. Footnotes are no longer frequently used, except in cases when you need to clarify or add information that might otherwise break the flow of your text or presentation.

Use in-text documentation to cite a source whenever you:

- use an original idea from one of your sources, whether you quote or paraphrase it
- summarize original ideas from one of your sources
- use factual information that is not common knowledge (Common knowledge is information that recurs in many sources. If you are not certain it is common knowledge, cite to be safe.)
- quote directly from a source
- use a date, fact, or statistic that might be disputed

Usually only the author's last name and the page number OR, in the absence of an author, the title and the page number are given. Do not use the word "page" or any abbreviations. Page numbers may be omitted if the article is a one-page article or one in an encyclopedia arranged alphabetically. Page numbers may also be omitted when citing Web resources, which do not normally include paging.

The purpose of this format is to give immediate source information without interrupting the flow of the paper. Usually parenthetical citations are placed at the end of a sentence, but they may be placed in the middle (see example 6). The academic world takes in-text documentation seriously. Inaccurate documentation is as serious as having no documentation at all.

RULES FOR USING IN-TEXT DOCUMENTATION

1. Use the author's last name and give the page number in parentheses. Do not use "page" or abbreviations for page, just write the number. In most cases you will be citing one or two pages, leading your reader to a specific piece of information. Allow one space before the parentheses but none after it if a period follows.

    EX: Arthur Miller's *The Crucible* "forces a revolution in our perception and definition of reality" (Martin 73).

2. If you are using more than one book by the same author, give the last name, comma, the title, and the page.

    EX: Animal imagery conveys the primitive, uncontrolled rage that the peasants feel. One person "acquired a tigerish smear about the mouth" (Dickens, *Tale of Two Cities* 33-34).

4-8A

3. There is a relationship between your writing and how you compose your in-text documentation. If you identify the author and title in the text, you do not need to repeat that information. Simply present the page number in your citation.

> EX: In *Understanding Why the Caged Bird Sings,* Megna-Wallace notes that Angelou's autobiography succeeds on two levels: "first, as a personal memoir . . . and second, as a representative narrative that exemplifies the struggle of many African American women against racial and sexual oppression" (10).

4. If there is no author, give the title and the page number.

> EX: A number of critics feel that Hemingway's journalistic style continued to influence writers through the end of the 20th century ("Hemingway Chronicle" 5).

5. If you are quoting a direct quotation from a secondary source, you must identify it as such.

> EX: According to Arthur Miller, "It was not only McCarthyism that moved me, it was as though the whole country had been born anew, without a memory even of certain elemental decencies" (qtd. in Budick 74).

6. If a quotation or information appears in the middle of your own idea, then insert the documentation immediately after the quotation.

> EX: Arthur's Miller's notion of a country "without memory of certain elemental decencies" (qtd. in Budick 74) resonates throughout *The Crucible.*

7. If the quoted material exceeds two lines in your text, use a comma or colon after the last word of text, indent and type the quotation without quotation marks. The parenthetical citation follows the punctuation at the end of the last sentence of the quote.

8. Web documents generally do not have fixed page numbers or any kind of section numbering. If your source lacks numbering, omit numbers from your in-text documentation and use only the main entry—author, or title, if there is no author—in parenthesis.

Note: For a Web document, the page numbers of a printout should NOT be cited, because the pagination may vary in different printouts.

> EX: A recent CNN.com review noted that the book's purpose was "to teach cultures that are both different from and similar to world status quo" (Allen).

Summarizing, Paraphrasing, and Quoting

You *can* borrow from the works of other writers as you research. Good writers use three strategies—summarizing, paraphrasing, and quoting—to blend source materials in with their own, while making sure their own voice is heard.

Summarizing involves putting the main idea(s) of one or several writers into your own words, including only the main point(s). Once again, it is necessary to attribute summarized ideas to the original source. Summarized ideas are not necessarily presented in the same order as in the original source. Summaries are significantly shorter than the original and take a broad overview of the source material.

Summarize when:

- You want to establish background or offer an overview of a topic
- You want to describe common knowledge (from several sources) about a topic
- You want to determine the main ideas of a single source

Paraphrasing means rephrasing the words of an author, putting his/her thoughts in your own words. A paraphrase can be viewed as a "translation" of the original source. When you paraphrase, you rework the source's ideas, words, phrases, and sentence structures with your own. Paraphrased text is often, but not always, slightly shorter than the original work. Like quotations, paraphrased material must be followed with in-text documentation and cited on the Works Cited page.

Paraphrase when:

- You plan to use information on your note cards and wish to avoid plagiarizing
- You want to avoid overusing quotations
- You want to use your own voice to present information

Quotations are the exact words of an author, copied directly from the source word for word. Quotations must be cited!

Use quotations when:

- You want to add the power of an author's words to support your argument
- You want to disagree with an author's argument
- You want to highlight particularly eloquent or powerful phrases or passages
- You are comparing and contrasting specific points of view
- You want to note the important research that precedes your own

---

SOURCE: Developed with Carol H. Rohrbach, K–12 Language Arts Coordinator, School District of Springfield Township, Erdenheim, PA.

Weaving Quotes into Your Writing

Effective writers use a variety of techniques to integrate quotations into their text.

When you use a quote in your writing, consider:

- What am I trying to say?
- Can a passage from the text say it for me?
- Have I explained the value of the quote?

Avoid "overquoting." It is important that your own voice is heard!

Discuss the effectiveness of the following writing samples:

Serious room for improvement:

William Golding's book *Lord of the Flies* is about kids stranded on an island. Some of the kids are good and some are bad. "Roger, with a sense of delirious abandonment, leaned all his weight on the lever" (Golding 180). So I ask you, what causes irresponsible behavior? Ralph is good, but Jack is bad.

Room for improvement:

There are bad kids on the island. One of them is Roger. He drops a boulder on Piggy and kills him. "Roger, with a sense of delirious abandonment, leaned all his weight on the lever" (Golding 180). This caused Piggy's death.

A possible revision:

The truest form of wickedness on the island is evident in Roger. He demonstrates his true depravity when, "with a sense of delirious abandonment, [he] leaned all his weight on the lever" (Golding 180). Well aware of Piggy's place beneath him, Roger willingly takes Piggy's life.

Another possible revision:

Roger's murder of Piggy clearly illustrates the depths children can sink to without appropriate supervision. As he stood high above Piggy on the mountain, "Roger, with a sense of delirious abandonment, leaned all his weight on the lever" (Golding 180). His willingness to welcome the moment with "delirious abandonment" clearly demonstrates the level of pleasure that Roger received by committing this horrific act.

SOURCE: By Ken Rodoff, English teacher, Springfield Township High School, Erdenheim, PA. Adapted by Joyce Valenza.

Copyright and Fair Use Guidelines for Teachers

This chart was designed to inform teachers of what they may do under the law. Feel free to make copies for teachers in your school or district, or download a PDF version at www.techlearning.com. More detailed information about fair use guidelines and copyright resources is available at www.halldavidson.net.

TECHNOLOGY & LEARNING

Medium	Specifics	What you can do	The Fine Print
Printed Material (short)	• Poem less than 250 words; 250-word excerpt of poem greater than 250 words • Articles, stories, or essays less than 2,500 words • Excerpt from a longer work (10 percent of work or 1,000 words, whichever is less) • One chart, picture, diagram, or cartoon per book or per periodical issue • Two pages (maximum) from an illustrated work less than 2,500 words, e.g., a children's book	• Teachers may make multiple copies for classroom use, and incorporate into multimedia for teaching classes. • Students may incorporate text into multimedia projects.	• Copies may be made only from legally acquired originals. • Only one copy allowed per student. • Teachers may make copies in nine instances per class per term. • Usage must be "at the instance and inspiration of a single teacher," i.e., not a directive from the district. • Don't create anthologies. • "Consumables," such as workbooks, may not be copied.
Printed Material (archives)	• An entire work • Portions of a work • A work in which the existing format has become obsolete, e.g., a document stored on a Wang computer	• A librarian may make up to three copies "solely for the purpose of replacement of a copy that is damaged, deteriorating, lost, or stolen."	• Copies must contain copyright information. • Archiving rights are designed to allow libraries to share with other libraries one-of-a-kind and out-of-print books.
Illustrations and Photographs	• Photograph • Illustration • Collections of photographs • Collections of illustrations	• Single works may be used in their entirety; but no more than five images by a single artist or photographer may be used. • From a collection, not more than 15 images or 10 percent (whichever is less) may be used.	• Although older illustrations may be in the public domain and don't need permission to be used, sometimes they're part of a copyright collection. Copyright ownership information is available at **www.loc.gov** or **www.mpa.org.**
Video (for viewing)	• Videotapes (purchased) • Videotapes (rented) • DVDs • Laserdiscs	• Teachers may use these materials in the classroom. • Copies may be made for archival purposes or to replace lost, damaged, or stolen copies.	• The material must be legitimately acquired. • Material must be used in a classroom or nonprofit environment "dedicated to face-to-face instruction." • Use should be instructional, not for entertainment or reward. • Copying OK only if replacements are

Medium	Examples	Guidelines
Video (for integration into multimedia or video projects)	• Videotapes • DVDs • Laserdiscs • Multimedia encyclopedias • QuickTime Movies • Video clips from the Internet	• Students "may use portions of lawfully acquired copyright works in their academic multimedia," defined as 10 percent or three minutes (whichever is less) of "motion media." • The material must be legitimately acquired: a legal copy (not bootleg) or home recording. • Copyright works included in multimedia projects must give proper attribution to copyright holder.
Music (for integration into multimedia or video projects)	• Records • Cassette tapes • CDs • Audio clips on the Web	• Up to 10 percent of a copyright musical composition may be reproduced, performed, and displayed as part of a multimedia program produced by an educator or students. • A maximum of 30 seconds per musical composition may be used. • Multimedia program must have an educational purpose.
Computer Software	• Software (purchased) • Software (licensed)	• Library may lend software to patrons. • Software may be installed on multiple machines, and distributed to users via a network. • Software may be installed at home and at school. • Libraries may make copies for archival use or to replace lost, damaged, or stolen copies if software is unavailable at a fair price or in a viable format. • Only one machine at a time may use the program. • The number of simultaneous users must not exceed the number of licenses; and the number of machines being used must never exceed the number licensed. A network license may be required for multiple users. • Take aggressive action to monitor that copying is not taking place (unless for archival purposes).
Internet	• Internet connections • World Wide Web	• Images may be downloaded for student projects and teacher lessons. • Sound files and video may be downloaded for use in multimedia projects (see portion restrictions above). • Resources from the Web may not be reposted onto the Internet without permission. However, links to legitimate resources can be posted. • Any resources you download must have been legitimately acquired by the Web site.
Television	• Broadcast (e.g., ABC, NBC, CBS, UPN, PBS, and local stations) • Cable (e.g., CNN, MTV, HBO) • Videotapes made of broadcast and cable TV programs	• Broadcasts or tapes made from broadcast may be used for instruction. • Cable channel programs may be used with permission. Many programs may be retained by teachers for years—see Cable in the Classroom (www.ciconline.org) for details. • Schools are allowed to retain broadcast tapes for a minimum of 10 school days. (Enlightened rights holders, such as PBS's *Reading Rainbow*, allow for much more.) • Cable programs are technically not covered by the same guidelines as broadcast television.

Sources: United States Copyright Office *Circular 21*; Sections 107, 108, and 110 of the Copyright Act (1976) and subsequent amendments, including the Digital Millennium Copyright Act; *Fair Use Guidelines for Educational Multimedia*; cable systems (and their associations); and *Copyright Policy and Guidelines for California's School Districts*, California Department of Education. **Note:** Representatives of the institutions and associations who helped to draw up many of the above guidelines wrote a letter to Congress dated March 19, 1976, stating "There may be instances in which copying that does not fall within the guidelines stated [above] may nonetheless be permitted under the criterion of fair use."

4-11B

Zippy Scenarios for Teaching Internet Ethics

Note to educators: Feel free to use any of the following scenarios for educational purposes. And please feel free to share your own ideas too! Send scenario suggestions to francey@uiuc.edu.

Describe the underlying netiquette/ethics issue(s) in each scenario. What is your opinion of the behaviors involved? What equitable solutions can you suggest? Describe a parallel situation in which computers are NOT involved.

1. Jules has walked away from a lab computer without logging off. Trish sits down and, still logged in as Jules, sends inflammatory e-mail messages out to a number of students and posts similar messages on the class newsgroup.

2. Lester sends e-mail to the entire student body inviting them to a BYOB party at his house while his parents are out of town. Lester receives a message from a system administrator calling him in for a meeting with school officials. He objects because he feels that his e-mail is his own private business.

3. Every time Abner posts a comment to a newsgroup, his posts are flamed by a group of "enemies." Abner has responded to each flame in turn, and a full-scale war is now in progress.

4. It seems like every time Melanie logs on to her account, Stanley knows about it and sends messages that cover her screen with text. At first she thinks it is funny, but now it's really starting to bother her. The messages reformat the text on her screen and, besides, it's kind of creepy the way he always knows she's logged on.

5. Sharon and Timothy are students at Big Suburban High School. They have designed a Web page devoted to their favorite rock band using their personal disk space on the school's Web server. They have posted song clips, lyrics, photographs of each band member, and articles they have found in various Web news sources. However, school authorities have asked them to shut down their site because of the obscene content of many of the lyrics. Sharon and Timothy object, noting that their First Amendment (free speech) rights are being violated.

6. A secretary on the campus of a tax-supported university has been requested to give her staff password to her supervisor. The supervisor would like to check the secretary's e-mail when she is not at work to see if departmental-related mail is coming in. The secretary is not comfortable giving her password to her supervisor, but is afraid to say no.

7. Tina's e-mail is being diverted and sent out to her entire class. The messages are quite personal and Tina is very embarrassed.

8. Sandy has been receiving 4 or 5 anonymous insults daily over e-mail. Because of the context of the notes, she has narrowed the suspect down to someone in her 4th hour class. She sends the entire class a nasty warning not to do it again.

9. Brad has posted a note on his class newsgroup stating his (highly unflattering) opinion of a new teacher. He wants to know what others think. Some of the responses that follow say nice things. Other comments are quite critical; a few are personal.

10. At Paradise High School, people can send e-mail messages to students-only mailing lists that no teachers or administrators can read. Teachers and administrators also have their own mailing lists. However, word leaks out that the answers to a sophomore-level test have been mailed to the sophomore student

mailing list, but no one is saying who is responsible for the posting. Now the school administration is rethinking the idea of student-only areas and the issue of whether the faculty should supervise them.

11. Paula and Ron went out for a few months. During that time, they sent each other some pretty personal e-mail. But their breakup was messy. The final straw came when Ron found out that Paula was sending copies of their old messages to his new girlfriend. Pretty soon, copies of the messages seemed to be all over the school and his new girlfriend wouldn't speak to him.

12. Russ has been an active participant at a chat site for teens. He knows a few of the people in "real life," but many live in other cities. One of them, Stuart, will be coming through town in a few weeks and wants to get together. He asks Russ for his home phone number and address. Russ suggests that they just meet at the mall, and Stuart agrees, but wants Russ's home info anyway in case he's delayed.

13. Word gets around that Sylvester maintains a web site on the Geocities web server. Besides containing sexually explicit references about a couple of girls at school, the web site links to hard-core porn sites. School officials find out about it and tell Sylvester that they plan to inform his parents about the web site.

14. Marla figures out that when she is logged into Mork, she can look at others' directories, make copies of files, and deposit new files. The Unix operating system was designed to allow this functionality so that programmers could share their work. Mr. Klausinsky objects when he observes Marla poking around in another student's directory. But Marla responds by saying, "If the system allows me to do it and there's no specific rule against it, what's the problem?"

15. After the September 11th terrorist attack, many students and teachers send related e-mail to the "all-student" or "all-faculty" mailing lists. Most of the messages contain information about the status of former students and about ways people can help in the crisis. But Penelope sends a long note with a heavy religious message. And Mr. Snidden sends out patriotic graphics and images. A small delegation of students takes their objections to the administration. They understood that these all-school mailing lists, which are screened by the school's system administrator, were supposed to be used for school related, informational purposes only.

16. Several students have discovered a web site that promotes anorexia as a lifestyle choice rather than an eating disorder. It includes tips for weight loss, pictures that glamorize the anorexic look, a discussion board members use to support one another, and other material that promotes "anorexic pride." School counselors have asked that this site and others like it be blocked on the school network. They point out that anorexia is a deadly disease and that some students are particularly susceptible to this type of misinformation.

17. Lynn advertises her club fund-raiser by sending out an e-mail to the club's discussion list, which has about 500 members. At the bottom of her message, she tells recipients they should reply to the message if they want to be taken off the list. But when recipients e-mail her back, their responses also go to the other 500 people on the list. Many of those people then send replies, asking: "Why did you send me this message? I can't remove you from the list!" Of course, many of these "cease and desist" messages also go to all 500 members. This e-mailing continues back and forth until people's mailboxes start filling to capacity. New messages start bouncing back to the server, which eventually crashes.

18. Joe uses e-mail/instant messaging/ weblogging to conduct a popularity poll. He asks, "Who are the people you like most in the sophomore class? Who are the people you like least?" A couple of names predominate on the "least liked" list. Suzy, who is one of those people, starts missing a lot of school. Her parents are puzzled because the doctor can find nothing physically wrong with her. School officials warn them that Suzy will have to repeat the year if her attendance doesn't improve.

INTELLECTUAL PROPERTY ISSUES

1. Tracy had a report to write on acid rain. She used several sources—books, magazines, newspaper articles, and a CD-ROM encyclopedia. She listed all these sources in her bibliography at the end of the report. She found the encyclopedia to be the most convenient source because she could highlight portions of the text and paste them into her word processing document.

2. Jason R. designed and posted a Star Wars web site. Once the site started receiving 40,000 hits a day, he received a phone call from Lucasfilm asking him to shut it down. Jason posted excerpts of the phone conversation on his web site. Lucasfilm was then flooded with angry e-mail messages from fans who felt the company was exerting totalitarian control over products to which they felt a deep personal connection.

3. Ms. Harris received e-mail from someone who liked the gargoyle image on the Uni High Library's web page and wanted to know if he could use it on his school library's web page. The art teacher, who created the image for the school, wrote back to him, explaining that the image belonged to the university and that, furthermore, it had special significance as the image that identifies Uni High. She thanked him for his interest, but told him that she could not grant permission for him to use it.

4. Richard asked Vicky if he could look at the essay she wrote for their history class. She told him "sure" and thought no more about it. Several days after the essays were turned in, the teacher asked her to stay after class. She showed Vicky that her essay and Richards were almost identical. She asked Vicky for an explanation.

5. Malcolm has a web page on the topic of sailboats. He has collected a truly astonishing amount of information and receives many complementary e-mail messages from sailing enthusiasts. He has downloaded numerous pictures and articles he finds on other web sites, and is always careful to give credit by citing the original sources.

6. Paramount pictures has cracked down on numerous Star Trek fans for printing synopses of the plots of just-released installments in the film series. In other media news, Fox TV sent a "cease and desist" letter to a woman whose Simpsons icons were starting to appear across various Web sites. She is quoted as saying that she felt she was giving Fox free publicity.

7. Roberta's family just got a new CD recorder for their home computer. She and Todd are the DJs for the next school dance, so Roberta invites Todd to her house and they surf the web for their favorite MP3 sites. They download several songs and burn them onto a CD they'll play at the dance. Some of the songs are from big name groups and others are from new artists who are using the web to build an audience.

8. Mr. Boxley asks the school librarian to check some references in Belinda's research paper. Mr. Boxley believes that the writing is far better than Belinda's usual work, almost spookily better. The librarian does a quick search and discovers that Belinda has copied whole paragraphs from the online articles she cites. However, in each sentence, at least two words have been changed. When confronted, Belinda argues that she has paraphrased and cited her sources. She does not believe she has plagiarized from other people's work.

9. Larry is a fan of a superheroes cartoon which has an accompanying web site. He particularly likes one of the characters. He copies the character's web page onto his own web page, but changes the name of the character to "Larry." Several weeks later, the school system administrator is contacted by the company that produces the show and the web page. They threaten to sue the school if the site is not immediately removed.

Puzzle: Which scenario in the top list also belongs in the second list under Intellectual Property Issues?

SOURCE: Reprinted by permission of Frances Jacobson Harris, University Laboratory High School Library, University of Illinois at Urbana-Champaign. http://www.uni.uiuc.edu/library/computerlit/scenarios.html.

USE CARRDSS TO HELP YOU EVALUATE YOUR SOURCES!

CREDIBILITY: Who is the author? What are his or her credentials?

ACCURACY: Can facts, statistics, or other information be verified through other sources? Based on your knowledge, does the information seem accurate?

RELIABILITY: Does the source present a particular view or bias?

RELEVANCE: Does this information directly support my hypothesis/thesis or help to answer my question?

DATE: When was this information created? When was it revised? Are these dates meaningful in terms of the subject matter?

SOURCES BEHIND THE TEXT: Did the author use reliable, credible sources?

SCOPE: Does this source address my hypothesis/thesis/question in a comprehensive or peripheral way? Is it a scholarly or popular treatment?

SOURCE: Developed in collaboration with Carol H. Rohrbach, K–12 Language Arts Coordinator, School District of Springfield Township, Erdenheim, PA.

Dewey Decimal Classification System and Highlighted Numbers of Interest to Students!

Nonfiction books in our Library Information Center, including reference, are organized by the Dewey Decimal Classification System.

000 Generalities

004, 005, 006 Computers
010 Bibliography
020 Library & information sciences
030 General encyclopedic works
040 Unassigned
050 General serials & their indexes
060 General organizations & museology
070 News media, journalism, publishing
080 General collections
090 Manuscripts & rare books

100 Philosophy and Psychology

110 Metaphysics
120 Epistemology, causation, humankind
130 Paranormal phenomena
    133 Parapsychology/occultism
    133.4 Witchcraft
    133.5 Astrology
140 Specific philosophical schools
150 Psychology
160 Logic
170 Ethics (moral philosophy)
    (Good area for debate material!)
180 Ancient, medieval, Oriental philosophy
190 Modern Western philosophy

200 Religion

210 Natural theology
220 Bible
230 Christian theology
240 Christian moral & devotional theology
250 Christian orders & local church
260 Christian social theology
270 Christian church history
280 Christian denominations & sects
290 Other & comparative religions
    292 Classical Mythology

300 Social sciences

Browse here for debate topics!
    305.4 Women
    305.8 Racial, ethnic, national groups
310 General statistics
320 Political science
    323 Civil and political rights
    324 Political process
    324.623 Women's suffrage
    325 International migration and colonization
    326 Slavery and emancipation
    327 International relations
330 Economics
    333 Economics of land and energy
340 Law
    342 Constitutional Law, Supreme Court
    345 Criminal law
350 Public administration
    355 Military science
360 Social services; associations
    364 Criminology
370 Education
380 Commerce, communications, transport
390 Customs, etiquette, folklore
    391 Costume and personal appearance
    394.2 Special occasions
    398 Folklore

400 Language	500 Natural Sciences and Mathematics
410 Linguistics	510 Mathematics
413 Dictionaries	512 Algebra
415 Grammar	513 Arithmetic
420 English & Old English	516 Geometry
430 Germanic languages, German	519 Probability
440 Romance languages, French	520 Astronomy & allied sciences
450 Italian, Romanian languages	523 Celestial bodies and phenomena (solar
460 Spanish & Portuese languages	system, moon, stars, planets)
470 Italic languages, Latin	525 Earth
480 Hellenic languages, Classical Greek	530 Physics
490 Other languages	540 Chemistry & allied sciences
	550 Earth sciences
	551.2 Earthquakes and volcanoes
	560 Paleontology, paleozoology
	570 Life sciences
	576 Genetics and evolution
	580 Botanical sciences (Plants)
	590 Zoological sciences (Animals)

600 Technology (Applied sciences)	700 The Arts and Recreation
600 General technology	709 Historical, geographic, biographic treatment
608 Inventions and patents	of art and artists
609 History of inventions	710 Civic & landscape art
610 Medical sciences and medicine	720 Architecture
612 Human body	730 Plastic arts, sculpture
614 Forensic medicine	740 Drawing & decorative arts
613.8 Substance abuse	745.5 Handicrafts
616 Disease	750 Painting & paintings (museums)
620 Engineering & allied operations	759 Paintings/Painters historic, geographic,
629.1 Flight	biographical
629.2 Motor land vehicles, cycles	760 Graphic arts, printmaking & prints, postage stamps
629.4 Astronautics	770 Photography & photographs
630 Agriculture	780 Music
636 Pets	782, 783 Vocal music
640 Home economics & family living	786.7 Electronic instruments
641.5 Cooking	786.9 Drums
650 Management & auxiliary services	789 Composers
660 Chemical engineering	790 Recreational & performing arts
670 Manufacturing	791.4 Movies, radio, television
680 Manufacture for specific uses	792 Stage presentations
690 Buildings	794 Indoor games
	796.323 Basketball
	796.332 Football
	796.342 Tennis
	796.352 Golf
	796.357 Baseball
	796.48 Olympics
	796.6 Cycling
	796.8 Combat sports
	796.9 Ice and snow sports
	796.91 Skating

800 Literature and Rhetoric	796.962 Hockey
	797.1 Boating
	797.2 Swimming and diving
	799 Fishing, hunting, shooting

800 Literature and Rhetoric	**900 Geography and History**
810 American literature	900 World History
811 American Poetry	910 Geography and travel
812 American Drama	920 Biography, genealogy, insignia
813 American Fiction (and Criticism)	930 History of the ancient world
817 American Humor	940 General history of Europe
820 English & Old English literatures	940.1 Middle Ages
821 English Poetry	940.3–4 World War I
822 English Drama	940.53–54 World War II
822.3 Shakespeare	950 General history of Asia, Far East
823 English Fiction	960 General history of Africa
830 Literatures of Germanic languages	970 General history of North America
840 Literatures of Romance languages	973 American History
850 Italian, Romanian literatures	973.2 Colonial period
860 Spanish & Portuguese literatures	973.3 Revolution and Confederation
870 Italic literatures, Latin	973.7 Civil War
880 Hellenic literatures, Classical Greek	973.9 1901–
890 Literatures of other languages	974–979 Specific states
	980 General history of South America
	990 General history of other areas

Web Page Evaluation Checklist

1. Go to Google and perform the search: **"stem cells" abortion**
2. Use this Checklist to try to evaluate systematically some of the search results.

	Title of page you are evaluating:	**Title of page you are evaluating:**
1. Look at the URL:		
Personal page or site?	☐ ~ or %, or *users, members,* or *people*	☐ ~ or %, or *users, members,* or *people*
What type of domain is it? Appropriate for the content?	☐com ☐org/net ☐edu ☐gov/mil/us ☐ non-US_____ ☐ other:	☐com ☐org/net ☐edu ☐gov/mil/us ☐ non-US_____ ☐ other:
Published by entity that makes sense? Does it correspond to the name of the site?	Publisher or Domain Name entity:	Publisher or Domain Name entity:
2. Scan the perimeter of page, looking for answers to these questions:		
Who wrote the page?	☐ E-mail ☐ Name:	☐ E-mail ☐ Name:
Dated?	Date _____ Current enough?	Date _____ Current enough?
Credentials on this subject? (Truncate back the URL if no useful links.)	Evidence?	Evidence?
3. Look for these indicators of quality		
Sources well documented?		
Complete? If 2nd-hand information, is it **not** altered or forged?		
Links to more resources? Do they work?		
Other viewpoints? Bias?		
4. What do others say?		
Who links to it? Hint: In Google search: *link:all.or.part.of.url*	Many or few? Opinions of it?	Many or few? Opinions of it?
Is the page rated well in a directory? http://lii.org or http://infomine.ucr.edu or http://about.com		
Look up the author in Google		
Does it all add up?		
Why was the page put on the Web?	☐ Inform, facts, data ☐ Explain ☐ Persuade ☐ Sell ☐ Entice ☐ Share/disclose Other:	☐ Inform, facts, data ☐ Explain ☐ Persuade ☐ Sell/entice ☐ Share/disclose Other:
Possibly ironic? Satire or parody?		

BOTTOM LINE: Is the web page as good as (or better than) what you could find in journal articles or other published literature that is not on the free, general web?

SOURCE: © 2002 Joe Barker, The Teaching Library, University of California, Berkeley, "The Best Stuff on the Web."

Why Should I Take This Author Seriously?

Remember the old saying: "Garbage in, garbage out!"

Students, you are information consumers! Before the Web, you had help in selecting information. Publishers, editors, librarians, and teachers contributed to ensuring the information you used was of high quality. In the self-publishing environment of the Web, you need to be a careful consumer. You want to be sure the sources you use are credible.

If you are unsure of an author's credentials, you might have difficulty defending use of his or her work in your documentation. Your teacher is likely to question you if you quote an expert who is unknown. Do a little legwork before you complete your project. If you run into any trouble at all finding sources, consult with your teacher-librarian!

CONSIDER

- Searching the Web for the author's résumé or C.V. (curriculum vita or vitae). A C.V. is a more formal, usually lengthier, résumé format, written by people in academic, research, or scientific environments. C.V.s generally include lists of publications, presentations, professional activities, and honors. If you cannot find a résumé or C.V., at the very least look for evidence of a university affiliation, or association with a major organization.

- Searching biographical reference tools—*Wilson Biographies, GaleNet's Biography Resource Center. Contemporary Authors*—in print or online, is extremely comprehensive and covers writers in all fields of knowledge from antiquity to modern day. Phone your nearest large public library and ask the reference librarian to check the **Who's Who** reference books in the appropriate subject area.

- Searching for news of them in a periodical database. Try using their names as keywords in sources like *EBSCOhost, Student Resource Center Gold,* or *bigchalk.*

- Doing a "link check." In either AltaVista or Google, perform the following search

<link:yoururl>. Your results will show who else has linked to the page you are evaluating. Would the pages that link to your page be considered reputable? Do they review or annotate the page you are examining?

- Checking to see if your page appears in a selective subject directory. For instance, has the page been included in Librarians' Index to the Internet?

- Examining the URL. Though there is no "etched in stone" rule, you can be guided by an address. A site ending in .gov is likely to be a reliable government site. A site ending in .org may be the work of a respected organization. A site ending in .edu might be created by a university, or a college or K–12 student. Sites which include a "~" are generally personal sites. While they may be appropriate for serious research, they are just as likely to be the product of a student (or faculty member) of a reliable institution who has a lot of free time!

- Truncating the URL, if no affiliation is available on the page you are examining. Your goal is to try to get to the "root" page that might contain information "about this site" or "about the author."

EDUCATION

- Does the person have an advanced degree? Are there impressive letters after the author's name—Ph.D.? Ed.D.? Is the degree related to the page you are evaluating? A professor of physics may not have particular expertise writing about the Holocaust.

- Is there evidence that the author is involved in significant research? Are there other studies by this author on the Web or in print?

- What evidence is offered of his or her knowledge? Be suspicious if the page lists no educational credentials.

- How well documented is the work they are presenting?

- Be skeptical. Remember, everyone has a bias.

EXPERIENCE

- How many years has the author been writing, teaching, studying, or researching?

- How active have they been in their area of specialty? Have others mentioned or cited them? (You might find this information in a Web search.)

- Can you find other respected or scholarly publications they have written?

- Do they offer any firsthand, primary source–type experiences? A soldier present during the D-Day invasion would not have to have a university degree to offer important perspective on the event you are studying!

- Is the person active in the area of study? If you are researching the Olympic Games, a page written by a noted gymnast, runner, boxer, or skater might have great value.

- Be skeptical. Remember, everyone has a bias.

AFFILIATION/REPUTATION

- What is the author's institutional or business affiliation? What title do they hold?

- Is the page sponsored by an organization?

- Is the person involved with a university? Is it one you have heard of? Does it matter if they are involved with a major university or a community college?

- Is this person well known?

- In what type of journal is their work published? Popular? Trade? Scholarly? Peer reviewed?

- What do others say about them? Has their work been reviewed or criticized?

- Is their involvement commercial? Someone representing Philip Morris might attack the issue of smokers' rights in a way quite different from a representative of the American Cancer Society.

- Be skeptical. Remember, everyone has a bias.

Why Take Notes?

Objective: To learn the importance of taking concise, pertinent notes

The lesson requires a cooperating teacher who will role-play with you. Tell the students that you are a teenager who has to take a phone message for her parents from a family friend who is at the mall, calling from a pay phone. The other teacher plays the calling-friend.

Setting the scene: The teacher stands at one end of the room and the library information specialist at the other. The calling friend (teacher), using an imaginary phone, keys in a phone number. The phone rings and the "teenager" picks up.

Peggy: Hi Sheila, this is Peggy. I know your parents aren't home right now but could I leave them an important message about tonight?

Sheila: Sure.

Peggy: Ok, they were going to pick me up at the theater on State Street at 5:30, but my cat got hit by a car and I had to take it to the vet's, so that is where I'll be until 5:30, and they will have to pick me up there instead. But they can't get there the normal way because the road got washed out with all the rain, so they closed it down. So I'll have to give you directions on how to get to the vet's another way. So tell them to get on the Memorial Bridge and take the first left off the bridge, then go through the next two traffic lights. At the third light they will take a right onto Oak Street and drive for about a mile. When they pass Oakhurst Dairy Farm, which will be on the left, they will come to an intersection with a four-way stop. Take a right onto Parkhurst Drive, and the vet's will be at the end of that street. Got that?

Sheila: Yes, I'll tell them.

Peggy: Ok, thanks, bye.

Sheila: *(hangs up the phone and immediately panics because she has forgotten the directions. After a few worried moments, phone rings again.)* Hello.

Peggy: Hi, Sheila, it's me again. I forgot to tell you to let your mom know that she has to bring a loaf of French bread tonight. Ok?

Sheila: Yes, sure, but am I glad you called back! I can't remember the directions you gave me. Could you run that by me again?

Peggy: Sure.

Sheila: Let me get a pencil first and a piece of paper. Ok, I'm ready.

Peggy: I had to take my cat to the vet's, so your folks will have to pick me up there at 5:30 tonight. But the usual route to the vet's is washed out by all the rain we had, so tell them to get on the Memorial Bridge and take the first left off the bridge, then go through the next two traffic lights.

Sheila: *(writing notes on the chalkboard)* Wait, wait! Slow down, I'm not getting all this.

Peggy: Sheila, you're not writing down EVERYTHING I'm saying are you? I'm on a pay phone, just get the important facts down. Ok? Ok, let me start with . . . tell them to get on the Memorial Bridge and take the first left off the bridge. Then they go through the next two traffic lights. At the third light they will take a right onto Oak Street and drive for about a mile. When they pass Oakhurst Dairy Farm, which will be on the left, they will come to an intersection with a four-way stop. Take a right onto Parkhurst Drive, and the vet's will be at the end of that street. Got that?

Sheila: Yes, I've got it this time. Thanks.

Peggy: And don't forget the bread!

After the script rewrite the notes you took on the board. Then let the class reconstruct the message from the notes.

SOURCE: Adapted by permission of Claire Simpson and Jane Perry.

Group Project Plan

Tentative thesis or question: _____

Names of group members	**Responsibility/task**
1.	
2.	
3.	
4.	
5.	

The goal of our project is:

Questions we hope to answer:

Project format:

Resources we plan to use:

Date we expect to complete first draft _____ Final product: _____

Questions for teacher/library information specialist (For more space use the back of this sheet):

Group Project Planning Chart

Teacher _____ Class _____

Unit _____ Date Due _____

Group 1 Assignment:

Student	Responsible for:	Student	Responsible for:
1.		4.	
2.		5.	
3.		6.	

Group 2 Assignment:

Student	Responsible for:	Student	Responsible for:
1.		4.	
2.		5.	
3.		6.	

Group 3 Assignment:

Student	Responsible for:	Student	Responsible for:
1.		4.	
2.		5.	
3.		6.	

Group 4 Assignment:

Student	Responsible for:	Student	Responsible for:
1.		4.	
2.		5.	
3.		6.	

Group 5 Assignment:

Student	Responsible for:	Student	Responsible for:
1.		4.	
2.		5.	
3.		6.	

Library Scavenger Hunt

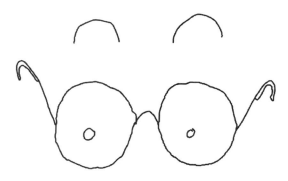

This scavenger hunt is meant as a basic introduction to the library services—both online and off—you will be using over the next few years. You will be given a quiz grade for the activity, but remember that the goal is for you to explore and get familiar with resources so you can better decide which to use when research projects come up in any of your classes.

Record your answers on a separate sheet of paper or use a word processor. Please staple any of the requested printouts to your answer sheet. You do not have to work on the questions in order. If you are using a word processor, remember to leave yourself plenty of time to print your work before the activity is over.

Please remember to work quietly and efficiently!

On the library floor,

1. Politely introduce yourself to one or both of our library staff members. List both their names.

2. Locate and browse through the biography section and list one title you'd like to read. (List one for each partner.)

3. Which Dewey number do you think has the most titles in our reference area? Why do you think there are so many books in this area?

4. How much does it cost to make a copy in our library?

5. List three of our bound magazine titles. Which magazine goes back the furthest? How far back does it run?

6. List the titles of three magazines you didn't know the library had.

7. Browse through the fiction section, and list the name of one famous author who shares your last initial (the first letter of your last name).

8. Locate a dictionary in the reference section. Find a word and definition that will stump the class.

9. On the library map, locate and label the following:
   - a. circulation desk
   - b. automated catalog
   - c. print encyclopedia
   - d. reference area
   - e. nonfiction area
   - f. fiction area
   - g. pencil sharpener
   - h. copy machine
   - i. book drop
   - j. research workstations
   - k. student supply box

In the lab area, locate the Virtual Library online and answer the following:

1. In the OPAC, find a book on any of the following topics and copy the name of the author, the title, and call number. Can you tell if it is available?
   a. basketball
   b. rap music
   c. Civil War
   d. mythology

2. Using the AP Photo Archive (in Catalogs and Databases) print a picture of an event that happened the year that you were born. (One image per team, please!)

3. List four different databases included in EBSCOhost (in Catalogs and Databases).

4. List three "resource centers" included in our GaleNet subscription (in Catalogs and Databases).

5. Use any of the library's online databases to print a citation for an article about one of the following:
   a. AIDS
   b. bullying
   c. Tiger Woods
   d. Israel
   e. robotics
   f. your favorite musical group or artist

6. What are the names of the two biographical databases in the library's online collection (in Catalogs and Databases)?

7. List two encyclopedias available from the Catalogs and Databases page.

8. Using Facts.com (in Catalogs and Databases), list one important event from either the 1940s or 1950s.

9. How would you document an image you find online in a Works Cited page? Write a formal citation for an image. (How did you find your answer?)

10. What is the difference between a search engine and a subject directory? Give an example of each.

11. Name three Internet search tools (search engines or subject directories) you have never used. (Check under Search Here)

12. Almost every database offers you the opportunity to search by keyword or subject. What is the difference? Give an example of when each approach would be the best way to start.

13. What is the best strategy for searching a phrase on the Web? Give an example.

14. Do a search and list the types of materials available in the Gale's Student Resource Center. (See Catalogs and Databases—GaleNet.)

15. Locate the summer reading lists on the Virtual Library. Which book, on next year's list, are you most interested in reading? Where are these books located on the library shelves?

16. What is the URL for the library's Web page?

17. What is the name of your teacher-librarian? Discover one interesting fact about him/her. (You may use his or her home page or ask him or her personally.)

BONUS

On the Web print an item of *breaking news* from a major online news source. Make sure the URL of the source appears on the printout.

Or locate a local online newspaper. Print a recent article about an issue of local interest.

4-20B

Library Skills Game

1. Books that are used mainly for quickly looking up facts and information are called _____.

   a. fiction
   b. autobiographies
   c. reference books
   d. catalogs

2. You can find a listing of all books in the resource center by looking in the _____.

   a. vertical file
   b. OPAC (online catalog)
   c. book depository
   d. periodical indexes

3. A _____ prints and distributes books.

   a. publisher
   b. author
   c. editor
   d. vendor

4. Books that are created from the author's imagination are called _____.

   a. fiction
   b. nonfiction
   c. biography
   d. anthologies

5. A book with the call number 796.3 N is definitely a _____.

   a. fiction book
   b. trade paperback
   c. nonfiction book

6. A book with the number 920 FRA is a _____ .

   a. fiction book
   b. collection of stories
   c. collective biography

7. A list of books on a particular subject is called a(n) _____.

   a. bibliography
   b. biography
   c. autobiography
   d. catalog

8. A book about a person's life written by someone else is called a(n) _____.

   a. biography
   b. bibliography
   c. historical fiction
   d. autobiography

9. To find the current population of Illinois, your best source (online or offline) is an _____.

   a. encyclopedia
   b. almanac
   c. atlas

10. A book that contains the life stories of more than one person is called _____.

    a. individual biography
    b. collective biography
    c. bibliography
    d. memoirs

11. elibrary, SIRS, and GaleNet are indexes and full text sources for:

    a. magazine articles
    b. reference materials
    c. newspaper articles
    d. all of the above

12. In the online catalog or OPAC, you may look for materials under which of the following?

    a. author
    b. title
    c. subject
    d. keyword
    e. call number
    f. all of the above

13. Call numbers for fiction materials are composed of _____.

    a. the letter F plus shelf location
    b. place of publication and publisher
    c. author's initials plus the letter F
    d. The letter F plus the first three letters of the author's last name
    e. none of the above

14. A biography of Abraham Lincoln by Carl Sandburg will be found on the biography shelves under _____.

    a. Abraham
    b. Carl
    c. Lincoln
    d. Sandburg
    e. the title

15. The call number of nonfiction material is composed of _____.

    a. place of publication and publisher
    b. Dewey Decimal number plus the first letters of the author's last name
    c. author's initials and shelf location
    d. the letters NF and subject letters

16. The copyright date for a book is usually found _____.

    a. on the spine
    b. on the back of the title page
    c. in the index
    d. on the last page of print

17. The introduction to a book is sometimes called its _____.

    a. title page
    b. glossary
    c. preface
    d. epilogue

18. Under the Dewey Decimal system _____.

    a. books on the same subject are grouped together
    b. no two books can have the same number
    c. only letters and no numbers are used

19. (Display a transparency or an online entry of a Stephen King criticism from the catalog, for example.)

    a. What's the title?
    b. What are the subjects?
    c. Copyright?
    d. Publisher?
    e. Call #?

20. Put these fiction call numbers in order. (Use manipulative cards with oversize numbers or actual books.)

21. Put these nonfiction call numbers in order. (Use manipulative cards with oversize numbers or actual books.)

22. Where could you look to find contemporary ("when it happened") accounts of the Kennedy assassination?

23. Why might you want to use a print index even though we have online databases?

24. Why should you keep a record of your sources as you search?

25. Why should your work have footnotes, endnotes, or parenthetical notes?

26. In a database what is an abstract? (Why is an abstract helpful?)

27. If you are searching an online database and you find that you have 2,000 possible articles relating to your subject, what should that signal to you about your search? (How might you narrow a search?)

28. Name three types of material you might find in the SIRS Researcher database.

29. What are two synonyms for the word *magazine?*

30. On the Web, what is the difference between a subject directory and a search engine?

31. *True* or *false.* Search engines can find any page on the Web.

32. *True* or *false.* Web masters can fool a search engine into listing a site higher in its result lists.

33. What is the *Invisible or Deep Web*?

34. What is a database? Give two examples.

35. What are some ways you might evaluate a book before reading it?

36. What is a primary source?

37. Your general encyclopedia doesn't give the brief definition you need for a specific term in electronics and you don't want to read a whole book. What's your next step?

38. You are planning to buy new stereo equipment. How can you use the library to help you decide what to purchase?

39. You are writing a theme and find yourself frequently using the same word. What tool can you use to help improve your writing?

40. What does "paraphrase" mean? Do you have to cite what you paraphrase?

41. What do you think the term "search strategy" means?

42. What is a style sheet? What style sheet does our school use?

43. Name three places you might go to find magazine articles on a current topic.

44. Identifying keywords (or synonyms) can mean the difference between success and failure in your work with online databases. See if you can identify the keywords or helpful synonyms for the following research questions: (Display these statements.)
    a. Describe the legal problems involved with using DNA fingerprinting in criminal investigations.
    b. What testing measures and disciplinary actions are being taken to control the use of drugs by professional athletes?
    c. In what ways does the behavior of animals change to adapt to particular changes in weather conditions?

45. Which of the following research questions is more focused? (Sometimes preliminary research is needed to develop a question.)
    a. Should women serve in the military?
    b. Do the Afghanistan and Iraq wars strengthen the case for having women on the front line in combat?

46. In searching, sometimes you need to broaden or narrow your keywords. Number each term in the following items from 1 for the most broad to 3 for the most narrow. (Put on laminated cards for the student to manipulate.)
    a. DDT, toxic chemicals, insecticides   c. disasters, volcanoes, Mt. St. Helens
    b. crime, espionage, Rosenbergs   d. diseases, STDs, herpes

47. A thesis statement declares what you believe and what you intend to prove in your project. Which of the following sentences are acceptable preliminary thesis statements? Which are simple facts? (The thesis statements here are not yet fully developed.)
    a. Logging is destroying America's forests.
    b. The first U.S. women's rights convention was held in Seneca Falls in 1848.
    c. The United Nations has been ineffective in settling international disputes.
    d. The surrealist movement was dominated by the works of artists Salvador Dali and Joan Miró.

48. Besides the actual words in a question, how else can you find good keywords to use in a search?

49. Give other searchable keywords for these terms.
    a. air
    b. child
    c. country

50. What "three little words" are most important in the logic of database searching?

51. What is a URL?

52. Why is it important to keep track of your URLs as you research?

53. What are three ways you can evaluate a Web site for its usefulness to your research?

54. Your first search doesn't work exactly as you planned. Describe three strategies for refining your search.

55. You need to find information about the current situation in the Middle East on the Web. Devise a good strategy for your first search.

56. What is a search engine? Name one.

57. What is truncation? How would you truncate the word *adolescent?*

58. What do the letters AUP stand for? What is its purpose?

59. What are three activities that are encouraged under our district's AUP?

60. What are three activities that are not permitted under our district's AUP?

61. Which of the following should you do if you cannot find material on your question or thesis?
    a. give up
    b. get depressed
    c. ask your teacher-librarian for advice
    d. consider using another library

62. Which of the following are appropriate reasons to visit the library?
    a. to find a quiet place to study
    b. to read ESPN magazine
    c. to research a class assignment
    d. to find a cookie recipe
    e. to view a video from our collection
    f. to search an online database
    g. to goof off

63. What's my name?

SOURCE: By Joyce Valenza. Reprinted by permission from *Skills for Life: Library information Literacy for Grades 9–12,* Edited by Paul Rux. Copyright © 1993 by Linworth, Inc. All rights reserved.

700 and Nancy

This activity will help you get familiar with the layout of our shelves and to get a feel for the way the Dewey Decimal system works. Wander around the stacks and try to replace the underlined Dewey Decimal numbers with the words they represent. Have fun!

(1) 700 woke up from his nap with a start. Tonight was his big first date with Nancy. They'd met in (2) 371. Before they could go out, 700 would have to work at his uncle's (3) 629.2 shop. He wasn't looking forward to work. Uncle Alfonso was fond of telling 700 (4) 398.4 about past 629.2s he had serviced. You see, 629.2s have always held a certain (5) 793.8 for Alfonso. 700 arrived at the shop an hour late. After a long lecture on (6) 395, his uncle decided to send him to the library. (Alfonso was a (7) 900 buff!) "Go find me some new books on the (8) 973.7, and I'll call it even for work tonight," he said. So 700 eagerly headed for the library, past the attractive (9) 712s in their lovely (10) 974.8 town. Though 700 was easily distracted by the many books on (11) 133 and (12) 740, he asked the librarian for help and was directed to many new books on the 973.7. He thought Alfonso would be pleased.

When 700 began his short trip back to the repair shop, he encountered a bit of trouble. A formidable group of hooligans lurked ahead of him. 700 was no wimp, but he did not know if he could negotiate with this unruly (13) 302.3. He did know a lot about (14) 150. Fortunately, they too were fascinated by the 973.7 and were quite interested in 700's books. After a brief discussion of (15) 355 in (16) 973, 700 realized he was very late and raced back to the shop with the speed of a (17) 796 hero. 700 dropped the books off with his uncle and went home to prepare for his date. Then he hopped into his Volkswagen (18) 636.9 and drove over to Nancy's. He stared in awe at the clever (19) 720 of her house. How elegant the flying buttresses were! He rang the bell on the impressive front door. It produced lovely (20) 780.

A pudgy, middle-aged man opened the door. He had a tattoo of (21) 822.33 on his forearm. "Before you speak, I just want to warn you: Keep my Nancy away from the dangers of (22) 363.2 and (23) 616.86!" he said.

700 took a defensive step back and assured Nancy's father he was a (24) 553.8 of a guy, solid as a (25) 552, the salt of the (26.) 550. Why, he was into amateur (27) 770 and was planning a (28) 371.42 in (29) 610. His dad was employed in (30) 370 and his mom was a famous (31) 346!

Nancy's father invited 700 in just as Nancy was descending the winding staircase. She looked extremely lovely in her (32) 675 necklace. Her father sat down and began to watch (33) 791.45. A show on (34) 560 soon had him fully engrossed.

Nancy took 700's arm and escorted him to his 636.9. As much as they liked each other, they drove to the (35) 791.43 arguing over which film they would see. Nancy loved (36) 812 and 700 preferred (37) 817. They compromised, saw a (38) 882 and enjoyed their evening anyway. 700 asked Nancy how she liked the film. "It was (39) 480 to me," she said.

700 ♡ Nancy

On the way home 700 told Nancy how fond he was of her (40) 597.96 bracelet, made of (41) 669. He entertained her by trying to interpret her (42) 130. She promised she'd someday analyze his (43) 652.1.

At the door, 700 gave Nancy a peck on the cheek. There was certainly (44) 540 between them. The night was full of 793.8. Would they be able to (45) 599.78 being apart until they saw each other Monday in (46) 510 class?

ANSWERS (700 AND NANCY)

1.	700	art
2.	371	school
3.	629.2	car
4.	398.4	fairy tales
5.	793.8	magic
6.	395	manners/etiquette
7.	900	history
8.	973.7	Civil War
9.	712	landscape design
10.	974.8	Pennsylvania
11.	133	occult/paranormal
12.	740	drawing
13.	302.3	gang
14.	150	psychology
15.	355	warfare
16.	973	U.S. history
17.	796	sports
18.	636.9	rabbit
19.	720	architecture
20.	780	music
21.	822.33	William Shakespeare
22.	362.2	drugs
23.	616.86	alcohol
24.	553.8	gem
25.	552	rock
26.	550	earth
27.	770	photography
28.	371.42	career
29.	610	medicine
30.	370	education
31.	346	law(yer)
32.	675	leather
33.	791.45	television
34.	560	dinosaurs/paleontology
35.	791.43	movies
36.	812	drama
37.	817	comedy/humor
38.	882	Greek drama
39.	480	Greek
40.	597.96	snake/reptile
41.	669	metal
42.	130	dreams
43.	652.1	handwriting
44.	540	chemistry
45.	599.78	bear
46.	510	math

Search Tools Species:
A Field Guide

There's a relative jungle of search options out there! To help you choose the right species for your information needs, here's a field guide. (Remember you'll often want to use a combination of search tools.)

SEARCH ENGINES

Search engines offer a *keyword approach* to searching. Search engines are *large* databases of Web documents that rely on *robots, spiders, or crawlers,* automated programs to match words and phrases to Web documents, ignoring certain common "stop words" like "the," "of," "a," and "an." Search engines depend on *you* to do the work through the use of *syntax,* the particular protocol or the searching language of that unique search engine. Advanced search screens give you opportunities to search with greater precision—dates, file types, AND, OR, NOT, and searching in specific parts of documents.

Advantages

Search engines are large and offer broad databases of information. Good searchers can use strategies to create focused searches that will likely yield excellent results. Some "smarter" search engines use technologies to move high quality, relevant results up to the first few pages of your results lists.

Which are the smarter search engines?

Google offers "link relevance," or PageRank technology to move the sites people link to most to the top of your list.

Several newer search engines "autocategorize" or group results into subject hierarchies or concept clusters. These include Teoma, WiseNut, or Vivisimo (really a meta-search engine). Some of these new search engines combine two or more of these "smart" features.

Disadvantages

Search engines do little original thinking. They match the words and phrases you enter with little regard for the meaning of those terms, the synonyms you forgot to mention or the words you meant to exclude. They make no use of humans to organize or evaluate results. Searchers often get many irrelevant results in their first several pages. Search engines calculate relevance in a variety of ways. "Pay for placement" policies put lots of advertising (sponsored results) in front of searchers and may unfairly alter the real relevance of results. Searchers need to learn the strategies and the relevance habits behind their favorite search engines.

When to use a search engine:

- When you have a narrow topic or several keywords
- When you want to do a comprehensive search
- When you want to retrieve a large number of documents on your topic
- When you want to search for particular types of documents, file types, source locations, languages, date last modified, etc.
- When you want to take advantage of newer retrieval technologies such as concept clustering / autocategorization, popularity ranking, link ranking, thesauri

Examples of Search Engines

Google http://google.com

Alltheweb http://alltheweb.com

AltaVista http://altavista.com

Yahoo! (search engine) http://search.yahoo.com

Hotbot http://hotbot.com

Teoma http://teoma.com

WiseNut http://wisenut.com

META-SEARCH ENGINES

Meta-search engines have no databases of their own. They search across the databases of a variety of other search tools. More advanced meta-search engines collate your results, and eliminate repetitive hits. Some combine results into one unified list, others report each search engine's results separately.

Advantages

Meta-search tools offer a comprehensive search, an opportunity to take a broad look at what types of materials are out there on the Web. Some meta-search engines offer searches across databases you yourself would normally overlook. Some allow you to conveniently search all your favorite search engines in one blow.

Disadvantages

Bigger is not always better. Meta-search engines sometimes ignore more sophisticated search strategies. Search protocol is not standardized across search tools. When you search with a familiar search engine, you get to know how to exploit its particular syntax, or search language. Meta-search tools may take a little more time to display results. Because of the greater processing time required, you may get only partial results in the time it would have taken to get full results in standard search engine. Most meta-search engines limit the time they spend at each database and return only a small percentage of results from each of the search tools queried. Some meta-search tools lock you in their own frames. In order to see the URL of the results you want to visit, you must figure out how to toggle out of frames.

When to use a meta-search engine:

- When you have failed to find what you are looking for in your favorite search tools
- When you don't feel you need to use complex search strategies
- When you want to get a feel for "what's out there" on a particular topic

A word of advice: if the results of your meta-search are overwhelming, or mostly irrelevant, go back to using the individual search tools.

Examples of Meta-Search Engines

Vivisimo http://vivisimo.com

IxQuick Metasearch (collects "top 10" lists from the major engines) http://ixquick.com

Profusion (allows a subject-focused search) http://www.profusion.com

Ithaki http://www.ithaki.net

Dogpile http://dogpile.com

SUBJECT DIRECTORIES

Subject directories are catalogs of websites collected, organized, and maintained by HUMANS, not computer robots or spiders. Directories are usually arranged in "trees" or hierarchies, which attempt to organize information into large and progressively smaller subcategories. Subject directory editors generally review and select sites for inclusion based on established criteria. Subject directories base their databases on a thesaurus of terms. When directory editors index, they consider synonyms, linking together words like "car" and "automobile." Directories vary in type. To judge the usefulness of a subject directory, consider who selects and categorizes its resources, how its results are displayed, and whether its results are ranked, reviewed, or annotated.

Advantages

Though they may offer fewer results than search engines, subject directory results are generally of high quality and high relevance. They may offer valuable annotations and the ability to browse among related materials.

Disadvantages

Directories are much smaller in scope than search engines.

Unlike search engines, directories do not store databases of websites, they merely point to them. They search their own database structures. While this may limit results to higher quality links, it may also take a while for directory editors to recognize changes and the disappearance of links. Dead links are a drawback for many directories.

Tip: When you need to combine several concepts, or if you are looking for something very specific, you are better off starting in a search engine.

When to use a subject directory:

- When you are just starting out and want to examine a few quality sites
- When you have a broad topic or one major keyword or concept
- When you want to get quickly to the best sites on a topic
- When you are looking for a group of similar sites on the same topic
- When you want annotations before you visit sites
- When subject headings would be useful to regroup or retrieve relevant material
- When you want to avoid viewing "noise" documents frequently picked up by search engines

Examples of Subject Directories

Google Directory http://directory.google.com

Looksmart http://looksmart.com

Yahoo! Directory http://dir.yahoo.com (Yahoo! now functions as a search engine but maintains its traditional directory.)

About.com http://about.com

More Academic Directories

Librarians' Index to the Internet http://lii.org

WWW Virtual Library http://vlib.org

Infomine http://infomine.ucr.edu

Academic Info http://www.academicinfo.net/index.html

Noodlelinks http://www.noodletools.com/noodlelinks

INVISIBLE WEB

The Invisible Web is the term used to describe the huge amount of Web content that is difficult or impossible to find using traditional search tools. This content includes databases, special file types (like PDFs and spreadsheets), subscription databases and other sites that require password access, and sites that block robots or spiders.

How to find the Invisible Web:

- Use a standard search tool and enter your search terms and the term "database"
- Search Librarian's Index to the Internet and Infomine and pay particular attention to results labeled "database"
- Browse through special topical indexes designed especially for the Invisible Web

  Directories for the Invisible Web
  - Invisible Web Directory http://invisible-web.net
  - IncyWincy http://www.incywincy.com
  - Geniusfind http://www.geniusfind.com
  - Complete Planet http://completeplanet.com
  - Pinakes http://www.hw.ac.uk/libWWW/irn/pinakes/pinakes.html

- Use the subscription databases offered by you school and public libraries—EBSCOhost, GaleNet, Facts.com, WilsonWeb, CQ Researcher, LexisNexis, etc.

  Examples of Invisible Web Databases
  - GEM: Gateway to Educational Materials http://thegateway.org
  - Internet Movie Database http://imdb.com
  - Healthfinder http://www.healthfinder.gov
  - American Memory Collection http://memory.loc.gov/ammem/collections/finder.html
  - OAIster Search Interface http://oaister.umdl.umich.edu/index.html
  - NARA (National Archives and Records Administration) Search http://www.archives.gov/search/advanced_search.html

Database Worksheet

Name _____ Class _____ Date _____

What does this database do? _____
_____
_____

Is it full text?   ___ Yes   ___ No

What dates are covered? _____

Which types of resources are included?

    ___ magazines ___ newspapers ___ reference books

    ___ radio and television transcripts ___ government documents

    ___ other primary sources ___

    other _____

What search options are offered?

    ___ Topic/Subject ___ Keyword ___ fields ___ other _____

Is there an advanced search screen?   ___ Yes   ___ No

On the advanced search screen, are any search fields you would find useful?

If both are available, compare a *topic/subject* search with a *keyword* search and comment on the benefits and drawbacks of each. Try a sample search with a question you are currently researching. Which is the best strategy for your particular search problem?

    Examine an entry. Are abstracts included?   ___ Yes   ___ No

    Is a subject field or are descriptors included?   ___ Yes   ___ No

Why might subject fields be useful to you? _____
_____
_____

Can you e-mail articles to yourself?   ___ Yes   ___ No

Is bibliographic formatting provided?   ___ Yes   ___ No

How does this database compare with the other databases you've used? _____

_____

_____

_____

Does this database have any special features? _____

_____

_____

_____

What are the best features of this database? _____

_____

_____

_____

How does this database compare with your favorite *free* Web search tool?_____

_____

_____

_____

SOURCE: Reprinted by permission from *Skills for Life: Library Information Literacy for Grades 9–12*. Edited by Paul Rux. Copyright 1993 by Linworth, Inc. All rights reserved.

4-24B

Mini-Documentary Assignment

Goal: Your goal is to expose and to challenge a current issue in a mini-documentary.

Role: You are a news director trying to gather, analyze, synthesize, and report in-depth information about an issue to the general public. You will write and direct this documentary.

Audience: Your audience is the general public who have limited awareness of this issue.

Situation *(Choose one)*

- *Issue in Television:* Select an issue surrounding the television shows we watch or the technology we use to watch them. The program director at your station charged you with breaking a story about one of those issues.

- *Current Event:* Select one of the national or international issues affecting us today. The program director at your station charged you with breaking a story about one of those issues.

Product

You will script and direct a 3–5 minute studio production. You will use PowerPoint or other visual content to supply at least 10 graphics during your show.

With a clear opening and thesis, body, and conclusion, define the issue, summarize current practice through a survey of current literature, and discuss possible future developments surrounding this issue.

List at least 5 sources of information (3 of which should be journal or magazine articles). Refer to the *Research Paper Guide* on the School District's *Virtual Library* for citing your sources.

❐ Discuss topic and essential question with instructor   *Due* _____

❐ Research proposal with tentative thesis   *Due* _____

❐ Graphic organizer check-in   *Due* _____

❐ First draft of script   *Due* _____

   ☐ All narration or audio for your documentary

   ☐ All director's commands, camera shots, and graphics

   ☐ All times

❐ Final script   *Due* _____

❐ Studio Production   *Date* _____

Student: _____ Date: _____

Research **Tentative Thesis Due:** _____	1.0 In progress		2.0 Basic		3.0 Proficient		4.0 Advanced	
	S	T	S	T	S	T	S	T
Planning								
Researcher formulated a thoughtful hypothesis, question, or tentative thesis								
Question/hypothesis or thesis is focused								
Question/hypothesis or thesis did not lend itself to readily available answers								

Graphic Organizer Due: _____

Gathering								
Researcher gathered information from a full range of quality electronic and print sources, including appropriate licensed databases and primary sources								
Researcher evaluated resources								
Researcher effectively used graphic organizer for extracting information from sources								

Final Draft Due: _____

Organizing								
Researcher processed and synthesized ideas and information from various sources to answer question or prove thesis								
Researcher synthesized information to convey new understanding (researcher's voice is heard)								
Researcher used effective supporting evidence								
Documenting								
Researcher used information ethically								
Researcher credited all ideas, text, graphics, media not his or her own								
Researcher followed Works Cited/Works Consulted format correctly								
Reflecting								
Researcher reflected thoughtfully and specifically on the process								

Grade Point	4	3.5	3	2	1	0
Score	95	88	83	78	65	F

4-25B

Student: _____ Date: _____

	1.0 In progress		2.0 Basic		3.0 Proficient		4.0 Advanced	
	S	T	S	T	S	T	S	T
Audio Script								
Focus Sharp, distinct controlling point made about a single topic with evident awareness of task								
Content Substantial, specific, and/or illustrative content demonstrating strong development and sophisticated ideas								
Organization Sophisticated arrangement of content with evident and/or subtle transitions								
Has a clear, compelling opening (grabber), thesis, body, and conclusion								
Style Precise, illustrative use of a variety of words and sentence structures to create consistent original writer's voice and tone appropriate to audience								
Conventions Evident control of grammar, mechanics, spelling, usage, and sentence formation								

Video Script								
The script is written to be visually interesting using a variety of camera shots								
At least 10 graphics or other visual information is included								
Times are included								
All camera shots are included								
Music is included (copyright-free)								
Director's commands are included								

Grade Point	4	3.5	3	2	1	0
Score	95	88	83	78	65	F

4-25C

Studio Production: _____

	1.0 In progress		2.0 Basic		3.0 Proficient		4.0 Advanced	
	S	T	S	T	S	T	S	T
Preparation								
The script and storyboard are prepared and distributed								
All graphics are prepared								
The Producer/Director								
Is in control of the shoot								
Gives clear directions and answers all questions								
Approaches the project the most organized and efficient way possible								
Made all necessary adjustments								
Final Product								
Graphics are used effectively								
Graphics are easy for the audience to understand/read								
The production is done the most visually interesting way								
All project requirements are met								

SOURCE: Adapted from a unit developed by Dan Meder, Media Production Teacher, Springfield Township High School, Erdenheim, PA.

Multimedia/Web Page Research Rubric

Student(s) _____ Class _____ Date _____ Final Grade ____

	Assessment ___ Self __ Peer __ Teacher						Weight of Criteria (x 1, 2, 3)
Mechanical/Technical	**Scale**						**Score**
Project or page runs/loads smoothly. Student checked for all possible technical bugs.	5	4	3	2	1	0 *Comments:*	
Navigation is intuitive and logical for content. All links work. Titles, subtitles, and sections are meaningful.	5	4	3	2	1	0 *Comments:*	
Grammar, spelling, and punctuation are correct.	5	4	3	2	1	0 *Comments:*	
All technical requirements set by the teacher are met or exceeded Requirements:	5	4	3	2	1	0 *Comments:*	
Appearance/Creativity	**Scale**						**Score**
Screens or pages display elements of effective design. Choices of fonts, colors, and backgrounds are effective, tasteful, consistent. Text and media are artistically balanced, appropriately sized, and consistent with message.	5	4	3	2	1	0 *Comments:*	
All media carefully selected to enhance message, support thesis, convey meaning.	5	4	3	2	1	0 *Comments:*	
Project visually communicates student creativity. Student(s) used original art.	5	4	3	2	1	0 *Comments:*	

Organization and Presentation of Content	Scale						Score
Information is presented in logical sequence or structure. Project demonstrates evidence of use of an organizer or note taking strategy.	5	4	3	2	1	0	
	Comments:						
Project uses media to effectively structure information. Branching/hyperlinking or sections work to communicate information effectively.	5	4	3	2	1	0	
	Comments:						
Textual content is clearly and effectively written.	5	4	3	2	1	0	
	Comments:						
The work of others is effectively and selectively paraphrased, summarized, or quoted.	5	4	3	2	1	0	
	Comments:						
Evidence of Quality Research	Scale						Score
Student(s) developed a question or thesis worthy of research.	5	4	3	2	1	0	
	Comments:						
No research "holes." The most important sources were consulted.	5	4	3	2	1	0	
	Comments:						
Sources were critically evaluated. Student(s) used a full range of quality electronic and print sources, including appropriate databases and primary sources. Students consulted resources that showed a variety of perspectives.	5	4	3	2	1	0	
	Comments:						
Student(s) displayed original thought in analyzing material from a variety of sources, drawing conclusions, and displaying deep understanding. Project is not merely a rehash of data; "student voice is heard."	5	4	3	2	1	0	
	Comments:						

Documentation	Scale	Score
All ideas, text, and media are properly cited following MLA style.	5 4 3 2 1 0 *Comments:*	
For Web project or media broadcast, all permissions to use text, graphics, audio and video, not in the public domain, are obtained and clearly noted.	5 4 3 2 1 0 *Comments:*	

Group Work (if collaborative)	Scale	Score
Group members collaborated effectively. Each assumed appropriate roles and contributed in a significant ways.	5 4 3 2 1 0 *Comments:*	

Oral Presentation (if presented)	Scale	Score
Student(s) used effective presentation strategies—opening clincher, strong closing.	5 4 3 2 1 0 *Comments:*	
Students monitored audience for reaction, maintained eye contact, and projected voice to be clearly heard.	5 4 3 2 1 0 *Comments:*	
Presentation displayed evidence of rehearsal. Language was appropriate. Delivery was smooth.	5 4 3 2 1 0 *Comments:*	
Additional Project-Specific Criteria	5 4 3 2 1 0 *Comments:*	

Overall Comments:

Multimedia Project Evaluation Form
(Middle School)

Student _____   Class _____   Date _____   Grade _____

Evaluator: ☐ Self   ☐ Peer   ☐ Teacher   Total Points: _____

Poor ◄————————► **Excellent**

1. **Research problem/Thesis/Question**   1   2   3   4   5
   Comments:

2. **Research effort/Information access**   1   2   3   4   5
   Comments:

3. **Research accuracy/Supporting evidence**   1   2   3   4   5
   Comments:

4. **Organization: Is the project structured in a logical way?**   1   2   3   4   5
   Comments:

5. **Mechanics—grammar, spelling, punctuation**   1   2   3   4   5
   Comments:

6. **Use of media**   1   2   3   4   5
   Comments:

7. **Creativity**   1   2   3   4   5
   Comments:

8. **Communication**   1   2   3   4   5
   Comments:

9. **Documentation**   1   2   3   4   5
   Comments:

10. **Specific criteria for project**   1   2   3   4   5
   Comments:

Research CheckBric

PLANNING   5   4   3   2   1   0

_____ Researcher(s) formulated a thoughtful question/hypothesis, or tentative thesis.

Thesis: _____

     _____ question/hypothesis or thesis prompted a meaningful "how" or "why" exploration

     _____ question/hypothesis or thesis focused

     _____ question/hypothesis or thesis did not lend itself to readily available answers

Comments:

GATHERING   5   4   3   2   1   0

_____ Researcher(s) gathered information from a full range of quality electronic and print sources, including appropriate subscription databases and primary sources.

     _____ used effective search strategies for locating information

        _____ brainstormed key words, subject categories, related terms

        _____ used appropriate syntax for search tools

        _____ used appropriate search tools

     _____ evaluated resources (Sources defendable according to CARRDSS)

     _____ consulted balanced resources (print, journals, websites)

     _____ used structured format(s) for extracting information from sources

Comments:

ORGANIZING   5   4   3   2   1   0

_____ Researcher(s) processed and synthesized ideas and information from various sources to answer question or prove thesis.

     _____ avoided "research holes" (All important sources are included.)

     _____ paraphrased effectively

     _____ used "quotable" quotations (quotes truly worthy of quoting)

     _____ integrated researcher's own ideas with quoted and paraphrased material

     _____ synthesized information to convey new understanding (researcher's voice)

     _____ used effective supporting evidence

     _____ used structuring tool (graphic organizers, outlines)

Comments:

DOCUMENTING   5   4   3   2   1   0

_____ Researcher(s) used information ethically.

     _____ credited ideas, text, graphics, media

     _____ followed in-text documentation format correctly

     _____ followed Works Cited/Works Consulted format correctly

Comments:

REFLECTING   5   4   3   2   1   0

_____ Researcher(s) reflected thoughtfully and specifically on the process.

Comments:

SOURCE: Developed in collaboration with Carol H. Rohrbach, Language Arts Coordinator, School District of Springfield Township, Erdenheim, PA.

4-28B

Rubric for a Research Project

Student Name(s) _____ Teacher _____ Class _____ Final Grade _____

	Thesis/Problem/ Question	Information Seeking/Selecting and Evaluating	Analysis	Synthesis	Documentation	Product/Process
4	Student(s) posed a thoughtful, creative question that engaged them in challenging or provocative research. The question breaks new ground or contributes to knowledge in a focused, specific area.	Student(s) gathered information from a variety of quality electronic and print sources, including appropriate licensed databases. Sources are relevant, balanced, and include key readings relating to the thesis or problem. Primary sources were included (if appropriate).	Student(s) carefully analyzed the information collected and drew logical and inventive conclusions supported by evidence. Voice of the student writer is evident.	Student(s) developed appropriate structure for communicating the product, incorporating a variety of quality sources. Information is logically and creatively organized with smooth transitions.	Student(s) documented all sources, including visuals, sounds, and animations. Sources are properly cited, both in-text/in-product and on Works Cited/Works Consulted pages/slides. Documentation is error-free.	Student(s) effectively and creatively used appropriate communication tools to convey their conclusions and demonstrated thorough, effective research techniques. Product displays creativity and originality.
3	Student(s) posed a focused question involving them in challenging research.	Student(s) gathered information from a variety of relevant sources—print and electronic.	Student(s)' product shows good effort was made in analyzing the evidence collected. Student writer's voice is heard.	Student(s) logically organized the product and made good connections among ideas.	Student(s) documented sources with some care. Sources are cited, both in-text/in-product and on Works Cited/Works Consulted pages/slides. Work includes few errors.	Student(s) effectively communicated the results of research to the audience.
2	Student(s) constructed a "so what" or "who cares" question that lends itself to readily available answers.	Student(s) gathered information from a limited range of sources and displayed minimal effort in selecting quality resources. Research has "holes."	Student(s)' conclusions could be supported by stronger evidence. Level of analysis could have been deeper. Where is the student writer's voice?	Student(s) could have put greater effort into organizing the product.	Student(s) need to use greater care in documenting sources. Documentation was poorly constructed or absent.	Student(s) need to work on communicating more effectively.
1	Student(s) developed a question requiring little creative thought.	Student(s) gathered information that lacked relevance, quality, depth, and balance. Research has significant "holes."	Student(s)' conclusions involved simply restating information. Conclusions not supported by evidence. Where is the student writer's voice?	Student work is not logically or effectively structured. No transitions were made among ideas.	Student(s) clearly plagiarized materials.	Student(s) showed little evidence of thoughtful research. Product does not effectively communicate research findings.
Teacher/ Librarian Comments	Points: _____	Points: _____	Points: _____	Points: _____	Points: _____	Points: _____

What Is a Thesis?

A thesis statement declares what you believe and what you intend to prove. A good thesis statement makes the difference between a thoughtful research project and a simple retelling of facts.

A good tentative thesis will help you focus your search for information. But don't rush! You must do a lot of background reading before you know enough about a subject to identify key or essential questions. You may not know how you stand on an issue until you have examined the evidence. You will likely begin your research with a working, preliminary, or tentative thesis which you will continue to refine until you are certain of where the evidence leads.

The thesis statement is typically located at the end of your opening paragraph. (The opening paragraph serves to set the context for the thesis.)

Remember, your reader will be looking for your thesis. Make it clear, strong, and easy to find.

Attributes of a good thesis

- It should be contestable, proposing an arguable point with which people could reasonably disagree. A strong thesis is provocative; it takes a stand and justifies the discussion you will present.

- It tackles a subject that could be adequately covered in the format of the project assigned.

- It is specific and focused. A strong thesis proves a point without discussing "everything about . . ." Instead of music, think "American jazz in the 1930s" and your argument about it.

- It clearly asserts your own conclusion based on evidence. Note: Be flexible. The evidence may lead you to a conclusion you didn't think you'd reach. **It is perfectly okay to change your thesis!**

- It provides the reader with a map to guide him/her through your work.

- It anticipates and refutes the counter-arguments.

- It **avoids** vague language (like "it seems").

- It **avoids** the first person ("I believe," "In my opinion").

- It should pass the So what? or Who cares? Test. (Would your most honest friend ask why he should care or respond with "but everyone knows that"?) For instance, "people should avoid driving under the influence of alcohol," would be unlikely to evoke any opposition.

How do you know if you've got a solid tentative thesis?

Try these five tests:

1. Does the thesis inspire a reasonable reader to ask, "How?" or "Why?"
2. Would a reasonable reader NOT respond with "Duh!" or "So what?" or "Gee, no kidding!" or "Who cares?"
3. Does the thesis avoid general phrasing and/or sweeping words such as "all" or "none" or "every"?
4. Does the thesis lead the reader toward the topic sentences (the subtopics needed to prove the thesis)?
5. Can the thesis be adequately developed in the required length of the paper or project?

If you cannot answer "YES" to these questions, what changes must you make in order for your thesis to pass these tests?

Examine and evaluate these sample thesis statements, using the Five Tests.

- E-coli contamination should not happen.
- The causes of the Civil War were economic, social, and political.
- *The Simpsons* represents the greatest animated show in the history of television.
- *The Simpsons* treats the issues of ethnicity, family dynamics, and social issues effectively.
- Often dismissed because it is animated, *The Simpsons* treats the issue of ethnicity more powerfully than did the critically praised *All In The Family*.

Proficient vs. advanced

Proficient: Inspires the reasonable reader to ask "How?" or "Why?"

Advanced: Inspires the reasonable reader to ask "How?" or "Why?" and to exclaim "Wow!" This thesis engages the student in challenging or provocative research and displays a level of thought that breaks new ground.

Remember: Reading and coaching can significantly improve the tentative thesis.

Thesis brainstorming

As you read, ask yourself these questions:

- Are interesting contrasts or comparisons or patterns emerging in the information?
- Is there something about the topic that surprises you?
- Do you encounter ideas that make you wonder why?
- Does something an "expert" says make you respond, "No way! That can be right!" or "Yes, absolutely. I agree!"?

SOURCE: Developed by Carol H. Rohrbach and Joyce Valenza, School District of Springfield Township, Erdenheim, PA.

Thesis Generator

thesis

topic

IDEAS FOR HELPING STUDENTS DEVELOP BETTER THESIS STATEMENTS

1. **Equations:** Think about the thesis equations as you ask questions and move toward a tentative thesis.

   A tentative thesis should look something like this:

   Specific topic + Attitude/Angle/Argument = Thesis

   What you plan to argue + How you plan to argue it = Thesis

2. **Thesis Stems:** Consider using these stems to help students move from proficient to advanced thesis statements.

Rank with Justification

   Most important to least important

   Least important to most important

Contrasts (of Perspectives of Sources)

   Although newspapers at the time claimed X, the most significant cause/explanation/reason, etc., is . . .

   While So and So maintains that ...., more accurately/importantly, etc., #2's position is the stronger one. (Substitute "most historians" for So and So and the appropriate person or view or source for #2.)

Perception versus Reality

   Although Turner himself may have believed X, the real causes were Y and Z.

Good versus Bad Reasons

   Historians generally list six reasons as the cause for X, but among these are four that are valid and two that are not.

Cause and Effect

   Certainly, X was the cause and Y was its effect, but between the two are two other factors of equal importance.

   Separately the causes would have not necessarily led to a rampage; however, together their effect was inevitably murderous.

   Although the effects of the rampage were . . . , the causes were understandable/justifiable/inevitable.

   The more important effects of Nat Turner's rebellion went beyond those of the local rampage.

Challenge

   Nat Turner's rebellion was not a righteous response to the injustice of slavery; it was motivated purely by disturbing psychological issues.

3. **Question Stems:** Good questions help students brainstorm their possibilities and focus a thesis. These question stems should lead students toward developing thesis statements that would generate a variety of different structures for essays, papers, presentations.

- What should the audience/reader do/feel/believe?
- Who are the major players on both/each side and how did they contribute to?
- Which are the most important?
- What was the impact of?
- Can I compare? How is X like or unlike Y?
- What if? Can I predict?
- How could we solve/improve/design/deal with?
- Is there a better solution to?
- How can you defend?
- What changes would you recommend to?
- Was it effective, justified, defensible, warranted?
- Why did this happen? Why did it succeed? Why did it fail?
- What should be? What are/would be the possible outcomes of?
- What are the problems related to?
- What were the motives behind?
- Why are the opponents protesting?
- What is my personal response to?
- What case can I make for?
- What is the significance of?
- Where will the next move(s) occur?
- How is this debate likely to affect?
- What is the value or, what is/are the potential benefit(s) of?
- What are three/four/five reasons for us to believe?

SOURCE: Developed by Carol H. Rohrbach and Joyce Valenza, School District of Springfield Township, Erdenheim, PA.

VISUALIZING THE SEARCH PROCESS

PLANNING/THINKING	SEARCHING	REFINING/EVALUATING

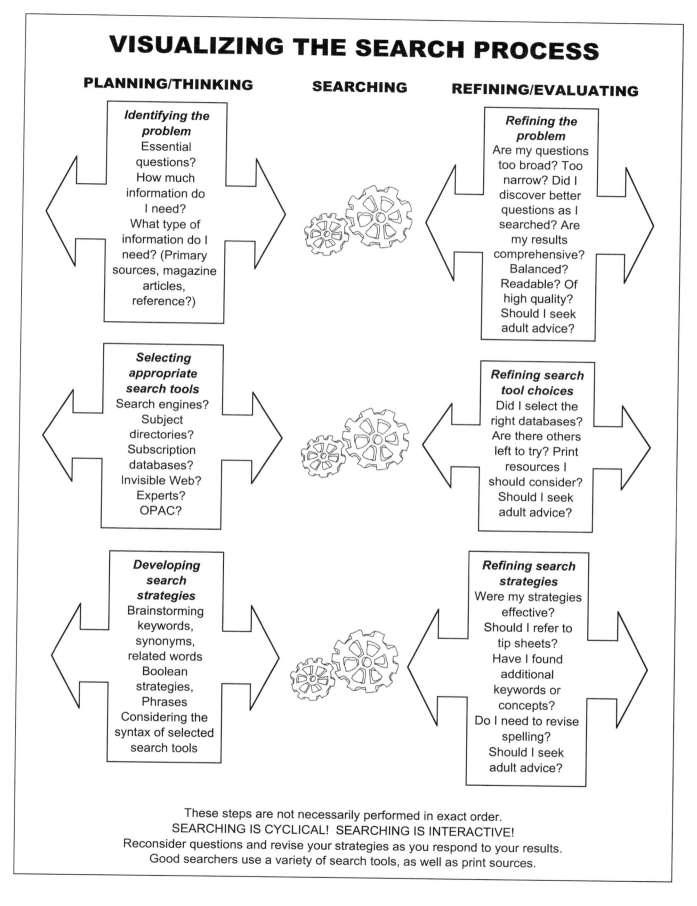

Identifying the problem
Essential questions?
How much information do I need?
What type of information do I need? (Primary sources, magazine articles, reference?)

Refining the problem
Are my questions too broad? Too narrow? Did I discover better questions as I searched? Are my results comprehensive? Balanced? Readable? Of high quality? Should I seek adult advice?

Selecting appropriate search tools
Search engines?
Subject directories?
Subscription databases?
Invisible Web?
Experts?
OPAC?

Refining search tool choices
Did I select the right databases? Are there others left to try? Print resources I should consider? Should I seek adult advice?

Developing search strategies
Brainstorming keywords, synonyms, related words
Boolean strategies, Phrases
Considering the syntax of selected search tools

Refining search strategies
Were my strategies effective?
Should I refer to tip sheets?
Have I found additional keywords or concepts?
Do I need to revise spelling?
Should I seek adult advice?

These steps are not necessarily performed in exact order.
SEARCHING IS CYCLICAL! SEARCHING IS INTERACTIVE!
Reconsider questions and revise your strategies as you respond to your results.
Good searchers use a variety of search tools, as well as print sources.

Student Tools for Information Literacy

This group of tools—handouts, checklists, note takers, and other scaffolding—is designed to guide students toward more thoughtful reading and research, toward better-structured projects. The tools demonstrate the supporting thinking and organizational skills necessary at the various in-process steps of their work to help students transform the raw material they locate into original work displaying high levels of synthesis and analysis, work that highlights the student's unique voice.

After sufficient practice and application, the skills should become internalized; the scaffolding can be removed, and the cognitive skills and habits should stand on their own. The tools can be used in conjunction with specific assignments or kept at the circulation desk for students to use as they themselves determine a need.

5-1/5-2
Evaluative Annotated Works Cited
(Middle School and High School Versions)

Asking students to annotate their sources automatically raises the research bar. Annotations require students to use critical research and evaluation skills. Use these guidelines as a starting point. You might ask student to use annotations only for *free* Web resources, or you might ask them to annotate their best sources. This handout reminds them of the criteria you require in a thoughtful annotation.

5-3A/5-3B
Changing the Questions (Question Organizer and Some Sample Responses)

This "brainstormer" can be assigned before students begin a research project. It is designed to move students beyond topical research to the types of questions that inspire critical thought. Teachers and librarians can conference with students to help them select the most promising questions to research. Though students are likely to use the form to brainstorm topics related to the area they are studying, the samples here were written for two unrelated topics to demonstrate a greater variety of question options.

5-4
Before You Log On: Planning Your Search

This planning chart ensures students consider their keywords and strategies prior to logging on and enables you to assess their understanding of search strategies. Students may use the organizer to record additional keywords they discover or "mine" during the search process. Assign this as a homework project the day before a visit to the library or lab.

5-5
Research Task Requirements Checklist

This checklist analyzes the small pieces of a major project and their due dates. You may ask a class to take notes on the template as you describe a new project, or you may edit and complete it for the class yourself prior to announcing the project.

5-6
Ask Yourself Questions As You Evaluate the Information You Find on the Web . . .

This student handout could be displayed and distributed during an initial class discussion of the importance of evaluating web pages.

5-7/5-8
Thesis Project Organizer and Project Outline

Thesis statements drive most of the commonly assigned projects in our program. These organizers, also usable for in-process assessment, will help students clarify their arguments and focus them on gathering solid evidence to support them.

5-9
Student Project Proposal

Have individual students or small groups organize their ideas and formalize their plans with this proposal form. After the first planning visit, teachers can evaluate the proposal, add comments, and accept, refine, or reject the plans.

5-10
Current Events (Template)

Experienced one too many "so what" current events presentations? You *can* encourage more student thought and reflection. Use this organizer with students to help them prepare to present a news item to the class. The questions are designed to move students beyond the simple summary, to reflect on the impact of the event, and to explore their personal reactions. You might examine these organizers prior to presentation time to evaluate students' level of preparation, or collect them for use as an assessment tool.

5-11
Speech Organizer

This organizer should help students fight their fear of speaking by ensuring they prepare compelling opening and closing statements and carefully consider the major points they need to make.

5-12
Debate Organizer

Avoid debating disasters and ensure that students walk into class ready to argue. This organizer may be used as a formative assessment tool to ensure students are prepared enough to participate and as an organization tool to supplement debaters' note cards.

5-13
Persuasive Documentary Organizer

This tool, designed in collaboration with Theater/Communication Arts teacher Marlene Thornton, helps students prepare video documentaries to broadcast over the school cable network. It forces students to carefully plan how they will grab the attention of their audience, focus their thesis, and dismiss conflicting opinions.

5-14
Student Self-Evaluation Checklist

By asking students to sign and attach this form to their finished product, you ensure that procrastinators will think one last time about the quality of their work and planners will think more carefully about the criteria you value most.

5-15
Research Conference Form

Research is a process, and as a process, *its steps* should be evaluated and refined. If we examine only finished products, we often find ourselves faced with research disasters and we ignore important learning opportunities. Research conferences provide opportunities to guide students before they hit the disaster stage. They show students that we value the process as well as the product. They involve the special expertise of the teacher-librarian and allow students valuable opportunities to consult with information professionals.

5-16
Reflecting on the Research Process

This tool, developed with Language Arts Coordinator Carol Rohrbach, asks students to focus and reflect on their process. When students know upfront they will be graded on the process as well as the product, they take the process more seriously. Reflection encourages the serious consideration that will improve students' future research.

5-17
Checklist for Research

Many students don't realize the large variety of choices open to them. Adapt this list to match your own resources, and distribute it to students for their notebooks. Post it strategically around the library. I photocopy this sheet and print it on the back of the Search Planner and distribute it as a student handout.

5-18
Checklist for a Research Interview

A personal interview can be an exciting tool for research and can really make a topic come alive. Before conducting an interview, students should develop a plan and be aware of some of the "people skills" they might employ to make their interview a more successful and pleasant experience.

5-19
How to Score More Points with Your PowerPoints

Distribute and discuss this handout prior to assigning a multimedia product. It will guide students toward focusing on what's truly important in delivering an effective presentation.

5-20
Library Visit Log

Some classroom teachers may like to assess students' progress and ensure that students stay on task by requiring them to report the progress made during a library visit with a short form such as this.

5-21
E-mail Netiquette

These guidelines are probably outlined in your Acceptable Use Policy. I discuss appropriate behavior with students at the beginning of the school year. You might choose to post these rules near your workstations.

5-22
Storyboard for a Multimedia Presentation

Have lots of these on hand as students begin to structure their multimedia productions. Consider requiring well-planned storyboards from students before they even touch a keyboard or a camera.

5-23
Search Planner

Ask students to keep this form in their notebooks as an organizer, as well as an in-process assessment tool, for any major research project.

5-24
Note Taker

This general note-taking device might be copied in quantity and made available to students as they read and research. Ideally, each sheet would help a student collect notes for each major subheading. Teachers should remind students to look

for quotes and solid evidence, to cite their sources, and discern main ideas worth remembering.

5-25
Steps in Online Searching

There are some smaller steps students need to master when they approach electronic databases. I usually introduce or reinforce these steps before a class begins a major project. It may be useful to focus on each step individually in a ten-minutes mini-lesson before students begin their hands-on work. To illustrate these steps more clearly, make transparencies from printouts of searches that didn't work and have students evaluate the problems.

5-26
Big6 Organizer

Students may use this form to plan a project using the Mike Eisenberg and Bob Berkowitz Big6 model. It might also serve as an attachment to a finished product, ensuring that students have carefully thought about each step of the research process. As an overhead, it might be used to introduce the steps while the class and the library information specialist brainstorm a sample project.

5-27
Keyword Search Plan

Before a unit begins, remind students of the importance of brainstorming keywords and developing a list of synonyms ("ORs") and a list of ideas they will need to connect with "ANDs." This form helps them organize their searches before they go online.

5-28
Compare and Contrast Outline

Use this form to aid students in writing essays that ask for comparisons. It helps them clearly identify similarities and differences and might be used, for instance, to compare two elements on the periodic table. Perhaps both might be metals and might share certain properties, but there would be differences in their chemical and physical properties. Students might also compare and contrast two presidencies with regard to economic policy, domestic affairs and foreign policy, or cultures; two philosophies; or two fictional characters.

5-29
Time Line/Chronology

This chart could be used to prepare a project that is organized around a sequence of events, or it might be used as a note-taking device so that students are cued to record the key incidents leading up to an historic event. Use the chart also to help show cause/effect, process/product, or problem/solution. Time lines can be helpful in understanding the biographical events in a person's life, histories of countries, or complex plots in a novel or play.

5-30
Essay Outline

This chart might be used to support main ideas of an essay or speech or to describe parts of a whole. It should help students sort information into logical paragraphs or sections as they read and research.

5-31A–5-31C
Source Cards

The source card samples represent a few of the most-cited resource types. They are meant to be used as "super index cards," cuing students to gather the information they will need from each source to make preparing their works cited or works consulted pages far easier. They are also useful for noting main ideas and valuable quotes. We print each type of source card on different-

color paper so students can quickly identify the forms they need.

5-32
Note Cards

Have students use these note cards to record quotes or paraphrases they'll later cite, making sure they carefully list source and page numbers to refer back to the references in their source cards.

5-33
Power Searching Tips for the Web and Online Databases

This "cheat sheet" describes most of the common strategies used by search engines and databases. Use this handout for more advanced students, emphasizing the unique syntax of each search tool. Though you cannot teach every interface, it helps to understand and have students look for these broad concepts. Knowing that these strategies exist, and discovering how they are expressed in students' favorite search tools, especially in advanced search screens, will significantly focus and improve student searches.

5-34
URLs as Clues to Context

When students better understand the URLs they see on their result lists, they can quickly identify sites worthy of visiting and sites not likely to be citable. This handout helps students understand URL suffixes. Use it in connection with Hey There! Have You Evaluated? in the presentation section, chapter 6.

Evaluative Annotated Works Cited
(Middle School)

Your teacher may ask you to justify the quality of a source with an annotation. Good annotations clearly prove the value of the source to your research.

When preparing an annotation, the most challenging task may be locating the credentials of an author who is not well known. Consult *Current Biography, Contemporary Authors, Book Review Digest,* or some of our periodical databases for biographical information. You may also choose to do a Web search of the author's name and the words *profile, biography,* or *curriculum vitae,* or *C.V.*

Answer four questions relating to your source

1. How: How did you locate it? What database, search tool did you use?
2. Who: Who wrote it? Can you determine anything about the author's credentials?
3. Where: Where did it come from: the site of a major organization, university, public television station, a journal, etc.?
4. Why: Why did you choose this source over the many others available?

Example

Skiba, Russ and Kevin Dwyer. "School Violence: Listening to the Students."
   NASP Communiqué. Volume 28, No. 2 Oct. 1999.
   <http://www.nasponline.org/publications/cq282violence.html>

This article appeared on my Google result list when I used the keywords "cliques" AND "middle school." Skiba, a Ph.D., is on the faculty of the School Psychology Program at Indiana University and is Director of the Institute for Child Study at Indiana University. Dwyer, the president of the National Association of School Psychologists, is an author and retired school psychologist. The article is posted on the site of the National Association of School Psychologists and discusses the serious relationship of cliques to school violence. The argument directly supports my thesis.

Evaluative Annotated Bibliography (High School)

Your teacher may ask you to justify the quality of a source with an annotation. Good annotations clearly prove the value of the source to your research. Sometimes assigned as a project in itself, an annotated bibliography requires the same research and evaluation techniques as a traditional term paper.

When preparing an annotation, the most challenging task may be locating the credentials of an author who is not well known. Consult *Current Biography, Contemporary Authors, Book Review Digest,* or our periodical databases for biographical information. You may also choose to do a Web search of the author's name and the words *profile, biography,* or *curriculum vitae* or *C.V.* A C.V. is a resume for an academic that usually includes publications and presentations.

Use the following criteria to evaluate books, articles, Web sites, and reference materials. If you feel the work would be difficult to defend in your works cited or works consulted, it would be best not to include it.

Elements to include in an evaluative annotation (check with your teacher to see which criteria are necessary for any specific project):

1. Author's credentials
2. Scope and purpose of the work: Is it an overview, persuasive, editorial, scholarly, popular?
3. Comparison of the work with others dealing with the same topic or others in your bibliography
4. Intended audience
5. Brief summary of contents
6. Evaluation of research: Is the work logical, clear, well documented, based on solid evidence?
7. Evaluation of scope: Has the topic been adequately covered or analyzed?
8. Evaluation of author bias
9. Relative value of the work to the thesis

Example of an evaluative annotation

Katz, Jon. "The Rights of Kids in the Digital Age." *Wired* July 1996: 120+.

Katz, former contributing editor of *Wired* and the author of Netizen's "Media Rant" on HotWired, presents a compelling argument for safeguarding the rights of children online. The article is aimed at a general, but computer-savvy, audience. Katz offers a far more liberal perspective than recent pieces in such major news journals as *Newsweek,* which continue to warn the public of the dangers children face in electronic environments. Katz advocates the idea of preparing the "responsible child" and outlines the rights of such a child. He claims that our new "digital nation" requires a social contract similar to the one proposed by philosopher John Locke and adopted by the founders of our own country to protect the rights of all citizens. This unique liberal view added needed balance to my project.

Changing the Questions (Question Organizer)

	Topic #1 _____	Topic #2 _____
Which one? (Collect information to make an informed choice.) *E.g.,* Which 20th-century president did the most to promote civil rights?		
How? (Understand problems and perspectives, weigh options, and propose solutions.) *E.g.,* How should we solve the problem of water pollution in our neighborhood?		
What if? (Use the knowledge you have to pose a hypothesis and consider options.) *E.g.,* What if the Declaration of Independence abolished slavery?		
Should? (Make a moral or practical decision based on evidence.) *E.g.,* Should we clone humans?		
Why? (Understand and explain relationships to get to the essence of a complicated issue.) *E.g.,* Why do people abuse children?		

Brainstorm two topics related to the unit we are studying. Use the cues to develop essential questions that will help you focus your research. You don't need to fill in every box.

Changing the Questions (Some Sample Responses)

	Topic #1 Civil War	Topic #2 Shakespeare
Which one? (Collect information to make an informed choice.) *E.g.,* Which 20th-century president did the most to promote civil rights?	Which Civil War general was the best military strategist?	Which of Shakespeare's tragedies has the most relevance for today's politicians? Which of the characters in *Romeo and Juliet* is most worthy of punishment?
How? (Understand problems and perspectives, weigh options, and propose solutions.) *E.g.,* How should we solve the problem of water pollution in our neighborhood?	How did the scientific advances of the 19th century affect the outcome of the Civil War? (Students might choose among advances in communications, transportation, weaponry, etc.)	How does Shakespeare's subplot help us better understand the themes of _____?
What if? (Use the knowledge you have to pose a hypothesis and consider options.) *E.g.,* What if the Declaration of Independence abolished slavery?	What if General Lee had better intelligence at Gettysburg?	What if Brutus had made the final funeral oration in *Julius Caesar?*
Should? (Make a moral or practical decision based on evidence.) *E.g.,* Should we clone humans?	Should Confederate symbols be used in official state flags and logos today?	Should Hamlet have minded his own business?
Why? (Understand and explain relationships to get to the essence of a complicated issue.) *E.g.,* Why do people abuse children?	Why did Great Britain favor the South during the Civil War?	Why do Shakespeare's plays continue to have meaning for today's students? Why does Shakespeare use so many references to the natural and unnatural in *Macbeth?*

Brainstorm two topics related to the unit we are studying. Use the cues to develop essential questions that will help you focus your research. You don't need to fill in every box.

Before You Log On: Planning Your Search

	concept #1	concept #2	concept #3	concept #4
Sample question: How effective are drug abuse prevention programs for young people?				
Connect with "ANDs"				
	concept #1	concept #2	concept #3	concept #4
OR	teen*	"drug abuse"	prevention	effective*
OR	adolesc*	marijuana	programs	success
OR	children	alcohol	treatment	
Potential problem words (if any) to exclude or "NOT": medic*, prescription				

Plan your own search using the strategies outlined above. Consider Boolean operators, phrases, and truncation. Remember to brainstorm synonyms or related words.

	concept #1	concept #2	concept #3	concept #4
Question/Tentative Thesis:				
Connect with "ANDs"				
	concept #1	concept #2	concept #3	concept #4
OR				
OR				
OR				
Potential Problem words (if any) to exclude or "NOT":				

Research Task Requirements Checklist

Project title: _____

1. What is the due date for the completed project? _____

2. In-process steps/research package requirements. Are specific materials due during different stages of the research process?

	Date
Preliminary or working thesis due	_____
Pre-write/first draft due	_____
Second draft due	_____
Note cards/source cards due	_____
Storyboard/outline/organizer due	_____
Working bibliography/works cited/consulted due	_____
Research conference form due	_____

3. What are the format requirements for the project? Must it be a formal paper, oral presentation, video, multimedia project? May I choose the format?

4. What is the required length in words or pages? _____

   Are there specific word processing requirements?

5. Are a specific number of sources required? _____

6. Are specific source types required? For instance, magazine articles, newspaper articles, primary sources (speeches, letters, legislation, interviews, etc.) websites, books, scholarly journals.

   Other _____

7. Are there any source types my teacher prefers that I do not use? (encyclopedias, SparkNotes, etc.?)

8. What form should my documentation take? Works Cited and/or Consulted? Annotations? In-text or in-project documentation?

9. Will your teacher require you to formally defend your research? (explain your conclusions, your choice of sources and how and why they were used)

10. Will you have to include a reflection on the research process as part of your final product? This might take the form of a cover sheet or journal and should describe the strategies you used, the successes and frustrations you experienced in your writing and your research, which research tools were most effective, and what you might do differently next time.

Ask yourself questions as you evaluate the information you find on the Web and consider it for use in your projects:

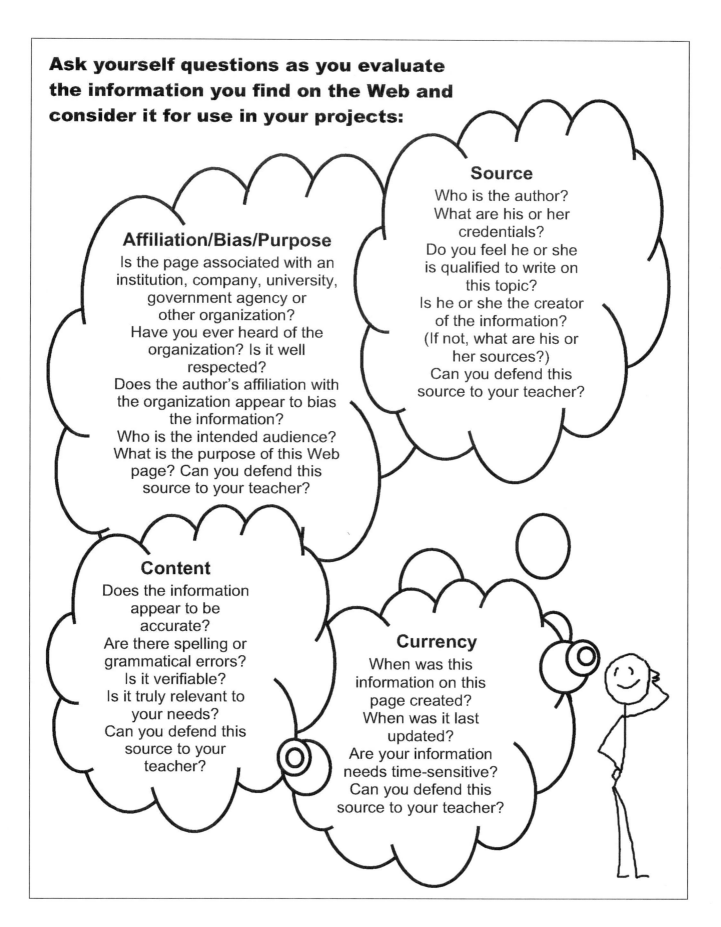

Affiliation/Bias/Purpose
Is the page associated with an institution, company, university, government agency or other organization?
Have you ever heard of the organization? Is it well respected?
Does the author's affiliation with the organization appear to bias the information?
Who is the intended audience?
What is the purpose of this Web page? Can you defend this source to your teacher?

Source
Who is the author?
What are his or her credentials?
Do you feel he or she is qualified to write on this topic?
Is he or she the creator of the information?
(If not, what are his or her sources?)
Can you defend this source to your teacher?

Content
Does the information appear to be accurate?
Are there spelling or grammatical errors?
Is it verifiable?
Is it truly relevant to your needs?
Can you defend this source to your teacher?

Currency
When was this information on this page created?
When was it last updated?
Are your information needs time-sensitive?
Can you defend this source to your teacher?

Thesis Project Organizer

Preliminary/Working Thesis: What is the argument you plan to prove in your project?
Avoid a "so what" thesis!

Supporting Argument:

Evidence/Quotes:

Transition:

Supporting Argument:

Evidence/Quotes:

Transition:

Supporting Argument:

Evidence/Quotes:

Transition:

Examination and
Refutation of Possible
Opposing Arguments:

Evidence/Quotes:

Reconfirmation of
Position/Thesis —
Main Points

Projected Conclusion: Powerfully restate the stance of your thesis in light of the evidence you presented.

Project Outline

Problem/Thesis:
(Quote or attention grabber)

_____

1. Topic:

    a. Detail/Evidence:

    b. Detail/Evidence:

    c. Detail/Evidence:

Transition:

_____

2. Topic:

    a. Detail/Evidence:

    b. Detail/Evidence:

    c. Detail/Evidence:

Transition:

_____

3. Topic:

    a. Detail/Evidence:

    b. Detail/Evidence:

    c. Detail/Evidence:

Transition:

_____

4. Topic:

    a. Detail/Evidence:

    b. Detail/Evidence:

    c. Detail/Evidence:

_____

5. Conclusion (powerful restatement of thesis, summary of evidence, clincher sentence):

Student Project Proposal

Proposed thesis or problem to be solved:

Project format: ___ research paper   ___ video   ___ multimedia   ___ oral presentation

___ other (please describe) _____

Search tools and databases I (we) plan to use:

Keywords and subject headings I (we) plan to use:

Five potential sources

1. _____

2. _____

3. _____

4. _____

5. _____

I (We) will complete the project by: _____

Student(s') signature(s): _____

_____

Project accepted: ___ Yes   ___ No   Date _____

Suggestions for refining:

Teacher/librarian comments:

Classroom Teacher's signature: _____

Current Events

Complete the following to help you analyze the event you've selected:

ARTICLE CITATION:

WHO?

WHAT?

WHERE?

WHEN?

PRIOR KNOWLEDGE? What did you already know about this topic?

MAIN POINTS: Use keywords and "bullets," not full sentences.

AUTHOR BIAS? support/opposes/neutral

QUOTE: Identify a quote to back up your assessment of the author's view or a quote that sums up the essence of the article.

SO WHAT? (Why is this news important? Who is likely to feel the impact of this news? What difference does it make?)

REACTION: What is your personal reaction to this news? How does the new information change your understanding this topic?

QUESTIONS: What issues remain unanswered? What else would you like to know? What bothers you about this article?

Speech Organizer

Opening: attention-getting device (story, humorous anecdote, compelling fact or statistic)	
Preview of what's to come and/or transition from opening to body of speech	
Body of speech (note any statistics, quotes, evidence, or visual aides that fit in with each point)	Point 1
	Point 2
	Point 3
Conclusion (a.k.a. clincher, wrap-up, point you want to restate)	
Final statement (What is the very last thought you want to leave with your audience?)	

Debate Organizer

Resolved/Position:

Make sure you include quotations and note sources as part of your evidence.
Bring index cards including full versions of your important quotes!

Argument 1:	Evidence:
Argument 2:	Evidence:
Argument 3:	Evidence:
Argument 4:	Evidence:

Anticipate! Be prepared to counter the arguments of your opposition.

Opposing Position:

Refuting Arguments

Argument 1:	But:
Argument 2:	But:
Argument 3:	But:
Argument 4:	But:

Clinch your argument with a strong summary, your most compelling evidence, a powerful quote.

Closing:

Persuasive Documentary Organizer

Hook:

Thesis:

Essential background for viewers:

Argument 1:	Evidence/Quotes:
Argument 2:	Evidence/Quotes:
Argument 3:	Evidence/Quotes:
Argument 4:	Evidence/Quotes:

Include here the opposing arguments you plan to briefly dismiss.

Opposing Viewpoint	**Response**
1.	1.
2.	2.
3.	3.

How will you clinch your argument? What are your final words for the audience?

Conclusion:

Student Self-Evaluation Checklist

Name _____ Teacher _____ Course _____ Date _____

Please attach this sheet to your finished project.

1. Clearly state the hypothesis, question, or problem your research attempts to address or answer.

2. Write a three- to five-sentence abstract summarizing your research.

3. I have fulfilled all the requirements listed on the assignment sheet. ☐ Yes ☐ No
4. My thesis or question is adequately answered and supported by evidence ☐ Yes ☐ No
5. My evidence is logically organized. ☐ Yes ☐ No
6. My introduction and conclusion clearly explain my question/thesis. ☐ Yes ☐ No
7. I have carefully checked spelling, grammar, and punctuation. ☐ Yes ☐ No
8. My verb tense is consistent throughout. ☐ Yes ☐ No
9. I have varied sentence structure to make the text more readable. ☐ Yes ☐ No
10. My paragraphs have topic sentences. ☐ Yes ☐ No
11. Transitional sentences link my paragraphs. ☐ Yes ☐ No
12. I have effectively and responsibly quoted, paraphrased, and summarized
    (All facts not commonly known are documented.) ☐ Yes ☐ No
13. My documentation is correctly formatted. ☐ Yes ☐ No
14. I have used a *balanced* and adequate number of relevant resources. ☐ Yes ☐ No
15. My project is neatly published and appealing to the reader. ☐ Yes ☐ No
16. I have chosen an effective method of presentation. ☐ Yes ☐ No
17. My own voice, as a writer, is clearly heard. ☐ Yes ☐ No
18. I have not plagiarized any of the material in this project.

Signature _____

Please list your comments about the research process on the back of this form.
What would you do differently next time?

Research Conference Form

The purpose of this conference is to avoid research "holes," to ensure you have identified quality sources and haven't overlooked any significant sources or strategies before you complete your project. Schedule an appointment with your teacher-librarian to discuss your progress and bring your sources to discuss. Be sure to schedule this appointment at least a week before your final project is due. *This conference is a project requirement. Return this form to your teacher following your conference with the teacher-librarian.*

Complete this section prior to your conference. Attach a working draft of your Works Consulted and/or Works Cited pages or bring along your note and source cards.

Preliminary/Working Thesis:

Subscription databases searched:

Search engines/Subject directories used:

Keywords/Subject headings searched:

Best three sources so far (print or online):

1.

2.

3.

Other valuable sources:

Problems you have encountered so far:

Complete this section during the conference

My plan for the next step:

Teacher-Librarian's suggested strategies:

Student's signature _____ Class _____ Date _____

Teacher-Librarian's signature _____ Date _____

Reflecting on the Research Process

On a separate sheet please reflect on the challenges and successes you faced during the research process. Make reference to each of the categories below, but focus on those issues that are most relevant to you.

Planning: Reflect on the process of focusing your research. What challenges did you encounter in developing a question, hypothesis, or thesis?

Gathering: Describe any problems or successes you had as you searched. Did any particular search strategies work well or disappoint you? Which databases and search engines worked well? What were the major barriers to your search for balanced and credible resources?

Organizing: How did you ensure that your information comprehensively addressed the question, hypothesis, or thesis? How and why did you modify your original question, hypothesis, or thesis? What strategies did you use to reorganize the information? Did these strategies lead you to connections, patterns, etc.? Discuss your thinking process as you decided how to structure the final product.

Synthesis: Describe your experiences reaching conclusions, culling and integrating information from the various sources you found, and finding your own voice as a writer regarding this assignment.

Documenting: Did any issues arise as you documented your sources both in-project and in your Works Cited/Works Consulted? Do you feel you ethically documented all your quotes, paraphrases, and summaries?

Evaluating: How would you describe your effort for this project? How effective was the product? What could you have done to improve your research next time around?

SOURCE: Developed in collaboration with Carol H. Rohrbach, K–12 Language Arts Coordinator, School District of Springfield Township, Erdenheim, PA.

Checklist for Research

Are you doing a thorough job researching? (You may ignore rows if you are certain they are not appropriate to your research.) Attach this form to the first draft of your project. Remember to list the most promising results you find in each area.

My thesis or question: _____

Did you use?		Best Result
Relevant reference books (to get a topic overview) ☐ yes ☐ no *Comments:*		
The online catalog to search for books, videos, CD-ROMs, DVDs, selected links ☐ yes ☐ no *Comments:*		
The statewide catalog, available catalogs of nearby public libraries, universities ☐ yes ☐ no *Comments:*		
Subscription services for magazine, journal, newspaper, reference materials ☐ yes ☐ no Please check all used. *SIRS* _____ *GaleNet* _____ *EBSCOhost* _____ *Facts.com* _____ *bigchalk* _____ *LexisNexis* _____ *Historical Newspapers (ProQuest)* _____ *CQ Researcher* _____ *Other* _____ *Comments:*		

A variety of subject directories, search engines, web-based databases? Which? Please list. _____ _____ *Comments:*	❑ yes ❑ no	
What were your best search terms and strategies? _____ *Comments:*	❑ yes ❑ no	
Bibliographies of the books and articles you already had to find new leads *Comments:*	❑ yes ❑ no	
Readers' Guide or other print indexes (especially for pre-1990 events) *Comments:*	❑ yes ❑ no	
Interviews? Experts, organizations, associations via e-mail? *Comments:*	❑ yes ❑ no	
Primary sources (speeches, documents, legislation, letters, songs, photographs, surveys, statistics, polls)? *Comments:*	❑ yes ❑ no	
Perspective, advice, and feedback from the teacher-librarian, classroom teacher, other adult? *Comments:*	❑ yes ❑ no	

Name: _____ Date: _____ Class: _____

Comments of Teacher/Librarian: _____

_____

_____

_____

Checklist for a Research Interview

Before conducting an in-person interview, make sure you

- are dressed neatly and appropriately
- introduce yourself
- welcome your guest with a smile and a handshake
- make your guest comfortable (offer a seat and water)
- explain the scope and purpose of your interview
- ask permission *first* if you plan to tape responses

Remember to record the date and verify spelling of names.
(You will need this information for your bibliography.)

FACTS

1. Full name and spelling: _____ Date: _____

2. Position/company/organization: _____

3. Can you tell me who/what/where/how?

_____
_____
_____
_____
_____

PERSONAL PERSPECTIVE

1. What was that experience like for you?

_____
_____
_____
_____
_____

2. What did you think/like/dislike about it?

_____
_____
_____
_____
_____

3. *Points of view:* What is your opinion of . . . ? How did you feel about . . . ? How did others feel?

_____

_____

_____

_____

_____

4. *Conclusion:* Summarize the main points of

_____

_____

_____

_____

_____

Can we conclude that . . . ?

_____

_____

_____

_____

_____

So you believe that . . . ?

_____

_____

_____

_____

_____

5. *Ending the interview:* You might say, "I was wondering if I missed anything important about. . . . Can you think of anything you'd like to add?"

_____

_____

_____

_____

_____

6. Before you say goodbye, thank your guest for his or her time and cooperation. Ask if he or she may be contacted if you have any additional questions.

_____

_____

_____

_____

_____

Phone: _____   E-mail: _____

How to Score More Points with Your Powerpoints

TIPS FOR IMPROVING YOUR MULTIMEDIA PRESENTATIONS

1. *Content* counts big time!

   - Begin by preparing a storyboard or use the program's outlining tool to help make sure your project is logically structured and that it effectively delivers your message.

   - Focus on your content. Make sure your presentation shows evidence of solid research and your own high level thought.

   - Know your message. What is the essential question? What is your thesis? Your audience does not need to know "everything you know about X."

   - Spelling errors look even worse when projected! Proofread like crazy.

   - Respect copyright by citing every piece of borrowed text, as well as every piece of media you use, other than copyright-free clip art. Unless items are cited throughout, the last slide should list your Works Cited, no matter how informal the presentation. Use only small portions of media elements. The Fair Use Guidelines for Educational Multimedia sets limits for the amount of borrowed material acceptable for use in student and teacher products.

2. Present powerfully! PowerPoint is most powerful in the hands of an effective speaker.

   - Practice! Rehearse even if it feels silly. Use family, friends, pets, as well as your mirror.

   - Engage your audience by making frequent eye contact.

   - Tell stories. Personal anecdotes and relevant examples are far more compelling than bullets, no matter how they fly in.

   - Grab your audience by starting with a hook—a powerful quote, story, anecdote, statistic, or a surprising fact.

   - Speak clearly and slowly. Avoid using slang and filler words (Uh . . . Ya know, etc.)

   - Look good. Dress appropriately. Dress like you care what others think.

   - Be flexible. Do not read straight from your notes and slides.

   - Keep it simple. Summarize rather than cram. Limit the number of points per slide, so the audience does not struggle, reading to keep up. Unless you are quoting, full sentences and paragraphs have no place in your presentation.

   - End with the exact point you want your audience to remember.

- Convey your own excitement and enthusiasm for your presentation. Consider every presentation as a valuable present, a gift for your audience. What you give them should change them in some way. There are no magic bullets.

3. *Design* matters

   - All graphic elements are messages. Your medium should match your message. Choose a consistent look that enhances rather than detracts from your theme. All slides and transitions should look as if they are part of the same presentation. Understand both your message and the audience and adjust your text and art accordingly. A presentation on the Holocaust would be destroyed with cute fonts and silly cartoons.

   - Use sounds and animations cautiously. They can distract from your message. Reserve multimedia for emphasizing important points.

   - All bullets should be readable from the back of the room. Check your font size. Check for text on the top and bottom of your slides. Combinations of upper- and lowercase letters are the most readable.

   - Create and use original art. Your own drawings and digital photographs pack far more punch than tired clip art. Why spend hours searching for the perfect image of a flower when you could far more effectively draw one or shoot one with a digital camera? If you must use clip art, consider combining it with other elements—for instance, incorporating clever thought bubbles.

4. Consult your teacher's rubric to make sure you understand exactly what he or she expects.

Library Visit Log

Name: _____ Teacher: _____

Class: _____ Date: _____

Progress Made during Today's Visit to the Library Information Center: _____
_____

Topic/Question/Tentative Thesis: _____
_____

Selected: ❑ Yes ❑ No   **Investigated:** ❑ Yes ❑ No

  1. Question(s) explored:

  2. Keywords/subject headings (original and new discoveries):

  3. New questions developed:

  4. Best sources found today:

  5. Databases and free Web search tools used:

  6. Plan for next visit:

  7. Evaluation of my efforts today:

E-mail Netiquette

- Be polite. Show respect for others and their feelings.

- Never reveal your personal address or phone number.

- Check your e-mail daily.

- Do not use inappropriate language.

- DO NOT SHOUT! (Using all capital letters is considered annoying and impolite.)

- Do not assume that your e-mail is private.

- Do not waste online time.

- Delete suspicious messages before you open them. Be aware of potential virus attachments.

- Delete any inappropriate e-mail promptly. Notify an adult if the mail is on the school server.

- Never impersonate another user. Never peek in the files of others.

- Think carefully before you hit the "send" command.

- Do not forward someone else's message without the writer's permission.

- Be aware that your humor may not be understood on the other end. Sarcasm is easily misinterpreted. Use smileys to be clear.

- Delete mail regularly.

- Keep messages short and to the point.

- When posting to a group, use clear subject lines.

- Thank people who take time out of their busy lives to help you.

Storyboard for a Multimedia Presentation

Name _____ Page no. _____

Slide/Card	Slide/Card/Image and/or Description	Story/Text/Source
#_____		
#_____		
#_____		

Search Planner

Brainstorming Keywords

Question/Thesis:

OR   +   OR   +   OR

OR   +   OR   +   OR

OR   +   OR   +   OR

OR   +   OR   +   OR

Databases to search:

Descriptors found while searching:

Synonyms/Related terms:

Broader/Narrower:

Proper nouns (names, places, organizations, companies):

Alternate spellings:

Preliminary/Working Thesis

Topic/Argument:

Topic/Argument:

Topic/Argument:

Evidence:

Evidence:

Evidence:

Working conclusion:

Promising Dewey (call) numbers:

Promising major websites:

Note Taker

Sheet # _____ Student _____ Teacher _____

Subject Heading/Question:

Idea/Subtopics	Detailed Notes, Exact Quotes, Evidence	Source #/Pages

Steps in Online Searching

Note: These steps are not necessarily performed in the following exact order but "interactively," as you revise your strategies and adapt them to your search results. You may need to go back to some questions several times.

1. **Identify the problem**
   a. Can I state my search problem in a clear question?
   b. What type of information do I need? (overview, scholarly, news, point of view, documents)
   c. How much information do I need? (term paper, essay, speech, definition)

2. **Select appropriate databases/search tools**
   a. Does it cover my subject?
   b. Does it contain the formats I need to answer my questions? (newspapers, magazines, primary sources, encyclopedia)
   c. Are there abstracts that help me decide if the text will be useful?
   d. Does it cover the time period I am interested in?
   e. Can I understand the information contained in it? (If I can't understand the abstracts, the full text may be even tougher!)
   f. Is it full text? If not, can I access the materials it indexes through interlibrary loans, other libraries, or fax?

3. **Brainstorm keywords**
   a. What are my major concepts?
   b. What synonyms, broader or narrower terms, or related ideas could I use?
   c. How will I express keywords with Boolean operators (AND, OR, NOT)?
   d. Should I be concerned about plurals or other forms of words? (Are there truncation or wildcard features?)
   e. Are there any proper names (people or places) that would focus my search?
   f. Should I adjust my strategy for a full-text database?
   g. Is there a thesaurus or controlled vocabulary?
   h. Are some words meaningless in this database? (for example, "company" in a business database)
   i. Have I spelled everything correctly?

4. **Subject vs. keyword search** (Subject directory vs. Search engine)
   a. Do I have more than one concept to search?
   b. Am I browsing for a topic or looking for a way to narrow a broad topic?
   c. Can I spell all the vocabulary correctly?
   d. Can I search by field?

5. **Refine the search online** (Searching is an interactive process!)

    a. Are my hits relevant, readable, accessible?

    b. Have I used all the strategies I planned to use?

    c. Have I tried different combinations of keywords?

    d. Should I use broader or narrower terms?

    e. Have I *mined* the most promising hits for better vocabulary (especially in the "subject" or "descriptor" fields)?

    f. Did I spell my search terms correctly?

    g. Do I need to ask the teacher-librarian information specialist for advice?

    h. Should I try another database?

    i. Is my topic really not "doable"? Should I consider another?

6. **Evaluate the search offline; examine that printout; ask, "What if?"**

    a. How relevant were my hits?

    b. Which of the hits are the best? (most relevant, timely, credible, readable, available, and promote the point of view I support)

    c. Which of my strategies worked best? Should I try them in another database?

    d. Are there additional keyword clues in my printouts?

    e. Did I select the best possible databases?

    f. What is my next step?

Big6 Organizer

Directions: Use this sheet as a worksheet to organize your project. It is intended to aid you in your research; not all questions require a written response.

1. Task Definition

What am I supposed to do?

What is the problem I need to solve?

What are the questions I should answer?

What type of information do I need?

How much information do I need?

Should I narrow my topic?

What will my finished product look like?

Notes:

2. Information-Seeking Strategies

What are my possible sources? Books, websites (portals, search engines, subject directories, subscription databases), periodicals, e-mail, interviews, television, video?

Which search tools and subscription databases should I use? Should I use the OPAC?

Which are the best sources?

Notes:

3. Location and Access

Where will I find my best resources?

Who can help me find the materials I need?

Can I mine the sources I have for alternate keywords?

Within my sources, how will I locate information? (Print: tables of contents, indexes, headings, subheadings, bold print, scanning text. Electronic: database strategies, keyword vs. subject, keyword identification, find on page, search within a search)

Should I investigate other libraries or use interlibrary loan?

Notes:

4. **Use of Information—reading, hearing, viewing, interacting**

    Which information is relevant?

    How will I record the information I find—note cards, organizers?

    What is the most logical structure for organizing what I have collected?

    Are there appropriate quotes? Paraphrases? Ideas to summarize?

    How will I give credit to my sources? Do I need permissions for Web publishing or broadcasting?

    Notes:

5. **Synthesis**

    How will I organize information from multiple sources?

    Can I eliminate information that does not answer my questions or help prove my thesis?

    How will I present the results of my research? Format? Structure?

    How will I make sure my own voice as a writer is heard?

    What conclusions have I made?

    Notes:

6. **Evaluation**

    Have I completed the requirements of the assignment?

    Is it logically organized, carefully proofread, ethically documented?

    How could I have improved the project? What will I do differently next time?

    Did I really answer the questions I posed?

    Did I use quality evidence to support my argument?

    How effective was my research process?

    How effective is my product?

    Is this my best work?

    Notes:

SOURCE: Adapted with permission from Michael B. Eisenberg and Robert E. Berkowitz, The Big6 Model. Big6 website http://www.big6.com.

Keyword Search Plan

Before you begin your search it is important to have a plan. Brainstorm your main concepts across, connected with "and." Synonyms and related terms ("ors") can be listed in the vertical columns.

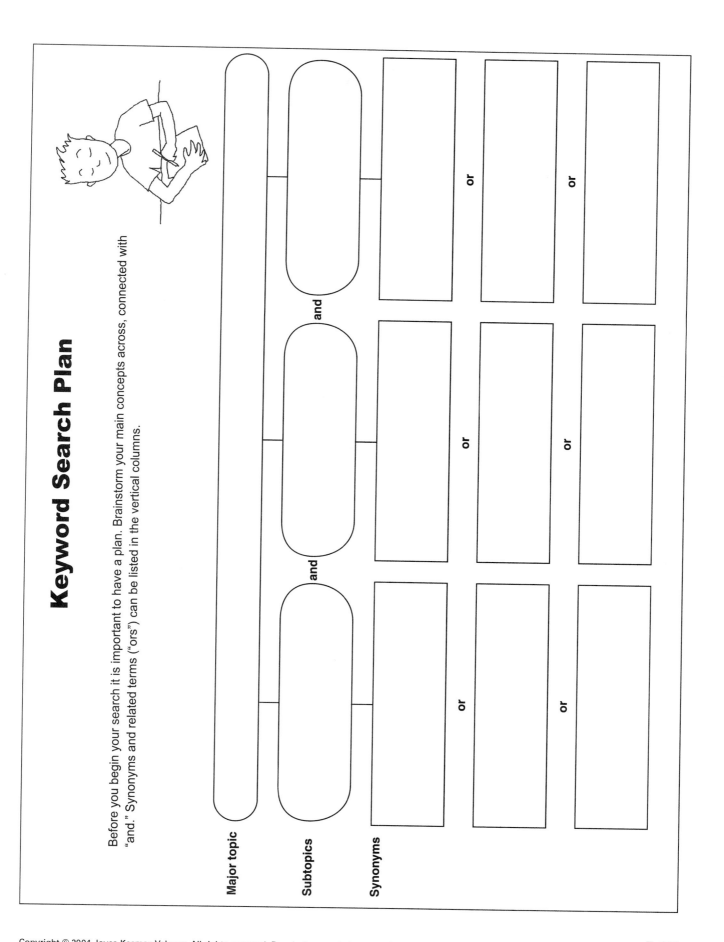

Major topic

Subtopics

Synonyms

and

and

or

or

or

or

or

or

Compare and Contrast Outline

Idea 1:

Idea 2:

How alike?

How
different?

Issue 1 ←→

Issue 2 ←→

Issue 3 ←→

Issue 4 ←→

Conclusion:

Time Line/Chronology

THEME:

Major dates:	Events:

Conclusion/Analysis:

Essay Outline

Thesis (statement of problem, grabber, or quote):

Introductory sentence: _____

Topic sentence	Supporting idea	Details

Conclusion (restate thesis, clincher):

Source Cards

Name _____

Source #

Magazine Article in an Online Database (Source Card)

Author(s) _____

Title of Article _____

Magazine _____

Date _____ Page nos. _____

Database Name _____ Publisher _____

Name of Providing Library, Consortium, or Library System _____

Date of Access _____

URL (shortened form) _____

Notes/Quotes _____

Author. "Article Title." <u>Periodical Title</u> Date of print publication (if available): pages. <u>Database Name (if any)</u>.
  Publisher (if appropriate). Name of Providing Library, Consortium, or Library System. Date of Access.
  <http://addressofdatabase>.

- -

Source #

Name _____

Reference Article in an Online Database (Source Card)

Author(s) _____

Title of Article _____

Book Title/Original Source _____

City of Publication _____ Publisher _____ Date of Publication _____

Page nos. _____

Database Name _____

Publisher _____

Name of Providing Library, Consortium, or Library System _____

Date of Access _____

URL (shortened form) _____

Notes/Quotes _____

Author (if provided). "Article Title." <u>Specific Database/Reference Work on Larger Database</u>. Date. <u>Title of
  Database or Online Service</u>. Publisher (if appropriate). Name of Providing Library, Consortium, or Library
  System. Date of Access. <http://addressofdatabase>.

Source Cards 2

Source #

Name _____

General Web Site (Source Card)

Author(s) if noted _____

Title of Page or Document _____

Title of Larger Site _____

Date of Electronic Publication/Last update/Posting _____

Name of Any Associated Institution _____

Date of Access _____

URL _____

Notes/Quotes _____

_____

Author. "Title of Page." <u>Title of Larger Site</u>. Date of Publication. Name of Associated Institution. Date of Access.
    <http://addressofsite>.

- -

Source #

Name _____

Online Image/Sound/Video Clip (Source Card)

Artist/Creator (if noted) _____

Description or Title of Media _____

Date image/sound/clip was created _____

(Online image/Online sound/Online videoclip) _____

Date of Electronic Publication/Last update/Posting _____

Title of Larger Site _____

Date of Access _____

URL _____

Notes _____

Author. "Description or Title of Media." Date created. Online image/sound/videoclip. <u>Title of Larger Site</u>. Name
    of Providing Library, Consortium, or Library System (if from a database). Date of Access.
    <http://addressofsite>.

Source Cards 3

Name _____

Source #

Book (Source Card)

Author(s) _____

Title _____

City of Publication _____ Publisher _____

Publication Date _____

Notes/Quotes _____

_____

_____

Author(s). "Title." City of Publication: Publisher, Date.

- -

Source #

Name _____

CD-ROM, Diskette, DVD (Source Card)

Author(s) _____

Title of Article/Document/Part of Work _____

Title of Product _____

Editor/Compiler/Translator (if appropriate) _____

Publication Medium (CD-ROM, diskette, DVD) Edition or Release _____

City of Publication _____ Publisher _____ Date of Publication _____

Notes _____

_____

_____

Author (if provided). "Article/Document Title." Title of Product. Ed. John Smith. CD-ROM. 2004 ed. Date. Title of Database or Online Service. Publisher. Date of Access. <addressofdatabase>.

Note Cards

Subtopic: **Source #**   **Page(s) #**

Notes/Quotes:

Name: _____   **Class:** _____

Subtopic: **Source #**   **Page(s) #**

Notes/Quotes:

Name: _____   **Class:** _____

Power Searching Tips for the Web and Online Databases

If you are not happy with your results, try another search engine, check your spelling, or try synonyms or related, broader, or narrower terms. *Mine* your results for new keywords. By all means, use some strategy. Though they have many quirks, most engines allow users the following advanced techniques. Check the "search tips," "cheat sheet," or "help" pages of your favorite search tools for the proper way to express these strategies. Remember: You can use these strategies more easily in the advanced search screens.

Boolean Operator/ Strategy	Why You'll Use It

+
AND
all the words
 	
	limits your search, requiring that all words appear
	    Vietnam AND protest AND students
	    +Japan +cooking
	    +eagles +habitat +endangered
	In Google, use + to include common words overlooked by search engines
	A growing number of search engines assume an AND. You still need to express AND in databases!

OR
any of the words
~
 	
	is used to capture synonyms or related words
	    car OR automobile
	    coronary OR heart
	    Google uses ~ to expresses synonyms

-
NOT
AND NOT
exclude
 	
	eliminates possibilities that will cause problem results
	    Martin Luther NOT King
	    + eagles -Philadelphia -football

(Most search engines allow you to use "+" and "-" for AND and NOT. These characters must appear immediately before your search terms. Do not separate them with spaces.) Some search engines allow you to exclude words in their advanced search screens.	

Wildcards, Truncation, Stemming	Many search tools allow you to use an asterisk (*) to stand for any character or string of characters. This method is especially useful if you are uncertain of spelling or if you want to pick up various forms of a word or word endings.
	    teen* (picks up teenage, teenagers, or teens)
	    Herz* (for Herzegovina)

Phrases	Very often you will want words to appear together in specific order. Quotation marks (" ") set words off as phrases to be searched as a whole. A great strategy for names and titles too!
	    "vitamin A"
	    "raisin in the sun"
	    "George Washington Carver"

Proximity	Words are often not meaningful in a search unless they appear near each other in a document. In large documents, words separated by lots of text are generally unrelated.
	NEAR/25 specifies that two words appear within 25 words of each other (Used in AltaVista and AOL Search)
	Eric Clapton NEAR/10 Cream
Field Searching	This strategy restricts searches to certain portions of Web documents. It allows you to specify that search terms appear, for instance, in the title or URL of your results. (Used in a variety of ways in AltaVista, Alltheweb, and Google and often easier to use in the advanced screen.)
	title: cancer
	URL: epa
	domain: edu + "graphic organizers"
	inurl: nasa (used in Google)
	filetype: pdf
Case Sensitivity	Most search engines are case *insensitive* by default; that is, they treat upper- and lowercase letters the same. However, there are some that recognize uppercase and lowercase variations. It is good practice to search using lowercase letters unless you have a specific strategy in mind. In *case sensitive* search tools:
	Baker (retrieves name and eliminates most references to cake and bread makers)
	AIDS (eliminates reference to helpers)
	China (eliminates references to dishes)
Combining Strategies	Check to see if the search tool allows you to combine strategies. For instance, you might find it helpful to combine Boolean operators. Use ( ) to nest, or group your ORs and ANDs in more sophisticated searching. Like in algebra, what's in parentheses gets processed first.
	+dolphins +(behavior OR behaviour) -miami
	Sample using Google syntax:
	inurl: nasa +saturn
Searching within Your Search	If you have a long result list, and even if you don't, you might choose to search for targeted words within your search. Several search engines offer a handy feature to help you narrow your result lists. After you perform your first search, look for a "search within results" feature. If no such feature exists, you can use your browser's own "find" feature to search within each page.
Natural Language Searches	Some search engines (Ask Jeeves or IxQuick, for instance) allow you to type questions as you would think or speak them.
	"Why is the sky blue?"

TIP ABOUT TIPS

Every search engine is slightly different. For instance, Google uses an automatic AND. Some search engines allow for "natural language" searching. Remember to carefully read the "tips page" of the search tools you use most frequently. These pages discuss the syntax, or the specific search language, used by that particular search engine or directory.

URLs as Clues to Content

How can I assess the validity of a source in my result list?

You can use the end, or suffix of a domain name, to help you judge the validity of the information and the potential bias of a website.

Remember, this strategy is only a guideline. People can easily purchase domains that do not reflect their actual purpose

- .com=commercial sites (vary in their credibility)
- .gov=U.S. government site
- .org=organization, often nonprofit. (Some .orgs have strong bias and agendas)
- .edu=school or university site (Was it created by a K–12 class? By a college student? By a university department? By a scholar?)
- .store=retail business
- .int=international institution
- .ac=educational institution, usually higher education (like .edu)
- .mil=U.S. military site
- .net=networked service provider, Internet administrative site
- .museum=museum
- .name=individual Internet user
- .biz=a business
- .pro=professional's site
- ~=personal site (Be a little suspicious of personal sites. They are not endorsed by the institution on whose server they reside. For example, many college students have personal websites posted on their college's site.)

If the page you are on gives few clues about its value, truncate (or cut back) the URL to each of the next slash marks to see where the site originates.

Also be on the lookout for sponsored, or paid results. The creators of these sites pay to have their sites listed more prominently in search engine results.

Be wary of documents from free hosting sites: Geocities, AOL Members, and Tripod. Recognized institutions generally host reliable sites and professionals tend to pay for their Web hosting services. Your teacher will likely question such sites in your works-cited pages.

Presentations

(All presentations are in PowerPoint format. If you do not own the applications, they may be viewed but not edited in free downloadable viewer format.)

6-A   Teacher-Librarians and School Libraries: A Field Guide

       Audience: School Boards, Administrators, Parents

6-B   What Is Plagiarism? (And Why You Should Care!)

       Audience: Students, Teachers

6-C   Never-Ending Search: What You Really Need to Know about Online Searching and Search Tools!

       Audience: Students, Teachers

6-D   Thoughtful Research: Moving beyond the Topic

       Audience: Students, Parents

6-E   Uncovering the Invisible Web

       Audience: Students, Teachers, Parents

6-F   Hey There! Have You Evaluated?

       Audience: Students, Teachers, Parents

As teacher-librarians we are always presenting. We are teaching, in-servicing, advocating, communicating evidence. These presentations are generally too lengthy for most occasions. Use the slides you really need. Personalize the presentations for your unique audiences. Use your own digital photographs to tell the local story. Use my notes if you need to add "patter" to the show. They suggest questions for audience interaction. Feel free to include your own notes. Add and delete slides. Go forth and communicate powerfully!

6-A
Teacher-Librarians and School Libraries: A Field Guide

This presentation is useful for those constituents who might be less aware of the library's role in the learning culture of the school. Purposely light on illustrations, this presentation would be particularly effective using photographs displaying your own facility at its best and busiest!

Note: This presentation is too long for most purposes. Delete slides that do not add meaning for your particular audience.

6-B
What Is Plagiarism? (And Why You Should Care!)

If your school is concerned about developing a climate of academic integrity, this presentation will help you define *plagiarism*, present a strong rationale for ethical behavior in the face of a culture that promotes cheating, and offer students review materials to clarify how and when to document. For teachers, the last several slides offer tips on preventing and detecting classroom plagiarism. You may combine this with the model Academic Integrity Policy for Student Research (2-8), the Cheating and Plagiarism Survey (3-8), MLA Bibliographic Style: A Brief Guide (4-5), and several of the other documentation tools in chapter 4.

6-C
Never-Ending Search: What You Really Need to Know about Online Searching and Search Tools!

Though most students and teachers feel very confident about their abilities to search the Web, they may not be aware of all their options. This presentation introduces (or reinforces) search strategies and the importance of choosing the right search tool for a particular information task. Further information is provided in Search Tool Species: A Field Guide (4-23) and Visualizing the Search Process (4-32).

6-D
Thoughtful Research: Moving beyond the Topic

This little "pep talk" encourages students to move beyond topical research, to ask good questions, and to develop strong thesis statements. Students are guided through criteria and five tests for a solid thesis. This presentation would work to explain to parents the shift away from report writing to your school's expectations for more thoughtful, inquiry-driven work. Further advice for parents is offered in A Letter to Parents: Ch-ch-ch-ch-changes . . . (1-4), and much more thesis support is located in chapters 4 and 5.

6-E
Uncovering the Invisible Web

How many of your classroom teachers and students reach beyond their search engine of choice in their quest for information? With so many in search engine ruts, the teacher-librarian must remind constituents of their searching options and promote some of the tools they can use to dig a little deeper. This presentation is also designed to help promote your high-quality subscription databases and to help students uncover the secrets of the Invisible Web.

6-F
Hey There! Have You Evaluated?

This presentation reviews the criteria students should consider as they evaluate cites to visit from their results lists and as they evaluate documents for inclusion in their works cited pages. More support in helping students evaluate sources is presented in Use CARRDSS to Help You Evaluate Your Sources! (4-13), Web Page Evaluation Checklist (4-15), Why Should I Take This Author Seriously? (4-16), and Ask Yourself Questions As You Evaluate the Information You Find on the Web . . . (5-6).

Teacher–Librarians and School Libraries: A Field Guide

①

Why a field guide?

②

Libraries and librarians are evolving!

③

Many educators and administrators have not seen a working model of today's dynamic, wired library media center!

④

Today's Library Information Center

* The "brain" of the school
* The center of engaged, active, authentic, inquiry-driven learning
* Where information professionals, with educational credentials, teach critical 21st century skills

⑤

Habitat

* School building
* But *the library* is not just a place!
* The library's virtual reach is extensive (anywhere, anytime through its Web presence!)
* This reach may be long-lasting, and demonstrated in:
  – Love of reading, viewing, listening
  – Lifelong, transferable skills relating to information literacy and critical thinking

⑥

The teacher-librarian is critical in the learning ecosystem!

(7)

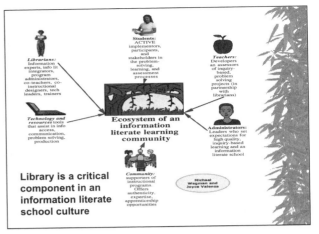

Library is a critical component in an information literate school culture

Ecosystem of an information literate learning community

Michael Wagman and Joyce Valenza

(8)

Changes in the learning ecosystem are supported by the evolved library media center!

* Explosion in information and communication technologies
* Brain research (multiple intelligences)
* Constructivism--students creating knowledge
* Standards, learning outcomes, evidence-based practice
* Differentiating learning
* Inquiry-based, resource-based, project/problem-based, interdisciplinary learning, driven by essential questions

(9)

The teacher-librarian is the *point person* for:

* Knowledge of the whole curriculum
* Teaching of literacies for all media
* Intellectual property / fair use guidance
* Effective pedagogical strategies
* Intellectual freedom: assuring access to information
* Technology integration
* Reviews / suggestions of software and print resources for content areas
* Literature in all formats

(10)

What goes on in today's library information center?

Students:
* discover, engage in, discuss, and borrow literature in traditional and emerging formats
* learn to effectively use ideas and information
* use information technologies to access, evaluate, and communicate information

(11)

What does this habitat look like?

On any given day you might see students . . .

(12)

- Preparing multimedia presentations and websites
- Learning how to improve their Web searches
- Using high quality subscription databases, highlighted on the library website
- Learning how to evaluate information sources
- Learning how to ethically document resources
- Defending a thesis in a thoughtful presentation
- Reading books, browsing through magazines, viewing DVDs, listening to audio-books

⑬

Teacher-Librarians, guided by National and State standards, ensure:

- Students develop information literacy skills
- Students know how to use current technology applications
- Equity! That all students have guidance and access (physical, intellectual, and flexible) to high-quality information sources on- and offline

⑭

Library Media Centers are where skills are *applied!*

School libraries are where the rubber meets the road—

Where all the technology skills learned in computer labs, where all the process skills learned in language arts, are *applied* in research and communication efforts.

⑮

Are librarians an unnecessary expense in a digital information landscape?

NO!

⑯

Why not?

A good teacher-librarian is one of the best educational bargains in town!

⑰

In a wired school, teacher-librarians are Information specialists:

- *website developers*
- *partners in creating instruction— on- and offline*
- *database experts*
- *upholders of intellectual freedom*
- *protectors of intellectual property*
- *technology leaders and scouts*
- *trainers and integrators*

⑱

The Internet cannot replace libraries.

* The boxes and wires we put in our classrooms and labs will have little meaning unless information professionals select quality resources for them.

* Information technology has little value unless we teach students how to effectively and ethically locate, analyze, evaluate, synthesize and communicate information.

⑲

But, a librarian cannot do it alone!

But I am really good!

Even if he or she is really good!
Process standards must be integrated and assessed across disciplines and grade levels.

⑳

It takes a village!

Teacher–Librarian

Principal

Dept. chairs

Tech Director

Classroom Teachers

Community

To raise an information literate child!

School Library Journal, Nov. 2002

㉑

How do you recognize the evolved teacher-librarian in action?

㉒

Roles of this species:

* Promoters of literacy
* Information professionals
* Program administrators
* Instructional partners

㉓

As promoters of literacy, teacher-librarians:

* Advocate for intellectual freedom, (intellectual, physical, flexible access for learners)
* Motivate students to pursue individual reading interests
* Maintain lively interesting collections designed to meet the needs of all learners
* Promote lifelong learning
* Encourage professional and curricular reading and learning

㉔

As information professionals, teacher-librarians:

* Integrate technology and information literacy into the whole-school curriculum through curriculum design and direct instruction!
* Teach information skills critical in an information-rich landscape
* Use expertise in information management, and selection, storage, retrieval, and evaluation of electronic resources and service
* Train teachers and students to use new and emerging information technologies
* Model legal guidelines and information ethics
* Are human links between technology and knowledge

(25)

As Program Administrators, teacher-librarians:

* Provide management expertise, planning, and evaluation
* Advocate for the library program and for the learners it impacts
* Have the knowledge, vision, and leadership to steer the program creatively and energetically in the twenty-first century

(26)

As Instructional Partners, teacher-librarians:

* Collaborate with teachers to design authentic learning tasks and assessments required to meet subject area standards
* Teach literacy skills for all media
* Analyze learning and information needs and acquire resources to meet those needs
* Provide curricular leadership in information literacy
* Design professional development
* Function as critical member of the curriculum and technology teams

(27)

Born Free?

* A teacher-librarian's contribution (evolution) is hindered when he or she is tied to clerical duties and regular *coverages*
* Libraries should not be an opportunity to schedule teachers' prep.
* To create effective library programs, administrators must allow librarians to function as professionals by providing support staff and by scheduling classes around **students' needs** rather than **teacher planning time.**

(28)

Endangered status

* Teacher-librarians have been threatened in several states, despite evidence of their importance to the ecosystem
* Situation especially critical in poor, urban areas

(29)

It's a national problem:

[It's a] "form of theft that is too often irreversible . . . It is a conscious act of social demarcation: a shameful way of building barriers around a child's mind, of starving intellect, of amputating dreams."

Jonathan Kozol in *Ordinary Resurrections,* on New York City Schools dismantling its school libraries.

(30)

Research shows:

Strong school library programs have a measurable impact on student achievement

A well-supported school library media center, with an integrated curriculum, is likely to raise reading achievement scores by 10–20 percent.

Based on findings of LRS School Library Media Impact Studies http://www.lrs.org/

③①

Research also shows:

* Professionally-staffed, well-stocked, and well-funded library media programs are critical to the success of schools in helping every child to learn.
* Successful schools are those whose library media specialists exercise a strong leadership role, integrate library media resources into a standards-based curriculum, and most importantly, collaborate with classroom teachers.
* The more time library media specialists are able to spend teaching teachers as well as students to make more effective use of information resources, the more successful the school will be.

"Librarians, Teachers & Principals Agree." Fast Facts: Recent Statistics from the Library Research Service. ED3/110.10/No. 178. July 1, 2001.

③②

School libraries are key to learning!

The largest study of its kind to date revealed:

* 99.4 percent of students indicated that the school library and its services help them learn.
* Libraries are dynamic rather than passive agents of learning
* The school library has a strong role "as an agent for individualized learning, knowledge construction and academic achievement."

2004 Ohio study Ross Todd and Carol Kuhlthau http://www.oelma.org/SLFindings.html

③③

Libraries count!

Effective library media programs—when led by **active, involved** librarians—can have a discernible positive impact on student achievement *regardless of student, school and community demographics.*

Hartzell, Gary. "Why Should Principals Support School Libraries?" EDO-IR-2002-06. Nov. 2002.

③④

Outlook for survival of the species

* Some school librarians will thrive!
  – Critical to the ecosystem
  – Find resources and support
  – Information literate school culture valued by instructional team
* Some will fade
  – Not critical to the ecosystem
  – Unsupported
  – Undervalued by instructional team

③⑤

So, what is the future of the species?

Choose your own scenario!

③⑥

Future School Scenario 1

* Library services are under/unfunded, undervalued
* Students and teachers use *free* Web exclusively
* No one advocates for students' broad physical and intellectual access to information
* No one visits library. Print is not valued
* Information skills are not taught or valued

Result:
Students go off to college or workforce unprepared to effectively locate, evaluate, analyze, use, communicate information

 37

Future School Scenario 2

* Teachers and students recognize need for information skills instruction across curriculum
* Students and teachers use library's online databases and presentation resources
* School library webpage is dynamic and essential to student success
* School librarian is key trainer in development of online instruction
* Teachers value and assess process skills: information gathering, evaluation, synthesis, ethical use

Result:
Learners graduate fully prepared to effectively locate, evaluate, analyze, use information in an information-rich world!

 38

Teacher-librarians:

* Help learners learn!
* Help teachers teach!
* Manage knowledge and learning!
* Are the human links between technology and learning

 39

"What a school thinks about its library is a measure of what it thinks about education."

Harold Howe, former U.S. Commissioner of Education

 40

For more information on the library's impact on student achievement:

* **Library Research Service**
  – http://www.lrs.org/
* ***Information Power: Nine Information Literacy Standards for Student Learning***
  – http://www.ala.org/aasl/ip_nine.html
* **Colorado and Texas studies by Lance, Loertscher and Smith, summarized in: Hartzell, Gary. "Why Should Principals Support School Libraries?" EDO-IR-2002-06. Nov. 2002.**
* **Library Research Service**
  – http://www.lrs.org/School_lib.html

 41

Further Sources

Lance, Keith Curry. *Proof of the Power: Recent Research on the Impact of School Library Media Programs on the Academic Achievement of U.S. Public School Students.* ERIC Digest. (ERIC Document Reproduction Service No. ED 456 861), 2001.
  – http://ericit.org/digests/EDO-IR-2001-05.pdf

Lance, K. C., and David Loertscher. *Powering Achievement: School Library Media Programs Make a Difference –The Evidence.* San Jose, CA: Hi Willow, 2001.

Lowe, Carrie. The Role of the School Library Media Specialist in the 21st Century. ERIC Digest. (ERIC Document Reproduction Service No. ED 446 769). 2000.
  – http://ericit.org/digests/EDO-IR-2000-08.sht

 42

1

What is plagiarism?

(And why you should care!)

2

Definition:

Plagiarism is the act of presenting the words, ideas, images, sounds, or the creative expression of others as your own.

3

How serious is the problem?

"A study of almost 4,500 students at 25 schools, suggests cheating is . . . a significant problem in high school — 74% of the respondents admitted to one or more instances of serious test cheating and **72% admitted to serious cheating on written assignments. Over half of the students admitted they have engaged in some level of plagiarism on written assignments using the Internet.**"

Based on the research of Donald L. McCabe, Rutgers University

Source: "CAI Research." Center for Academic Integrity, Duke University, 2003 <http://academicintegrity.org/cai_research.asp>.

4

Students. If:

- you have copied, included, downloaded, the words and ideas of others in your work that you neglected to cite,
- you have had help you wouldn't want your teacher to know about,

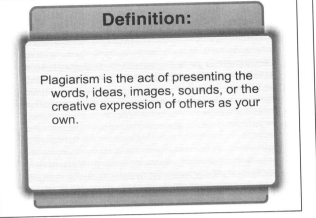

5

Two types of plagiarism:

- **Intentional**
  - Copying a friend's work
  - Buying or borrowing papers
  - Cutting and pasting blocks of text from electronic sources without documenting
  - Media "borrowing" without documentation
  - Web publishing without permissions of creators

- **Unintentional**
  - Careless paraphrasing
  - Poor documentation
  - Quoting excessively
  - Failure to use your own "voice"

6

Excuses

Rationale for academic integrity (as if it were necessary!)

- When you copy you cheat yourself. You limit your own learning.
- The consequences are not worth the risks!
- It is only right to give credit to authors whose ideas you use
- Citing gives authority to the information you present
- Citing makes it possible for your readers to locate your source
- Education is not an "us vs. them" game! It's about learning to learn!
- Cheating is unethical behavior

Is your academic reputation valuable to you?

Real life consequences:

- Damaged the reputation of two prominent historians, Stephen Ambrose and Doris Kearns Goodwin,
  - Kearns left television position and stepped down as Pulitzer Prize judge for "lifting" 50 passages for her 1987 book *The Fitzgeralds and the Kennedys* (Lewis)
- Senator Joseph Biden dropped his 1987 campaign for the Democratic presidential nomination. (Sabato)
  - Copied in law school and borrowed from campaign speeches of Robert Kennedy
- Boston Globe journalist Mike Barnicle forced to resign for plagiarism in his columns ("Boston Columnist . . .")
- Probe of plagiarism at UVA — 45 students dismissed, 3 graduate degrees revoked
  - *CNN Article* AP. 26 Nov. 2001
  - *Channel One Article* AP. 27 Nov. 2002

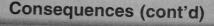

Consequences (cont'd)

- *New York Times* senior reporter Jayson Blair forced to resign after being accused of plagiarism and fraud.

  "The newspaper said at least 36 of the 73 articles he had written had problems with accuracy, calling the deception a "low point" in the newspaper's history."

  "New York Times Exposes Fraud of Own Reporter."
  ABC News Online. 12 May 2003.
  http://www.pbs.org/newshour/newshour_index.html

Consequences (cont'd)

A controversial New Jersey valedictorian was denied her seat as a Harvard freshman when it was discovered she plagiarized in a local newspaper.

Possible school consequences:

- "0" on the assignment
- Parent notification
- Referral to administrators
- Suspension or dismissal from school activities — sports and extracurricular
- Note on student record
- Loss of reputation in the school community

Is this important?

What if:
- Your architect cheated his way through math class. Will your new home be safe?
- Your lawyer paid for a copy of the bar exam to study. Will the contract she wrote for you stand up in court?
- The accountant who does your taxes hired someone to write his papers and paid a stand-in to take his major tests? Does he know enough to complete your tax forms properly?

(Lathrop and Foss 87)

(13)

Nope!

- Facts that are widely known, or
- Information or judgments considered "common knowledge"

Do **NOT** have to be documented.

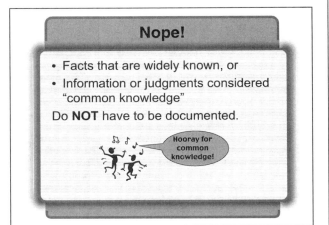

(14)

Examples of common knowledge

- John Adams was our second president.
- The Japanese attacked Pearl Harbor on December 7, 1941.

  If you see a fact in five or more sources, and you are fairly certain your readers already know this information, it is likely to be "common knowledge."

  But when in doubt, cite!

(15)

No need to document when:

- You are discussing your own experiences, observations, or reactions
- Compiling the results of original research, from science experiments, etc.

(16)

What's the big deal?

(17)

You can "borrow" from the works of others in your own work!

(18)

Use these three strategies,

- Quoting
- Paraphrasing
- Summarizing

But make sure you blend
source materials in with your own.
Make sure your own voice is heard.

 19

Quoting

Quotations are the exact words of an author, copied directly from a source, word for word. Quotations must be cited!

Use quotations when:
- You want to add the power of an author's words to support your argument
- You want to disagree with an author's argument
- You want to highlight particularly eloquent or powerful phrases or passages
- You are comparing and contrasting specific points of view
- You want to note the important research that precedes your own

Carol Rohrbach and Joyce Valenza

20

Paraphrasing

Paraphrasing means rephrasing the words of an author, putting his/her thoughts in your own words. When you paraphrase, you rework the source's ideas, words, phrases, and sentence structures with your own. Like quotations, paraphrased material must be followed with in-text documentation and cited on your Works-Cited page.

Paraphrase when:
- You plan to use information on your note cards and wish to avoid plagiarizing
- You want to avoid overusing quotations
- You want to use your own voice to present information

Carol Rohrbach and Joyce Valenza

 21

Summarizing

- **Summarizing involves putting the main idea(s) of one or several writers into your own words, including only the main point(s). Summaries are significantly shorter than the original and take a broad overview of the source material. Again, it is necessary to attribute summarized ideas to their original sources.**

Summarize when:
- You want to establish background or offer an overview of a topic
- You want to describe knowledge (from several sources) about a topic
- You want to determine the main ideas of a single source

Carol Rohrbach and Joyce Valenza

22

As you take notes:

- Include any direct quotes or unique phrases in quotation marks or mark with a big **Q** and make sure the speaker's/writer's name is identified.
- Make sure you note a paraphrase with the writer's name and mark it with a big **P**
- Include page numbers and source references so you can go back and check for accuracy as you write.

 23

In-text / in-project MLA documentation

- Purpose — to give immediate source information without interrupting the flow of paper or project.
- The academic world takes in-text documentation seriously.
- Inaccurate documentation is as serious as having no documentation at all.
- Brief information in in-text documentation should match full source information in Works Cited

24

Use in-text / in-project documentation when:

- You use an original idea from one of your sources, whether you quote or paraphrase it
- You summarize original ideas from one of your sources
- You use factual information that is not common knowledge (Cite to be safe.)
- You quote directly from a source
- You use a date or fact that might be disputed

25

How do I cite using MLA style?

- Parenthetical citations are usually placed at the end of a sentence, before the period, but they may be placed in the middle of sentence
- Cite the author's last name and the page number
- In the absence of an author, cite the title and the page number
- If you are using more than one book by the same author, list the last name, comma, the title, and the page
- If you identify the author and title in the text, just list the page number

26

But, what about the Web?

When citing a Web source in text, you are not likely to have page numbers. Just include the first part of the entry.

(Valenza)

or

("Plagiarism and the Web")

27

Typical example:

"Slightly more than 73% of Happy High School students reported plagiarizing papers sometime in their high school careers" (Smith 203).

For more information and specific examples see our school's Research Guide

28

Remember:

- Your teacher knows your work
- Your teachers discuss student work with each other
- Your teacher checks suspicious work against search engines and other student papers
- We expect honesty from our students

29

This next section is for teachers!

30

A list of paper mills

http://www.coastal.edu/library/mills2.htm

(31)

Preventing plagiarism

- Set a climate where academic integrity is valued
- Design thoughtful assignments
- Set up checkpoints throughout the process
  - Drafts, outlines, organizers, preliminary Works Cited
- Keep portfolios of student writing
- Vary assignments and topic suggestions each semester
- Describe the degree to which collaboration is acceptable to your students
- Require an annotated bibliography
- Shorter papers are okay

(32)

Preventing Plagiarism (cont'd)

- Make sure students understand what plagiarism is and how you expect them to document
- Make sure students know how seriously you personally take plagiarism as a violation of your trust and school and class rules of conduct.
- Make sure you are aware of how students plagiarize
- Make sure students know that you check for plagiarism

(33)

Prevention

- Ask for outlines and drafts
- Have students present research orally
- Ask the student under suspicion to read one or two difficult paragraphs and explain
- Have students present and defend their research orally
- Ask for photocopies of "best" sources

(Lathrop and Foss 163–166)

(34)

Prevention

- Require specific components
- Require drafts prior to due dates
- Require oral defense or presentation
- Include annotated bibliography
- Require up-to-date references
- Require a "meta-learning" essay in class after papers have been submitted

(Lathrop and Foss 194–195)

(35)

When you suspect plagiarism

- Ask librarian for help (other sources beyond free web)
- Pick an unusual string of words and search on Google, All the Web, AltaVista
  - "five or six words in quotation marks"
- Ask the student why certain phrases or words were used, or to identify location of a specific fact.
- Check to see if all citations are listed in Works Cited
- Check for inconsistencies in font, bibliographic format, text size, layout, and question them
- Does the paper not exactly match the assignment?
- Chat with other teachers about the student's work

(Lathrop and Foss 163–166, 194–195)

(36)

When you suspect plagiarism 2

- Ask to see drafts, outlines, etc. (Ask students to save them in advance!)
- Compare to other student work. Look for vocabulary, variation in sentence length, etc.
- Make a copy of a section, cut it into paragraphs and ask student to reassemble
- Discuss the paper. Ask student to defend opinions. Why he or she chose that specific evidence
- Ask student to read aloud paragraphs with unusual vocabulary or scholarly terms. Note fluency. Have student explain or paraphrase
- Does writing shift styles, especially in the middle?
- Ask where some items in the bibliography were located
- Ask student to relocate sources
- Ask why no recent sources were cited

(Lathrop and Foss 163–166)

(37)

Works Cited

"Boston Columnist Resigns Amid New Plagiarism Charges." *CNN.com* 19 Aug. 1998. 3 March 2003. <http://www.cnn.com/US/9808/19/barnicle/>

Fain, Margaret. "Internet Paper Mills." Kimbal Library. 12 Feb. 2003. <http://www.coastal.edu/library/mills2.htm>

Lathrop, Ann and Kathleen Foss. *Student Cheating and Plagiarism in the Internet Era.* Englewood, CO: Libraries Unlimited, 2000.

Lewis, Mark. "Doris Kearns Goodwin And The Credibility Gap." *Forbes.com* 2 Feb. 2002. <http://www.forbes.com/2002/02/27/0227goodwin.html>

"New York Times Exposes Fraud of own Reporter." ABC News Online. 12 May 2003. <http://www.pbs.org/newshour/newshour_index.html>

Sabato, Larry J. "Joseph Biden's Plagiarism; Michael Dukakis's 'Attack Video' – 1988." *Washington Post Online.* 1998. 3 March 2002. <http://www.washingtonpost.com/wpsrv/politics/special/clinton/frenzy/biden.htm>

(38)

Neverending Search:

What you really need
to know about
online searching
and search tools!

①

Search, don't surf!

It's a trillion page Web!

②

We already know how to use the Web!

Just because you *live* on the Web, doesn't mean you can't learn how to use it more effectively and more powerfully!

③

Effective searching

Brainstorming/ Questioning/ Planning

Understanding strategy/ syntax

Choosing the right type of search tool

Staying up to date

Evaluating results!

④

Four tips: FSRE (for sure?)

- **Focus**—What is your mission or question?

- **Strategize**—Which search tools will you use? Which keywords and search terms will you use and how will you express them?

- **Refine**—How might I improve my search results?

- **Evaluate**—Which results will you visit? Which sites or documents are worthy enough to use? Did I do good work?

⑤

Good searchers also:

- Use peripheral vision—they *mine* their results for additional search terms
- Consult several search tools
- Make use of advanced search screens
- Search the free Web and subscription databases
- Use appropriate syntax (the language specific to the search tool they are using)
- Use search strategies
- Modify or refine their searches (Searching is recursive!)

⑥

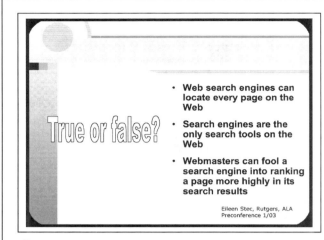

(7)

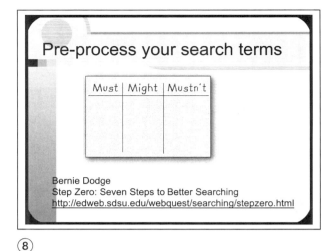

(8)

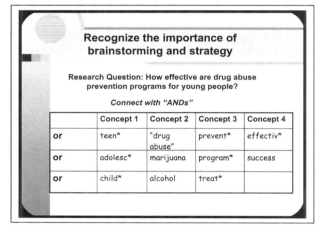

(9)

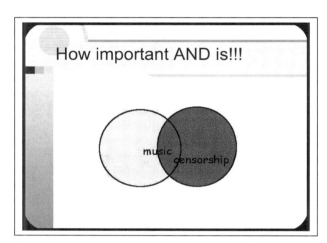

(10)

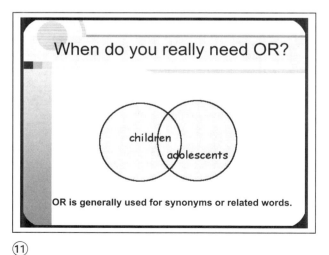

(11)

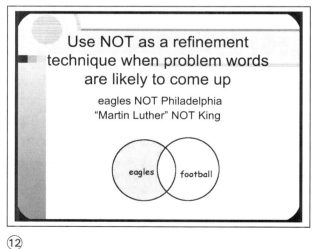

(12)

Rockwell Schrock's Boolean Machine

http://kathyschrock.net/rbs3k/boolean/

⑬

Let's play Boolean Aerobics!

- Stand up if you have brown hair AND brown eyes
- Remain standing if you have brown hair AND brown eyes AND are wearing glasses
- Remain standing if you have brown hair AND brown eyes AND are wearing glasses AND are wearing something blue

⑭

"Phrase searching"

- One of your best searching tools!
- Use only for legitimate phrases, names, titles
  - "vitamin A"
  - "John Quincy Adams"
  - Titles "An Officer and a Gentleman"
- Phrase searching is sometimes overused: Remember: not every group of words is a phrase
- Sometimes "ANDing" or "NEARing" are better strategies

⑮

Advanced Search Screens

- Google
- All the Web
- AltaVista
- HotBot

⑯

Tricks for advanced searchers seeking a needle in a haystack

- Word stemming:
  - wom*n
  - lesson* NEAR plan*
- Search within
  - Google, AlltheWeb
  - Also use "find" to search within a page full of text!
- Field Searching
  - Search for keywords in titles, subject tags, file formats rather than just words anywhere in the text
- Search Engine Features Chart
  http://searchenginewatch.com/facts/ataglance.html

⑰

Field searching is usually easier in the Advanced Search area

- title:
- Link check (Google, AltaVista) Helps in evaluating sites!
  - link:mciu.org/~spjvweb
- Media or filetype:pdf or ppt (Google) Great for finding documents, papers, and presentations!
- domain:
  - domain:jp +edu

⑱

Just as I wouldn't ask my contractor friend to prepare my will, I wouldn't ask my lawyer friend to build my new kitchen.

Search tools have specialties too.

(19)

A hammer won't do it all . . .

(20)

"People who are only good with hammers see every problem as a nail."

Abraham Maslow, psychologist

(21)

Choosing the right search tool is an important strategy!

search engines

annotated/rated directories

subject directories

subject guides/gateways

meta-search tools

specialized directories

(22)

A field guide to the search tools

Search engines
Databases of billions of Web pages, gathered by automated "robots," allowing broad, often overwhelming searches. Search engines vary in the ways they collect sites and organize results

Metasearch Engines
Search across a variety of search tools and organize the collected results. Good for a broad sweep type search

Subject directories
Links to resources arranged in subject hierarchies, encouraging users to both browse through, and often search for, results. Subject directories are often annotated. They are selected, evaluated, and maintained by humans.

Specific Subject Guides or Gateways
The work of a subject specialists, subject gateways usually result in carefully selected and annotated links

Specialized search engines
Search engines that focus their searching in a particular area of knowledge or interest.

Subscription Databases Pay services often provided by states or libraries offering premium content in the form of reference materials, journal and newspaper articles, broadcast transcripts, etc.

(23)

Subject directories: When to use them

- When you are just starting out, or have a broad topic or one major keyword or phrase (example: "Civil War")

- When you want to get to the best sites on a topic quickly

- When you value annotations and assigned subject headings which may help retrieve more relevant material

- When you want to avoid viewing the many *noise* documents picked up by search engines

(24)

Two Essential Directories

Librarians' Index to the Internet
http://lii.org

> Well-organized, selective, and continually updated collection, also known as "the thinking person's Yahoo." Maintained by a team of librarians at Berkeley Public Library

Kids Click
http://kidsclick.org/

> Great starting point for kids. Annotations are carefully written. Offers grade levels and describes how illustrated a site is.

 25

Subject directories to count on

INFOMINE: Scholarly Internet Resource Collections
http://infomine.ucr.edu/
A large collection of scholarly Internet resources

About.com http://www.about.com
Offers a surprising number of guide pages, maintained by paid experts. Not scholarly but very handy for everyday, practical topics

Academic Info: Your Gateway to Quality Educational Resources
http://www.academicinfo.net/
Great for high school and college research

BUBL Link http://bubl.ac.uk/link/
This UK project leads to carefully selected and annotated resources

WWW Virtual Library http://www.vlib.org/
The first subject directory on the Web. Features comprehensive, well-annotated subject collections maintained by experts around the world

 26

Subject directories—Popular

- Google Directory http://directory.google.com/

- Yahoo! Directory http://dir.yahoo.com

Both Yahoo! and Google offer popular directories. They are not very selective, but they offer some wonderful subject collections.

Examples:
> Yahoo! Full Coverage
> http://fullcoverage.yahoo.com/fc/

> Google Social Issues
> http://directory.google.com/Top/Society/Issues/

 27

Search Engines: When to use them

- When you have a narrow topic or several keywords
- When you are looking for a specific site
- When you want to do a comprehensive search and retrieve a large number of documents on your topic
- When you want to make use of the features in an advanced search screen or search for particular types of documents, file types, source locations, languages, date last modified, etc.
- When you want to take advantage of newer retrieval technologies, such as concept clustering, ranking by popularity, link ranking, etc.

 28

Search engines are powerful but they have limitations!

- They do not crawl the web in "real time"
- If a site is not linked or submitted it may not be accessible
- Not every page of a site is always searchable
- Few search engines truly search the full text of Web pages
- Special tools needed for the Invisible/Deep Web
- Paid placement/sponsored results distract from *real* results

 29

When using a search engine

Your goal is to get the best stuff to appear on the first two or three pages.

 30

Relevance rocks!

Search engines determine relevance in different ways.

Second Gen Search Tools

Approach relevance in helpful ways:

- Google ranks by link popularity
- Teoma ranks by subject-specific popularity
- Vivisimo offers concept-clustered results
- Surfwax uses human generated indexes—Focus Words and summaries
- Ixquick Metasearch uses the ranking schemes (top ten lists) of other search tools

U. Albany Laura Cohen
http://library.albany.edu/internet/second.html

Some search tools present results horizontally, not in long lists!

- Query Server (metasearch)
  http://www.queryserver.com/web.htm

- Vivisimo (metasearch)
  http://vivisimo.com

Your Goal as a Searcher: "Upping" the best results

Traditional
- Text relevance

Second generation
- Link analysis
- Popularity
- Thesauri
- Visualization/Mapping
- "More like this"
- Concept clustering/ Autocategorization

Trends to look for

- SurfWax and Ask Jeeves use indexes or thesauri. The burden of coming up with precise or extensive terminology shifted from searcher to the engine.
- Google, Teoma, Wisenut rank results based on the behavior of millions of Web users.
- Vivisimo,Teoma, and WiseNut use concept clustering/autocategorization/horizontal display
- Kartoo maps results visually
- Ixquick Metasearch compiles "top ten" lists of the major engines

Specialized Search Tools

- Scirus (science search)
- Search.edu (searches only edu domains)
- Biography Center (profile aggregator)
- SearchEric.org (education)
  http://searcheric.org
- SOSIG (Social Sciences)
  http://www.sosig.ac.uk/
- HUMBUL (Humanities)
  http://www.humbul.ac.uk/

Invisible/Deep/Hidden Web

- The Web's largest growing resource
- Estimated to be 40 times size of the visible Web
- Most not subject to fees
- Includes topic-specific databases

③⑦

Why is some of the Web invisible?

- The material is on the Web but it is a *proprietary* database
- The material is on the Web but is in a *free* database
- Content appears past the page size reach of the crawler
- The crawler does not search a particular file format or non-text interface
- The page is available only after registration
- The page is available by some engines but not others. No two engines are the same

③⑧

Why is some of the Web invisible? (2)

- Time lag exists between posting, crawling, and searching (Spiders do not crawl in real time). Site may have been unavailable during the last crawl
- Firewall prevents access
- Page must be accessed or searched in a special way
- Page is not linked to from any other page
- Page was not submitted to the search engine you are using

③⑨

Tools for seeing the Invisible Web

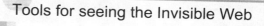

- Invisible Web Directory
  http://invisible-web.net/
- Complete Planet
  http://completeplanet.com
- Librarian's Index to the Internet
  http://lii.org
- Pinakes
  http://www.hw.ac.uk/libWWW/irn/pinakes/pinakes.html
- OAIster
  http://oaister.umdl.umich.edu

④⓪

Examples of *Free* Databases

- Find Articles
  http://www.findarticles.com
- MagPortal
  http://magportal.com
- ERIC
  http://searcheric.org
- American Memory Collection Finder
  http://lcweb2.loc.gov/ammem/collections/finder.html
- NARA
  http://www.archives.gov/search/index.html
- Perry Casteñeda Map Collection
  http://www.lib.utexas.edu/maps/index.html

④①

The free Web is <u>not</u> enough!

④②

What's not on the free Web?

- Copyrighted fiction and nonfiction: biographies

- High quality reference: including literary criticism, science biography

- Full, searchable archives of journals, magazines, newspapers

- Most of our OPAC

43

(Show links to your subscription databases here)

44

Some special search tools for kids

- Ask Jeeves for Kids
  http://www.ajkids.com
  http://www.ajschools.com/

- KidsClick! (highly selective)
  http://kidsclick.org

- Yahooligans
  http://www.yahooligans.com/

- Multnomah County Library
  http://www.multcolib.org/homework/

- Ithaki Kids Metasearch
  http://kids.ithaki.net/

45

Don't forget to use online encyclopedias and databases as subject directories!

They select great links!

46

Tools to help you make search engine choices:

- Debbie Abilock's Choosing the Best Search For Your Purpose
  http://www.noodletools.com/debbie/literacies/information/5locate/adviceengine.html

- How to Choose a Search Engine or Directory (U. Albany)
  http://library.albany.edu/internet/choose.html

For more information (and for people who love searching):

Search Engine Watch
http://searchenginewatch.com

47

Okay, what did we learn?

Let's review

48

1

Thoughtful research:

Moving beyond the topic!

2

So, what's the big deal about research?

It's just another project!

3

Research is a real-life skill

Research projects are training grounds for adult problem-solving and decision-making

- Which car should I buy and how much should I pay?
- Which candidate will best represent my interests?
- How can I convince my boss to accept my proposal?
- How should we work together to rebuild Iraq?
- Who do I believe?

4

No more reports!

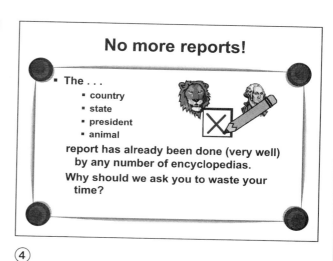

- The . . .
  - country
  - state
  - president
  - animal

report has already been done (very well) by any number of encyclopedias.

Why should we ask you to waste your time?

5

Thoughtful research asks you to:

- Analyze
- Judge
- Support or reject or critique
- Prioritize
- Evaluate
- Plan
- Debate
- Conclude
- Recommend
- Justify
- Argue
- Propose
- Invent

6

We are asking for . . . more meaningful, and more interesting research!

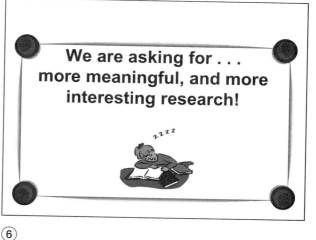

What exactly do we expect?

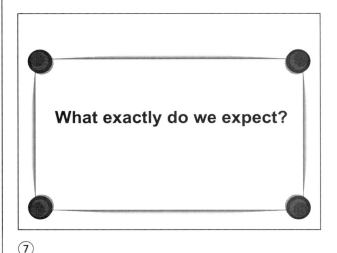

⑦

When you search:

Three tips:

- Focus—what is your mission? your question? Be specific!
- Strategize—select search tools and search terms with precision
- Refine—attempt to improve your search results
- Evaluate—which results to visit, which documents to use? Did I do good work?

⑧

Start with good questions

- ➤ "Which one"
- ➤ "How"
- ➤ "What if"
- ➤ "Should"
- ➤ "Why"

Brainstormer http://mciu.org/~spjvweb/questbrain.html

⑨

What your teachers expect:

- All research is inquiry-driven, based on good questions
- Perfect bibliographic format
- Defense of your source choices in annotations
- Quality, balanced sources. No research holes!
- Variety of access tools—search engines, subject directories, databases, books
- Original work, your own voice. No plagiarism!

⑩

Evaluate your sources!

- Are your sources from a variety of media formats?
- Have you considered the credibility, accuracy, currency, appropriateness, and relevance of all sources?
- Have you pursued sources energetically?
- Have you followed documentation guidelines?

⑪

Have you used print?

- Non-fiction books are filtered for quality!
- Non-fiction books are written not only by subject specialists, they are written by authors who know the cognitive and developmental needs of their audience.
- It may take a year or two of research and editing for an author to publish a book. Many web pages are "thrown up" in a very short time period.
- Probably 90% of this library's collection is NOT on the Web.
- You may need to *get up*. It's not all on the Web.

⑫

6D-2

Process for developing the thoughtful thesis

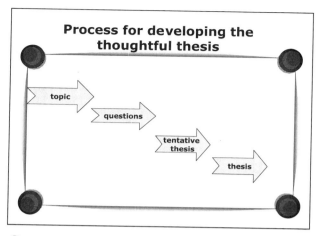

⑬

Why, a thesis?

- A thesis statement declares what you intend to prove.
- A thesis gives your work focus.
- A good thesis statement makes the difference between a thoughtful research project and a simple retelling of facts.
- It makes the work worth doing!

⑭

I have a thesis. Where do I put it?

The thesis statement is typically located at the end of your opening paragraph. (The opening paragraph serves to set the context for the thesis.)

⑮

How do I know if I have a solid tentative thesis?

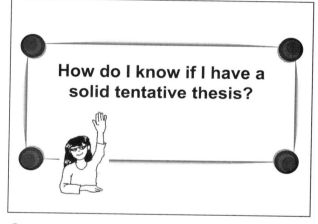

⑯

What does a thesis look like?

2 Simple equations:

Specific topic + Attitude/Angle/Argument = Thesis

(*or* 3 Ts: Topic + 'Tude = Thesis)

_____

What you plan to argue

+ How you plan to argue it

= Your thesis

⑰

Attributes of a good thesis:

Contestable—proposes an argument with which people could reasonably disagree.

Provocative—takes a stand and justifies the discussion you will present.

Coverable—could be adequately covered in the format of the project assigned.

Specific and focused—proves a point without discussing "everything in the world about ..."

Provable—asserts your own conclusion based on solid evidence.

⑱

Don't rush your thesis!

- A good tentative thesis will help you focus your search for information.
- You must do a lot of background reading before you know enough about a subject to identify the key or essential questions.
- You may not know how you stand on an issue until you have examined the evidence.
- You will likely begin your research with a working, preliminary or tentative thesis which you will continue to refine until you are certain of where the evidence leads.

(19)

Be flexible!

The evidence may lead you to a conclusion you didn't think you'd reach.

It is perfectly okay to change your thesis!

(20)

How will you find a thesis?

As you read look for:

- Interesting contrasts or comparisons or patterns emerging in the information
- Something about the topic that surprises you
- Ideas that make you wonder why?
- Priorities you can weigh
- Something an "expert" says that makes you respond, "No way! That can't be right!" or "Yes, absolutely. I agree!"

(21)

Try these five tests on your own tentative thesis:

1. Does the thesis inspire a reasonable reader to ask, "How?" or "Why?"
2. Would a reasonable reader NOT respond with "Duh!" or "So what?" or "Gee, no kidding!" or "Who cares?"
3. Does the thesis avoid general phrasing and/or sweeping words such as "all" or "none" or "every"?
4. Does the thesis lead the reader toward the topic sentences (the subtopics needed to prove the thesis)?
5. Can the thesis be adequately developed in the required length of the paper or project?

If you cannot answer "YES" to these questions, what changes must you make in order for your thesis to pass these tests?

(22)

Are these good thesis statements?
(Use the five tests to decide.)

1. Terrorism should not happen.
2. The causes of the Civil War were economic, social, and political.
3. *The Simpsons* represents the greatest animated show in the history of television.
4. *The Simpsons* treats the issues of ethnicity, family dynamics, and social issues effectively.
5. Often dismissed because it is animated, *The Simpsons* treats the issue of ethnicity more powerfully than did the critically praised *All In The Family*.

(23)

Now you are ready!
Go forth and do powerful, thoughtful research!

Remember, you are not alone. Check frequently with your teacher-librarian and classroom teacher for guidance!

(24)

Uncovering the

INVISIBLE

Web

①

Can your favorite search engine find all there is to find on the Web?

②

It finds all we need to find, right guys?

③

Think again.

- Search engines access a relatively small part of the Web, known as the "*free* Web"

- A large portion of the Web, inaccessible to the search engines, is known as the "Invisible Web"

④

What's not on the *free* Web?

- Around 90% of the books on our library's shelves, still under the protection of copyright
- The full-text of many magazine and newspaper articles
- Expensive reference and nonfiction books, like literary criticism, and in-depth biographical and historical works

⑤

Isn't the free stuff on the Web just as good?

And why can't we get this stuff for free?

⑥

Publishing is a business!

- Serious **authors** are in the business of earning money for their hard work
- **Publishers** also expect a return on their work and investment
- **Copyright** laws protect "intellectual property" from theft

⑦

Your teachers expect quality!

- Material from the **subscription services** is likely to be viewed by your teachers as more authoritative
- You may have to defend some of the sources you find on the *free* Web
- You may want to dig deep on the *free* Web for some harder to find sources.

⑧

I'd like to see an example of that!

⑨

Free Web databases!

For example:
Say you are looking for photographs of the Battle of Gettysburg

You may find some good ones through an image search on your favorite search engine

But did you know there is a database DEVOTED to Civil War photographs?

⑩

Search engines cannot pick up those photos of Gettysburg in that rich database because the database content is not searchable until you are actually in the database.

⑪

Try this database!

Selected Civil War Photographs
http://memory.loc.gov/ammem/cwphtml/cwphome.html

⑫

But how do you find a database like that?

- Use the word *database* with your search terms.
- Use a tool like Librarian's Index to the Internet (lii.org) to identify specialized databases
- Use a search tool specifically designed to pick up items the other search engines miss- a search tool for the Invisible Web
- Look for portals, or gateway sites, relating to your subject area

⑬

Other Web content may be *invisible* to your search engine:

- Files not written in html (some search engines can locate alternate formats)
- Sites requiring a login, like the free *New York Times Book Review*
- Longer files with content beyond the reach of robots or spiders
- Pages created by a search
- Private information owned by a company or organization
- Pages that are new or not frequently linked to

⑭

Some search tools for the *Invisible Web*

Invisible Web Directory
   http://invisible-web.net/

CompletePlanet
   http://www.completeplanet.com/index.asp

Incy Wincy
   http://www.incywincy.com/

OAIster Search Interface
   http://oaister.umdl.umich.edu/index.html

Pinakes Subject Launchpad
   http://www.hw.ac.uk/libWWW/irn/pinakes/pinakes.html

⑮

And . . .
The Invisible Web also includes *subscription*, or *proprietary* databases!

⑯

Presenting:
The subscription databases available to you here at school and through passwords at home!!!

⑰

[Insert icons, links, descriptions of your favorite subscription databases in the next few slides!]

⑱

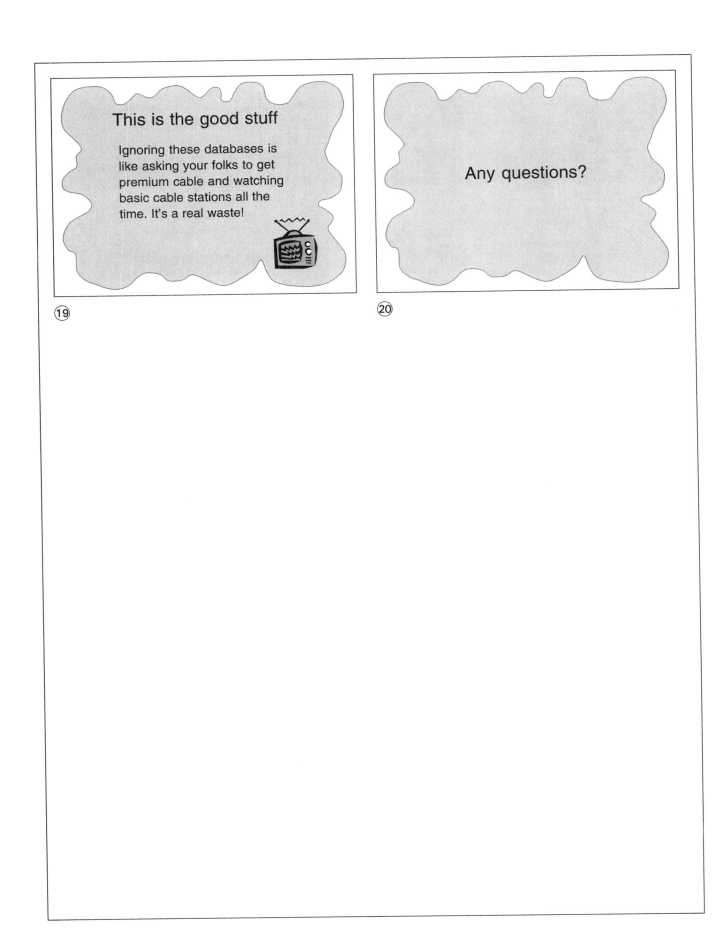

This is the good stuff

Ignoring these databases is like asking your folks to get premium cable and watching basic cable stations all the time. It's a real waste!

⑲

Any questions?

⑳

①

②

It's okay to be confused!

- There are billions of websites out there
- Many of them are not worthy of your time and don't belong in your bibliographies!
- Sometimes it's very hard to tell treasure from trash
- Sometimes Web developers don't want you to understand the difference

③

Remember: Anyone can publish anything on the Web!

It is your job, as a researcher, to look for quality!

④

⑤

Think of CARRDSS

CREDIBILITY / AUTHORITY

ACCURACY

RELIABILITY

RELEVANCE

DATE

SOURCES BEHIND THE TEXT

SCOPE AND PURPOSE

⑥

Slide 7

CREDIBILITY / AUTHORITY

Who is the author?

What are his or her credentials? Education? Experience? Affiliation?

Does the author's experience really qualify him or her as an expert?

Does he or she offer first-hand credibility? (For instance, a Vietnam veteran or a witness to Woodstock?)

Who actually published this page?

Is this a personal page or is it an endorsed part of a site belonging to a major institution? (Clues pointing to a personal page: ~ tilde, %, users, members)

Is the page hosted by a free server like AOL Members, Tripod, Geocities?

⑦

Slide 8

But what if I can't find any author information?

⑧

Slide 9

Look for credibility clues!

Words and phrases to look for:
- *About us, Who Am I, FAQs, For More, Company Information, Profiles, Our Staff, Home*

E-mail the author
- If you have no information other than an e-mail link, write a polite e-mail asking for more information.

⑨

Slide 10

More credibility clues
(What do others think?)

Do a *link check*
- In Google or AltaVista type link:siteaddress
- Your results will show which other sites have chosen to link to this page. If several respectable institutions have linked to a site, that provides a clue about the site's credibility.

Does the site appear in major subject directories like Librarian's Index to the Internet (lii.org)?

⑩

Slide 11

Truncate the URL

Delete characters in the address line up to the next slash mark to see if a main page offers more information about who is responsible for publishing the page you are interested in.

Go from:

http://www.statecollege.edu/history/middleages/chaucer/smith.htm

http://www.statecollege.edu/history/middleages/chaucer

http://www.statecollege.edu/history/middleages

http://www.statecollege.edu/history

http://www.statecollege.edu

⑪

Slide 12

Still more credibility clues

If you have an author's name but no further information about credentials,

- Search the name in quotation marks in a search engine or online database
- On the Web, include words like *profile, resume,* or *C.V.* (curriculum vitae—an academic resume) to narrow your name search
- You might also include the name of a college or association you can connect with the person
- Search the name in biographical sources on- and offline
- Ask your teacher-librarian for help

⑫

ACCURACY

- Can facts, statistics, or other information be verified through other sources?

- Based on your knowledge, does the information seem accurate? Is the information inconsistent with information you learned from other sources?

- Is the information second hand? Has it been altered?

- Do there appear to be errors on the page (spelling, grammar, facts)?

Practice checking for accuracy with a few of these sites!

California's Velcro Crop Under Challenge
http://home.inreach.com/kumbach/velcro.html

The Jackalope Conspiracy
http://www.sudftw.com/jackcon.htm4

Republic of Cascadia: Bureau of Sasquatch Affairs
http://zapatopi.net/bsa.html

Dihydrogen Monoxide Research Division
http://www.dhmo.org

Federal Vampire & Zombie Agency
http://www.fvza.org

For more examples:
http://mciu.org/~spjvweb/evaluating.html

RELIABILITY

Does the source present a particular view or bias?

Is the page affiliated with an organization that has a particular political or social agenda?

Is the page selling a product?

Can you find other material to offer balance so that you can see the bigger picture?

Was the information found in a *paid placement* or *sponsored result* from the search engine?

Information is seldom neutral. Sometimes a bias is useful for persuasive essays or debates.

*Recognizing bias
is important.*

Considering Bias

(Include here links to sites with bias. Preferably present more than one point of view.)

Multnomah County Library's Social Issues page offers links to sites on all sides of major issues:
http://www.multcolib.org/homework/sochc.html

RELEVANCE

- Does this information directly support my hypothesis/thesis or help to answer my question?

- Can I eliminate or ignore it because it simply doesn't help me?

DATE

- When was this information created?

- When was it last revised?

- Are these dates meaningful in terms of your information needs?

- Has the author of the page stopped maintaining it?

- (Be suspicious of undated material.)

SOURCES BEHIND THE TEXT

- Did the author bother to document his or her sources?
- Were those references reliable, popular, scholarly, reputable?
- Are those sources real? Have you or your librarian heard of or been able to verify them?
- Is the material reproduced (accurately) from another publication?
- What kind of links did the author choose?
- Are the hyperlinks reliable and valuable?

19

SCOPE / PURPOSE

- Does this source address my hypothesis/thesis/question in a comprehensive or peripheral way?
- Is it a scholarly or popular treatment?
- Is it material I can read and understand?
  - Is it too simple? Is it too challenging?
- Who is the intended audience?
- Why was this page created? To inform or explain? To persuade? To sell?

20

What can you learn from a URL?

- You can use the end, or suffix of a domain name to help you judge the validity of the information and the potential bias of a website.
- This strategy is only a guideline. People can easily purchase domains that do not reflect their actual purpose.

21

URLs as clues to content

.com=commercial sites (vary in their credibility)
.gov=U.S. government site
.org=organization, often non-profit.
    Some have strong bias and agendas
.edu=school or university site (is it K–12?
    By a student? By a scholar?)
.store=retail business
.int=international institution
.ac=educational institution (like .edu)
.mil=U.S. military site
.net=networked service provider, Internet
    administrative site
.museum=museum
.name=individual Internet user
.biz=a business
.pro=professional's site
~=personal site

22

What do their URLs reveal about these sites?

http://personal.statecollege.edu/~ejv114/

http://www.fi.edu/wright/index.html

http://www.house.gov/house/Legproc.html

http://aolmembers.com/joyciev328/civalwarsong

23

Remember, the *free* Web is not your only choice

- Did you use print sources?
- Did you search subscription databases?
- Did you check with your teacher-librarian for advice?

24

So, why should we care about all of this?

There are bigger questions in life! You will be using information to make important decisions!

- Which car should I buy?
- Which doctor should I choose?
- Should my child have this surgery?
- Should I take this medication?

You want to be able to ensure the information you choose is reliable, credible, current, balanced, relevant, and accurate!

Just as you evaluate your sources . . .

Your teacher will evaluate your work based on the quality of the sources you select.

Evaluate carefully. Don't settle for *good enough*!

Quality always counts!

Evaluation is important! Learn to be fussy!

㉕ ㉖ ㉗ ㉘

Appendix A
Library-Related Quotes

I cannot live without books.

—Thomas Jefferson

My library
Was dukedom large enough.

—William Shakespeare

I read because one life isn't enough, and in the
pages of a book I can be anybody.
I read because the words that build the story
become mine, to build my life.
I read not for happy endings but for new
beginnings; I'm just beginning myself, and I
wouldn't mind a map.
I read because every journey begins at the
library, and it's time to start packing.
I read because one of these days I'm going to
get out of this town, and I'm going to go
everywhere and meet everybody—and I want
to be ready.

—Robert Newton Peck

It is a tie between men to have read the same
book.

—Ralph Waldo Emerson

I have always imagined that paradise will be a
kind of library.

—Jorge Luis Borge

Books are the Carriers of Civilization.

—Barbara Tuchman

Reading is the work of an alert mind.

—E. B. White

A great book should leave you with many experiences, and slightly exhausted at the end. You live
several lives while reading it.

—William Styron

For what are the classics but the noblest recorded
thoughts of man? They are the only oracles which
are not decayed.

—Henry David Thoreau

There are worse crimes than burning books. One
of them is not reading them.

—Joseph Brodsky

The unread story is not a story; it is little black
marks on wood pulp. The reader, reading it, makes
it live: a live thing, a story.

—Ursula K. Le Guin

It's no use going to school unless the library is
your final destination.

—Ray Bradbury

349

Outside of a dog, man's best friend is a book; inside of a dog, it's too dark to read.

—Groucho Marx

I must say television is very educational. The minute someone turns it on, I go to the library and find a good book.

—Groucho Marx

Books were my path to personal freedom.

—Oprah Winfrey

The part of my education that has had the deepest influence wasn't any particular essay or even a specific class, it was how I was able to apply everything I learned in the library to certain situations in my life.

—Gloria Estefan

I cannot think of a time in my life when the library didn't exert a potent attraction for me, offering a sense of the specialness of each individual's curiosity and his or her quest to satisfy it.

—Scott Turow

My father gave me free run of his library. When I think of my boyhood, I think in terms of the books I read.

—Jorge Luis Borges

A house without books is like a room without windows. No man has a right to bring up children without surrounding them with books. . . . Children learn to read being in the presence of books.

—Heinrich Mann

A university is just a group of buildings gathered around a library.

—Shelby Foote

We cannot have good libraries until we first have good librarians—properly educated, professionally recognized, and fairly rewarded.

—Herbert S. White, *Library Journal* column

Mary Kay is one of the secret masters of the world: a librarian. They control information. Don't ever piss one off.

—Spider Robinson in *The Callahan Touch*

What can I say? Librarians rule.

—Regis Philbin on *Who Wants to Be a Millionaire?*

You wasted $150,000 on an education you coulda got for $1.50 in late fees at the public library.

—Matt Damon as Will in *Good Will Hunting*

Are all librarians this much trouble?

—From *The Mummy Returns*, 2001, spoken by Brendan Fraser as Rick O'Connell

He's like Super Librarian, y' know? Everyone forgets, Willow, that knowledge is the ultimate weapon.

—Nicholas Brendon as Xander Harris in *Buffy the Vampire Slayer*

I may not be an explorer, or an adventurer, or a treasure seeker, or a gunfighter, Mr. O'Connell, but I am proud of what I am. . . . I am a librarian, and I'm going to kiss you, Mr. O'Connell!

—Rachel Weisz as Evie Carnahan in *The Mummy*, 1999

What a school thinks about its library is a measure of what it thinks about education.

—Harold Howe, former U.S. Commissioner of Education

Ranganathan's Five Laws of Librarianship:
Books are for use.
Books are for all; or Every reader his book.
Every book its reader.
Save the time of the reader.
A library is a growing organism.

—Shiyali Ramamrita Ranganathan

Gorman's New Laws of Librarianship:
Libraries serve humanity.
Respect all forms by which knowledge is
    communicated.
Use technology intelligently to enhance service.
Protect free access to knowledge.
Honor the past & create the future.

—Michael Gorman (*American Libraries*, 9/95)

My mother and my father were illiterate immigrants from Russia. When I was a child they were constantly amazed that I could go to a building and take a book on any subject. They couldn't believe this access to knowledge we have here in America. They couldn't believe that it was free.

—Kirk Douglas

Since my family did not own many books or have the money for a child to buy them, it was good to know that solely by virtue of my municipal citizenship I had access to any book I wanted . . . from the branch library I could walk to in my neighborhood.

—Philip Roth

Do not forget. Remember and warn.

—Plaque fixed to the shell of
Sarajevo's National Library

I mourn the loss of the old card catalogs, not because I'm a luddite, but because the oaken trays of yesteryear offered the researcher an element of random utility and felicitous surprise through encounters with adjacent cards, information by chance that is different in kind from the computer's ramified but rigid order.

—Annie Proulx

Now, with my adolescence behind me and my daughter's still ahead, I am nearly speechless with gratitude for the endurance and goodwill of librarians in an era that discourages reading in almost incomprehensible ways.

—Barbara Kingsolver

A circulating library in a town is as an evergreen tree of diabolical knowledge! It blossoms through the year!

—Richard Sheridan

I'm of a fearsome mind to throw my arms around every living librarian who crosses my path, on behalf of the souls they never knew they saved.

—Barbara Kingsolver

You, as librarians, stand at the door beyond which this infinity resides. . . . As the 19th century French writer Victor Hugo said: "A library implies an act of faith." You are the keepers of that faith.

—Rita Dove

There is not such a cradle of democracy upon the earth as the Free Public Library, this republic of letters, where neither rank, office, nor wealth receives the slightest consideration.

—Andrew Carnegie

When I . . . discovered libraries, it was like having Christmas every day.

—Jean Fritz

The more that you read, the more things you will know. The more that you learn, the more places you'll go.

—Dr. Seuss

The man who does not read good books has no advantage over the man who can't read them.

—Mark Twain

Don't join the book burners. Don't think you are going to conceal faults by concealing evidence that they ever existed. Don't be afraid to go into your library and read every book.

—Dwight D. Eisenhower

The dirtiest book of all is the expurgated book.

—Walt Whitman

About Information Literacy

We are drowning in information but starving for knowledge.

—John Naisbitt

If students are to be the "workers" they absolutely require richly endowed libraries and the time to use them.

—Theodore Sizer

Not surprisingly, one good way to start designing an Essential school is to plan a library and let its shadow shape the rest.

—Theodore Sizer

Doing research on the Web is like using a library assembled piecemeal by pack rats and vandalized nightly.

—Roger Ebert

Information is the manager's main tool, indeed the manager's "capital," and it is he who must decide what information he needs and how to use it.

—Peter Drucker

A democratic society depends upon an informed and educated citizenry.

—Thomas Jefferson

Information is the currency of democracy.

—Thomas Jefferson

Data isn't information any more than fifty tons of cement is a skyscraper.

—Clifford Stoll

Show me a computer expert that gives a damn, and I'll show you a librarian.

—Patricia Wilson Berger

School library media specialists can and do exert a positive and significant effect on academic achievement.

Principal support of the LM program and teacher collaboration with the LMS are critical to making the LM program an integral part of teaching and learning.

For the LMS to be a pivotal player, support staff are essential. A professional LMS cannot do her job if tethered to the LMC.

The LMS has a teaching role—both as a co-teacher of information literacy to students and as an in-service trainer of teachers.

LM programs that contribute most strongly to academic achievement are those with the technology necessary to extend access to information resources beyond the LMC to classrooms and labs throughout the school.

—*Proof of the Power Key Common Findings, Fast Facts N. 164*, Keith Curry Lance, Marcia J. Rodney, Christine Hamilton-Pennell http://www.lrs.org/ffarchive.htm

Quotable Quotes about Libraries from ALA's Public Information Office

Libraries promote the sharing of knowledge, connecting people of all ages with valuable information resources. These dynamic and modern institutions, and the librarians who staff them, add immeasurably to our quality of life.

—President George W. Bush

Libraries are community treasure chests, loaded with a wealth of information available to everyone equally, and the key to that treasure chest is the library card. I have found the most valuable thing in my wallet is my library card.

—First Lady Laura Bush

Children know that if they have a question about the world, the library is the place to find the answer. And someone will always be there to help them find the answer—our librarians. (A librarian's) job is an important one. Our nation runs on the fuel of information and imagination that libraries provide. And they are in charge of collecting and sharing this information in a helpful way. Librarians inform the public, and by doing so, they strengthen our great democracy.

—First Lady Laura Bush

One of the greatest gifts my brother and I received from my mother was her love of literature and language. With their boundless energy, libraries open the door to these worlds and so many others. I urge young and old alike to embrace all that libraries have to offer.

—Caroline Kennedy

My encouragement to you is to go tomorrow to the library.

—Poet Maya Angelou, during a speech to a college audience that encouraged students to read voraciously and never stop learning.

Those who declared librarians obsolete when the Internet rage first appeared are now red-faced. We need them more than ever. The Internet is full of "stuff" but its value and readability is often questionable. "Stuff" doesn't give you a competitive edge, high-quality related information does.

—Patricia Schroeder, Association of American Publishers President

I used to go to the library all the time when I was kid. As a teenager, I got a book on how to write jokes at the library, and that, in turn, launched my comedy career.

—Comedian Drew Carey. Carey appeared on *Who Wants to Be a Millionaire?* where he announced that all of his winnings would go to Ohio public libraries. Carey donated nearly $600,000 to the Ohio Library Council.

I have a real soft spot in my heart for librarians and people who care about books.

—Ann Richards, former governor of Texas

In hard times, libraries are more important than ever. Human beings need what books give them better than any other medium. Since ancient nights around prehistoric campfires, we have needed myth. And heroes. And moral tales. And information about the world beyond the nearest mountains or oceans.

Today, with books and movies more expensive than ever, and television entertainment in free fall to the lowest level of stupidity, free circulating books are an absolute necessity. They are quite simply another kind of food. We imagine, and then we live.

For those without money, the road to the treasure house of the imagination begins at the public library.

—Columnist Pete Hamill, *New York Daily News*

My childhood library was small enough not to be intimidating. And yet I felt the whole world was contained in those two rooms. I could walk any aisle and smell wisdom.

—U.S. Poet Laureate Rita Dove

Libraries are places where we writers go after we die, if we're lucky. We're going to live on through libraries. But there is also something more. In addition to being a place that we go after we die, if we are lucky, libraries are also the place where a great many writers are born.

—Joe Klein, author of *Primary Colors* and *The Running Mate*

Being in the library is so addictive for me that I really have to exercise self-control so I can get some writing done at home.

—Janet Fitch, author of *White Oleander*

The library (in the migrant community) I grew up in was my only link to the outside world.

—Playwright and filmmaker Luis Valdez

When we build a public library, we don't have to pay to get in, but when we build a stadium, we have to pay the owner every time we go to a game.

—Former Minnesota governor Jesse Ventura

It was a great place to write a novel about book burning, in the library basement.

—Author Ray Bradbury on the writing of his classic novel *Fahrenheit 451* over 50 years ago

I would walk into the Carnegie Library and I would see the pictures of Booker T. and pictures of Frederick Douglass and I would read. I would go into the Savannah Public Libraries in the stacks and see all of the newspapers from all over the country. Did I dream that I would be on the Supreme Court? No. But I dreamt that there was a world out there that was worth pursuing.

—U.S. Supreme Court Justice Clarence Thomas

The public library is more than a repository of books. It's a mysterious, wondrous place with the power to change lives.

—*Chicago Tribune* literary editor Elizabeth Taylor

Many librarians perform their duties with a profound sense of responsibility: supporting the foundations of democracy by ensuring free access to information.

—*New York Times* reporter John Schwartz

Libraries are my passion in life. Before I became mayor [of Los Angeles], I used to sneak out here during lunchtime . . . and I'd go to a corner and take a book—any book almost—and read it for a while, and then feel rejuvenated.

—Richard Riordan

But despite the meek, shush-shushing stereotype, librarians are largely a freedom-upholding, risk-taking group. In the name of the First Amendment and anti-censorship, they have championed the causes of provocative writers and spoken out against banned and challenged books.

—Writer Linton Weeks, *Washington Post*

It's an essential fight librarians are making, an age-old fight; yours is a battle for civilization. It's a fight for our country's founding values.

—Radio talk-show host Jim Hightower

Books and reading saved a very lonely childhood. At the library I found people who took interest in me. From books, I learned about people and compassion.

—Nancy Slonim Aronie, Author of *Writing from the Heart*

You must live feverishly in a library. Colleges are not going to do any good unless you are raised and live in a library every day of your life.

—Author Ray Bradbury

Librarians. I give them all the credit in the book. The Mormon Family Library . . . was so generous and so kind to me. They are amazing . . . I would call them and say, 'Would you look up in the 1840 census the Henry family around Milton, Virginia?'

And . . . they would. . . . Librarians at Hunter College, the University of North Carolina library, and the Library of Congress as well.

—Harvard Professor Henry Louis Gates Jr., who edited a manuscript he purchased entitled, *The Bondswoman's Narrative*, by Hannah Crafts, the first known novel written by an African-American woman who had been a slave

As a child I was a very shy little blonde kid that didn't speak at all to anybody. . . . And what was wonderful about the library was that you didn't have to say a word. So it was my oasis. And you didn't have to ask for things in full sentences. You could just point to a shelf and say, "18th century dolls," and the librarians would lead you there. It was amazing. I felt like a queen.

—Adrienne Yorinks, award-winning illustrator and quilter

I find that when I come out of the library I'm in what I call the library bliss of being totally taken away from the distractions of life.

—Tracy Chevalier, Author of *Girl with a Pearl Earring*

My very identities as a reader and a writer began at the Walt Whitman branch library.

—Paula Spencer, *Woman's Day* Contributing Editor

I fell in love with libraries when I first walked into the school library in Falls City, Texas, population 462. It was tiny and I quickly read through almost everything, but it was a lifeline for a child starved for a larger world. In many ways I owe great chunks of the life I lead to libraries.

—Jane Chesnutt, Editor in Chief, *Woman's Day* Magazine

I liked reading and working out my ideas in the midst of that endless crowd walking in and out of the (library) looking for something. I, too, was seeking fame and fortune by sitting at the end of a long golden table next to the sets of American authors on the open shelves.

—Author Alfred Kazin

I have relied on the library to provide the research materials for five books and uncountable magazine articles. But what has always impressed me most forcefully is the institution's connection to the everyday life of New Yorkers, from giggling teenagers to the very old. . . . From its beginnings, this (library) building has served both as an insti-

gator and a mirror of social change. The Library is one of the last bastions of respect for those who try to carry on . . . independent scholarship. . . . As a writer, I can never get over the sense of being absolutely lucky to be able to get my hands (literally) on so many books.

—Writer Susan Jacoby

Going to the library builds a kid's imagination. Books help them discover themselves and the world.

—Baltimore Oriole All-Star shortstop Mike Bordick

Teenagers can discover the pleasures of reading and gain the power of knowledge by going to libraries. With that power, they will be invincible.

—NASCAR driver Ward Burton, winner of the Daytona 500

There is not such a cradle of democracy upon the earth as the Free Public Library, this republic of letters, where neither rank, office, nor wealth receives the slightest consideration.

—Andrew Carnegie

We must not think of learning as only what happens in schools. It is an extended part of life. The most readily available resource for all of life is our public library system.

—Author David McCullough

What is more important in a library than anything else—than everything else—is the fact that it exists.

—Poet Archibald MacLeish

Getting my library card was like citizenship; it was like American citizenship.

—Oprah Winfrey

When I was a kid and the other kids were home watching "Leave It to Beaver," my father and stepmother were marching me off to the library.

—Oprah Winfrey

What in the world would we do without our libraries?

—Katharine Hepburn

The richest person in the world—in fact. All the riches in the world couldn't provide you with anything like the endless, incredible loot available at your local library. You can measure the awareness, the breadth and the wisdom of a civilization, a nation, a people by the priority given to preserving these repositories of all that we are, all that we were, or will be.

—Publisher Malcolm Forbes

When you are growing up, there are two institutional places that affect you most powerfully—the church, which belongs to God, and the public library, which belongs to you. The public library is a great equalizer.

—Musician Keith Richards

My alma mater was books, a good library.

—Malcolm X

What libraries give you is all three tenses—the past tense—the present tense in which we live and the future that we can only imagine. These places have teachers who are living and dead and we are lucky to have them. If I sit here and read Aristotle, he is speaking to me across a thousand years—more than a thousand years. That sense that I am in the company of the great greatest people who ever lived is a humbling experience but a liberating experience.

—Columnist Pete Hamill, *New York Daily News*

A library is the delivery room for the birth of ideas, a place where history comes to life.

—Author Norman Cousins

As a child, I loved to read books. The library was a window to the world, a pathway to worlds and people far from my neighborhood in Philadelphia. And even today, as I travel around the world, I often visit places I used to dream about because of the books I'd read. The library made a difference in my life.

—Broadcaster Ed Bradley

The free access to information is not a privilege, but a necessity for any free society. One of my favorite things to do as a young man was wander through the stacks of my hometown library. I'd just browse until I found something interesting. Libraries have definitely changed my life.

—Actor Edward Asner

When I was young, we couldn't afford much. But, my library card was my key to the world.

—Actor John Goodman

We all love to hear a good story. We save our stories in books. We save our books in libraries. Libraries are the story houses full of all those stories and secrets.

—Actor Kathy Bates

I am here because libraries and museums are singular and important institutions with unique contributions to make to our nation. But more importantly, I am here as an advocate for children and families, for healthy communities, for economic development, for scholars and researchers, for individuals who seek educational and informational resources throughout their lives.

—U.S. Institute of Museum and Library Services Director Robert Martin

The day I discovered that one could go to the public library and take out books was one of the happiest of my life.

—Columnist Liz Smith

There are ways to recover one's perspective. You can wait for one of those periodic crises that summon the best of the decent men and women who toil at virtually every level of government. Or you can go to your local public library, where the democratic ideals of liberty, equality, and free inquiry are still burnished by daily use.

—Columnist Brian Dickerson, *Detroit Free Press*

I really didn't realize the librarians were, you know, such a dangerous group. They are subversive. You think they're just sitting there at the desk, all quiet and everything. They're like plotting the revolution, man. I wouldn't mess with them. You know, they've had their budgets cut. They're paid nothing. Books are falling apart. The libraries are just like the ass end of everything, right?

—Filmmaker and author Michael Moore

I think the New York Public Library is so, so amazing. It's literally the coolest place. It's good shelter from the sun and it's the most beautiful building. It's really, really fun.

—Actress Natalie Portman

Whatever the cost of our libraries, the price is cheap compared to that of an ignorant nation.

—Broadcaster Walter Cronkite

As a child, my number one best friend was the librarian in my grade school. I actually believed all those books belonged to her.

—Author Erma Bombeck

Public libraries have been a mainstay of my life. They represent an individual's right to acquire knowledge; they are the sinews that bind civilized societies the world over. Without libraries, I would be a pauper, intellectually and spiritually.

—Author James A. Michener

When I was a child in the Navy during World War II, I was perennially grateful to the armed services libraries for having on hand a good supply of those pocket-books, which were so common in that period. I must have read a couple hundred of them, and they did a lot to save my sanity."

—Author James A. Michener

Librarians have always been among the most thoughtful and helpful people. They are teachers without a classroom. No libraries, no progress.

—Broadcaster Willard Scott

Libraries store the energy that fuels the imagination. They open up windows to the world and inspire us to explore and achieve, and contribute to improving our quality of life. Libraries change lives for the better.

—Author Sidney Sheldon

The library is not only a diary of the human race, but marks an act of faith in the continuity of humanity.

—President, Carnegie Corporation,
Vartan Gregorian

The library is our house of intellect, our transcendental university, with one exception: no one graduates from a library. No one possibly can, and no one should.

—President, Carnegie Corporation,
Vartan Gregorian

We are not mere gatekeepers and doorkeepers of humanity's heritage. We also must protect its dissemination. We must beware of all censorship in whatever form it comes, because to censor, to tamper with truth, to tamper with our memory, is to commit a historical sin. We, as librarians, have a major duty that we must all share all over the world, in order not to allow anybody to control, to twist, and most important of all, to manipulate our human will and through it our free institutions.

—President, Carnegie Corporation,
Vartan Gregorian

The library is central to our free society. It is a critical element in the free exchange of information at the heart of our democracy.

—President, Carnegie Corporation,
Vartan Gregorian

Access to knowledge is the superb, the supreme act of truly great civilizations. Of all the institutions that purport to do this, free libraries stand virtually alone in accomplishing this mission. No committee decides who may enter, no crisis of body or spirit must accompany the entrant. No tuition is charged, no oath sworn, no visa demanded. Of the monuments humans build for themselves, very few say "touch me, use me, my hush is not indifference, my space is not barrier. If I inspire awe, it is because I am in awe of you and the possibilities that dwell in you.

—Author Toni Morrison

Here was one place where I could find out who I was and what I was going to become. And that was the public library.

—Author Jerzy Kosinski

When I got my library card, that's when my life began.

—Author Rita Mae Brown

A library book . . . is not, then, an article of mere consumption, but fairly of capital, and often in the case of professional men, setting out in life, is their only capital.

—Thomas Jefferson

Censorship, like charity, should begin at home; but unlike charity, it should end there.

—Clare Booth Luce

Throughout my formal education I spent many, many hours in public and school libraries. Libraries became courts of last resort, as it were. The current definitive answer to almost any question can be found within the four walls of most libraries.

—Tennis Champion–Human Rights Activist
Arthur Ashe

"Library"
Here is where people
One frequently finds
Lower their voices
And raise their minds

—Richard Armour

SOURCE: From *Quotable Quotes about Libraries* http://www.ala.org/ala/pio/availablepiomat/quotablequotes.htm

Appendix B
Librarian's Resources on the Web

Organizations

American Library Association
 http://www.ala.org
 50 East Huron Street
 Chicago, IL 60611
 800-545-2433
 312-280-4388

American Association of School Librarians
 http://www.ala.org/aasl

AASL Advocacy Toolkit
 http://www.ala.org/aaslTemplate.cfm?Section
 =aasladvocacytool

 A rich resource of documents, policy
 statements, and brochures to help support
 and promote your program

(YALSA) Young Adult Library Services
 Association
 http://www.ala.org/yalsa

IASL (International Association of School
 Librarians): School Libraries Online
 http://www.iasl-slo.org

ISTE (International Society for Technology in
 Education)
 http://www.iste.org

National Board for Professional Teaching
 Standards
 http://www.nbpts.org

Journals

American Libraries Online
 http://www.ala.org/alonline/index.html

Booklinks
 http://www.ala.org/BookLinks

Booklist
 http://www.ala.org/booklist/index.html

Bookwire
 http://www.bookwire.com

Horn Book
 http://www.hbook.com/mag.shtml

Journal of Youth Services in Libraries
 http://scholar.lib.vt.edu/ejournals/JYSL/jysl
 .html

Knowledge Quest
 http://www.ala.org/aasl/kqweb

Library Journal
 http://www.libraryjournal.com

Linworth Publishing/Library Media
 Connection
 http://www.linworth.com

LIS News
 http://www.lisnews.com

Multimedia Schools
 http://www.infotoday.com/MMSchools

Online Magazine
http://www.infotoday.com/online/default
.shtml

Publishers Weekly Online
http://publishersweekly.com

School Library Journal Online
http://www.schoollibraryjournal.com

School Library Media Research
http://www.ala.org/aasl/SLMR

Teacher Librarian
http://www.teacherlibrarian.com

VOYA
http://www.voya.com

Discussion Lists

AASL Electronic Discussion Lists (for members)
(to subscribe to any of the AASL lists)
http://www.ala.org/aasl/aasllist.html

YALSA (Young Adult Library Services
Association) Electronic Resources
http://www.ala.org/ala/ya/sa/
electronicresourcesb/electronicresources.htm

ALAWON (to receive messages from ALA's
Washington office)
http://www.ala.org/washoff/alawon

Big6
http://big6.com

LM_NET on the Web (subscribe to or search the
archives of one of the most popular
professional online mailing lists)
http://www.eduref.org/lm.net

Child Lit (unmoderated discussion list
maintained by Rutgers University)
http://www.rci.rutgers.edu/~mjoseph/childlit/
about.html

Information Skills and Standards

Big6 Skills
http://big6.com

Big6 Organizer
http://www.standrews.austin.tx.us/library/
Assignment%20organizer.htm

CyberSmart Curriculum
http://www.cybersmart.org/home

Developing Educational Standards: Library
Media
http://edStandards.org/StSu/Library.html

Do We Really Know Dewey?
http://www.columbia.k12.mo.us/dre/dewey/
index.html

Doug Johnson's Homepage
http://doug-johnson.com

Evaluation of Resources on the Internet
http://www.hi.is/~anne/webeval.html

IASL: School Libraries Make a Difference
http://www.iasl-slo.org/make-a-difference
.html

Information Literacy Page (Valenza)
http://mciu.org/~spjvweb/infolit.html

Information Literacy Lessons (Valenza)
http://mciu.org/~spjvweb/infolitles.html

Information Power: Building Partnerships for
Learning
http://www.ala.org/aasl/ip_toc.html

Kathy Schrock's Home Page
http://kathyschrock.net

LibrarySmart
http://www.librarysmart.com/working/home
.asp

LRS Library Research Service (research,
statistics, and much more!)
http://www.lrs.org

Mankato Schools Information Literacy
Curriculum Guidelines
http://www.isd77.k12.mn.us/resources/
infocurr/infolit.html

Media Literacy Clearinghouse
http://www.med.sc.edu:1081

NETS: National Educational Technology
Standards
http://cnets.iste.org

Neverending Search
http://joycevalenza.com

North Carolina Skills Curriculum
http://www.ncpublicschools.org/curriculum/
Information

OELMA (Ohio Research Study—Todd and
Kuhlthau)
http://www.oelma.org/StudentLearning

Texas Information Literacy Tutorial (TILT)
http://tilt.lib.utsystem.edu

Washington Library Media Association
Information Literacy
http://www.wlma.org/Instruction/infolit.htm

WLMA Information Skills
http://www.wlma.org/Instruction/
wlmaospibenchmarks.htm

School Library Web Pages

School Library/School Librarian Web Pages
http://www.school-libraries.net

School Libraries on the Web: A Directory
http://www.sldirectory.com

School Library Webpage WebQuest
http://mciu.org/~spjvweb/evallib.html

IASL School Library Webpage of the Month
http://www.iasl-slo.org/web_award.html

School Libraries and Librarians on the Web:
Online Models for Effective K–12 Internet Use
http://www.cusd.chico.k12.ca.us/~pmilbury/
ten.html

Innovative Internet Applications in Libraries
http://www.wiltonlibrary.org/innovate.html

Books and Literature

Aaron Shepard's World of Story
http://www.aaronshep.com

ALA Book/Media Awards
http://www.ala.org/Template.cfm?Section=
Book_Media_Awards&Template=/TaggedPage
/TaggedPageDisplay.cfm&TPLID=18&
ContentID=40667

Amazon
http://amazon.com

Author Spotlight (Houghton Mifflin)
http://www.eduplace.com/rdg/author/index
.html

Between the Lions
http://www.pbs.org/wgbh/lions

Barnes & Noble Book Browser
http://www.bookbrowser.com

Best Books for Young Adults (YALSA)
http://www.ala.org/yalsa/booklists/bbya

Book Club Resources
http://mciu.org/~spjvweb/bookclubs.html

Bookhive (children's reviews)
http://www.bookhive.org/bookhive.htm

Booktalks: Quick and Simple (Nancy Keane)
http://nancykeane.com/booktalks

Carol Hurst's Children's Literature Site
http://www.carolhurst.com

Children's Books
http://www.4childrensbooks.com

Children's Literature Web Guide
http://www.ucalgary.ca/~dkbrown

Children's Literature Comprehensive Database
http://www.childrenslit.com

Children's Literature and Language Arts
Resources
http://falcon.jmu.edu/~ramseyil/childlit.htm

Children's Theatre Plays
http://childrenstheatreplays.com

Database of Award-Winning Children's
Literature
http://dawcl.com

High School Literature Sites
http://www.multnomah.lib.or.us/lib/
homework/hslit.html

Kay E. Vandergrift's Special Interest Page
http://www.scils.rutgers.edu/~kvander

Teachers@Random
http://www.randomhouse.com/teachers/index
.html

Random House Reader Resources
http://www.randomhouse.com/reader_
resources/browsetitle

Reading Group Choices
http://www.readinggroupchoices.com

Reading Group Guides
http://www.readinggroupguides.com

Reading Rants! Out of the Ordinary Teen
Booklists
http://tln.lib.mi.us/~amutch/jen/index.html

Recommended Literature: Kindergarten through
Grade Twelve
http://www.cde.ca.gov/ci/literature

TeachingBooks.net
http://www.teachingbooks.net

Young Adult

Young Adult Librarian's Help Homepage
http://yahelp.suffolk.lib.ny.us

Internet Public Library TeenSpace
http://www.ipl.org/div/teen

Technical Services

SUNLINK
http://www.sunlink.ucf.edu

ACQWeb (for acquisitions)
http://www.library.vanderbilt.edu/law/acqs/acqs.html

Library of Congress MARC Standards
http://lcweb.loc.gov/marc

Library of Congress Online Catalog
http://catalog.loc.gov

LION: Cataloging Resources for School Libraries
http://www.libraries.phila.k12.pa.us/lion/cataloging.html

OCLC Bibliographic Format and Standards
http://www.oclc.org/bibformats

Books

Gibaldi, Joseph. *MLA Handbook for Writers of Research Papers.* New York: MLA, 2003.

Hartzell, Gary. *Invisible to Indispensable: Rethinking the Library Media Specialist-School Principal Relationship.* Worthington, OH: Linworth, 2004.

Hartzell, Gary. *Building Influence for the School Librarian: Tenets, Targets, and Tactics.* 2nd ed. Worthington, OH: Linworth, 2003.

Information Power: Building Partnerships for Learning. Chicago: ALA, 1998.

Johnson, Doug. *The Indispensable Librarian: Surviving (and Thriving) in School Library Media Centers in the Information Age.* Worthington, OH: Linworth, 1997.

Kaplan, Allison G. and Ann Marlow Riedling. *Catalog It! A Guide to Cataloging School Library Materials.* Worthington, OH: Linworth, 2002.

Lathrop, Ann and Kathleen Foss. *Student Cheating and Plagiarism in the Internet Era: A Wake-up Call.* Englewood, CO: Libraries Unlimited, 2000.

Loertscher, David V. and Blanche Woolls. *Information Literacy: A Review of the Research.* 2nd Ed. San Jose: Hi Willow, 2002.

Loertscher, David V. and Keith Curry Lance. *Powering Achievement: School Library Media Programs Make a Difference: The Evidence.* Worthington, OH: Linworth, 2001.

McKenzie, Jamie. *Beyond Technology: Questioning, Research, and the Information Literate School.* Worthington, OH: Linworth, 2000.

Simpson, Carol. *Copyright for Schools: A Practical Guide.* 3rd Ed. Worthington, OH: Linworth, 2001.

Valenza, Joyce Kasman. *Power Research Tools.* Chicago: ALA, 2002.

Photo by Jim Graham

Joyce Kasman Valenza is the librarian at Springfield Township High School Library in Erdenheim, Pa., and the techlife@school columnist for the *Philadelphia Inquirer*. Named a Milken Educator for 1997/98, she has also been a Library of Congress American Memory Fellow and participated in the Fulbright Japan program. Her video *Internet Searching Skills* (Schlessinger) became a YALSA Top Ten Award winner, and she won the IASL School Library Web Page of the Year Award in 2001.

In addition to having taught courses in library science and searching skills for Chestnut Hill College and Mansfield University, Joyce speaks nationally on issues relating to libraries, education, and information literacy skills.

Joyce is the author of *Power Tools* (ALA 1998) and *Power Research Tools* (ALA 2002). She is currently working on a new video series on information skills for teens.

The enclosed CD-ROM includes Microsoft® Word, Microsoft® PowerPoint, and Adobe® PDF files, which have been prepared by the author for your use. The files created in Microsoft® Word can be modified to suit the user's purposes. Several items, generously contributed by colleagues, are in Adobe® PDF format and should be used without editorial changes to maintain the integrity of the originator's work. These files are saved in Macintosh and Windows versions. The electronic files correspond to printed forms presented in *Power Tools Recharged*.

To open a file, place the CD-ROM in your computer and then browse the CD-ROM for the file you want to use. Each file name corresponds to its number in the print version. If you wish to modify one of the Microsoft® Word documents, copy the file to your hard drive where it can be opened and modified.

For help using Microsoft® Word or Microsoft® PowerPoint, please consult your manual or the Microsoft website at www.microsoft.com. For help with your Adobe® PDF files, please visit the Adobe website at www.adobe.com.

License Restrictions   You may not and you may not permit others to use the files in any manner that infringes the intellectual property or other rights of the authors or another party.

Limited Warranty and Limitation of Liability   For a period of 60 days from the date the Electronic Files are acquired by you, the Publisher warrants that the physical media upon which the Electronic Files reside will be free of defects that would prevent you from loading them on your computer. The Publisher's sole obligation under this warranty is to replace defective media, provided you have notified the Publisher of the defect within such 60-day period.

The Electronic Files are licensed to you "AS-IS" without warranty of any kind. THE PUBLISHER DISCLAIMS ALL OTHER WARRANTIES, EITHER EXPRESSED OR IMPLIED, INCLUDING, BUT NOT LIMITED TO THE IMPLIED WARRANTIES OF MERCHANTABILTY AND FITNESS FOR A PARTICULAR PURPOSE. THE PUBLISHER WILL NOT BE LIABLE FOR DIRECT, INDIRECT, OR CONSEQUENTIAL DAMAGES ARISING OUT OF OR RESULTING FROM YOUR POSSESSION OR USE OF THE ELECTRONIC FILES. SOME STATES DO NOT ALLOW THE EXCLUSION OF IMPLIED WARRANTIES, SO THE ABOVE LIMITATIONS OR EXCLUSIONS MAY NOT APPLY TO YOU. THIS WARRANTY GIVES YOU SPECIFIC LEGAL RIGHTS AND YOU MAY ALSO HAVE OTHER RIGHTS WHICH MAY VARY FROM STATE TO STATE.

It's back: recharged, better (and more needed!) than ever. *Power Tools Recharged* is a completely revised hands-on guide to address library media specialists' most pressing issues.

Affected by new technologies and information literacy standards, schools now face accountability, funding, and legislative issues that reshape daily practices. Library media centers are now crucial to assist schools in meeting new standards, while also educating students to deal with an information-saturated world.

Library media specialists have to communicate the benefit of their achievements to administrators, teachers, students, parents, and community leaders. Here are the tools to simplify your job and lead to change, even when time is at a premium. Use customizable forms, letters, brochures, hand-outs, and presentations to communicate the value of what you do to different audiences. Valenza has developed this must-have kit to help you administer everyday details and develop policies that work, support students with hands-on, project-based tools, and make powerful presentations, even on short notice.

School library media specialists, LIS educators, language arts teachers, and all owners of the previous *Power Tools* will welcome this recharged edition, complete with all the forms on CD-ROM, for easy customization.

ALAEditions

American Library Association
50 East Huron Street
Chicago, IL 60611

1-866-SHOP-ALA
(1-866-746-7252)
www.alastore.ala.org

ISBN 0-8389-0880-2

90000

9 780838 908808